un
tan
gle

How to Create Big Possibilities Through Small Changes

Angela McKinney

Printed in the United States of America
Print ISBN: 978-1-956019-41-4
eBook ISBN: 978-1-956019-42-1
Hardcover ISBN: 978-1-956019-43-8

Library of Congress Control Number: 2022902846

Published by DartFrog Blue, the traditional publishing imprint of DartFrog Books.

Publisher Information:
DartFrog Books
4697 Main Street
Manchester, VT 05255
www.DartFrogBooks.com

Advance Praise for *Untangle*

"With passion and personal engagement as well as psychological advice which is both classic and current, *Untangle* is an ambitious project, offering thoughtful and creative new directions."
— Marc Lewis, neuroscientist, author of *Memoirs of an Addicted Brain* and *The Biology of Desire*

"Angela McKinney's book is a joy and a revelation. She takes complex concepts and puts them in bite-sized pieces that do not overwhelm. *Untangle* is an invitation to the reader to step into their lives, their material, and their obstacles and navigate them in a new way. So grateful for McKinney's fresh approach."
— Lee Garlington, actress

"I have known Angela for many years through her work. She has been a loving contribution to all the people she helped reclaim their lives. Her methods are very accessible, combining experience, knowledge, and an artistic sensibility. I know this book will help readers find more self-regulation and growth."
— Sarah LaSaulle, PhD., MFT, SEP

"Angela has deep insights into how we get in our own way of thriving. With compassion and care, she writes from the heart."
— Helene Lerner, founder Womenworking.com

"What does it take for a reader to feel loved, inspired, and untangled by their own fear all at the same time? I don't know, but Angela McKinney sure does. Angela turns problems inside out, providing a working framework that shifts how you see your challenges and, by doing so, changes how you belong to the world. Brilliant. Poetic. Actionable."
— Jay Jacobs, NBC's *Biggest Loser*, weightloss expert, *Going Beyond The Scale*

"This book has the potential to change lives and the world. Angela's story is a triumph for anyone struggling. She has found true freedom and shows us how we can as well. Her work touches every part of us, offering a tender hand to navigate a new road of recovery."
— Carolina McFarland, CEO Discovery of You

"We all need to ask ourselves, 'Have I Untangled?' This book is a wake-up call for anyone wanting to become a better human. It shows us a path to stop creating our own suffering and obsessing over the past and land in the here and now. *Untangle* provides wisdom for building a better life and a brighter world."
— Rebecca Baldwin, founder of The Spiritual Compass

"In *Untangle: How to Create Big Possibilities Through Big Changes*, Angela McKinney presents a method of untangling the self from destructive patterns and emotions. She writes with clarity, warmth, and compassion, leading the reader, out of chaos wrought by trauma and addiction, onto a path of healing and integration."
— Jennifer Schneiderman, LSW

"*Untangle* is more than just a self-help book - it is a work of art."
— Deborah Henson-Conant, Grammy-nominated composer and performer

un-tan-gle
/ən-ˈtaŋ-gəl/

1. to free from a tangled or twisted state.
2. to bring order, light, and clarity to that which was dark and hidden.

This book is dedicated to my clients—past, present, and future—whose bravery seeds my inspiration.

I also acknowledge the overwhelmed parents and the underearners, the addicts and the hiders, the dreamers and the risk-avoiders. I am you, and you can do this.

Contents

Tangled Night of the Soul

Our world can fall apart in big ways and small ways. Crisis states take a sledgehammer to our lives, demanding total attention and a reckoning of our souls. But what about all the insidious little struggles happening right now? The real tragedies of our lives may be barely noticeable. The loss of our soul happens when we live inside opaque colors of vagueness—bonding with old, distorted perceptions that we reinforce day in and day out, leaving us unable to live fiercely.

These little moments, the everyday battles that entrap us in "invisible crisis," are what I tackle in this book. I want to rattle you to the truth of who you are in all your myriad colors, and help you find the confidence to handle life's ups and downs by entering every relationship with a more assertive spine, transparent modes of self-expression, and a vibrant heart. I want to show you that madness, terror, shame, self-hate, and confusion can dissolve through a process of untangling. Your life matters, and you can gather the skills needed to realize your best life.

I write to you today from a place of continued healing, peace, freedom, love, and thriving. For decades, I embodied what it means to be stuck, tangled, frozen. The absence of color. Part of me was so ashamed that it was as if I needed to bleach my nature, numbing my ambitions and creativity. I barely survived the endless loops of thoughts that squeezed my brain and pinched my heart. My colors smudged together like a used paintbrush had been plunged into a cup of water. Dirty. Heavy. Dull.

My tangled night of the soul was a long wrestle that twirled my body into one crisis after another until a crescendo in 2005. I was nine months pregnant with my first son. My husband and I were entangled in a raw separation, with financial troubles hanging in the wind. Everything inside and around me felt as fragile as an eggshell. And then I received a call that my father, who stood at the epicenter of my traumatic childhood, had had a horrific tractor accident and most likely would die. A week later, he did. Everything cracked. I stood in a shattered room, shattered life, shattered body. What could ever let me untangle from the complicated problems that stopped me in my tracks?

My father's death, and the complex tragedies that surfaced with his death, were too big for me to handle all at once. But the more I learned, the more I realized I didn't have to. It wasn't so much the big crises that needed my attention, but rather the smaller ones happening all the time, buried inside my body, devaluing me and destroying my life bit by bit. Tending to this internal angst, I went deeper, harnessing personal insights I had learned from my diverse range of expertise to build an integrative model. I befriended the triggering bonds that scratched my soul and took me hostage. I ruptured their destructive spells and found my purposeful place. This holistic understanding of the mind-body-spirit balance birthed the basic tenets of The Untangle Method.

Today, I spend most of my time helping people untangle destructive patterns to reclaim dignity and aliveness. I think about what it means to be untangled. How to take root, find balance, and restore trust within our system. How can we become remade by one trigger, one exchange, one vision? How can we integrate our varied experiences to birth something beautiful and release our inner songs to the world?

For the last twenty years, I have studied disorganized structures through multiple lenses: addiction and trauma, neuroscience and mindfulness, spirituality and creativity. I have drawn on the fields of biology, philosophy, psychology, the arts, and humanities to develop my coaching program, The Untangle Method. I work with trauma practitioners, medical directors, and neuroscientists, collaborating with renowned psychiatrists to build treatment plans and life skill programs for my clients. I have been an active participant in the evolving research on how the mind and the body recover from overwhelming experiences to reclaim life. While the experiences reported in this book were objectively organized, like all truths, they were first experienced personally. I learned skills to rebound from personal difficulties to become stronger in life, improve my mental health, cope with divorce, and recover from trauma.

These discoveries are my songs, my grit, my poetry. This book is part memoir, part how-to guide, and part artistry for disentangling from devaluing narratives so that we can move on from suffering to living life to the fullest.

Before we begin, let's get a few disclaimers out of the way. First, my privacy policy. I cite many examples of client experiences throughout the step work sections; however, I have changed details like names, careers, genders, and other identifying factors that were critical to protecting confidentiality. Any resemblance to actual people or events is purely coincidental. The use of these client stories is intended to demonstrate how to apply untangling skills.

I have also included my own narrative, shedding light on the roots of relational trauma and how I crawled my way out of it to build a thriving life. Though difficult, it has been meaningful and empowering for me to share how my own experience led me to develop the method I use to help others today. However, my story contains content that may be upsetting for some readers, particularly those who have experienced trauma of their own. Please feel free to engage with these sections of the book in the ways and to the extent to which you feel comfortable.

My hope is that in sharing my own vulnerability, you will feel *safe enough* to proceed earnestly and openly through the process as well.

As for the exercises included in the chapters, there are many ways you can do them: with a small group, with a friend, by yourself, or skip them. The activities and experiential exercises are designed to help you build a new relationship with your body and the things flying around both inside and outside of you. I suggest doing a chapter a week to integrate them into your everyday life. In any case, pace yourself. Please don't get caught up in the notion of having to do them "perfectly." The most important thing is to keep moving forward.

And finally, note that this book is not a substitute for professional treatment. It is meant to be used as a tool to help you regain joy and control in your life, but you may discover that it is just the first step in a greater untangling journey. Many of us need therapeutic support to untangle and thrive. Be kind, take care of yourself, and gather additional support as needed. At the end of the book, there will be solutions and suggestions, including books, therapy resources, group programs, and treatment options.

The ideas for this book were sparked from a discussion I had with a rabbi during Passover more than twenty years ago, as we explored different methods to help people recover from personal bondage and access freedom. Our exchange lit fireworks in my body, fertilizing a vision for my life's work. This book was lost and wrestled back to life over and over again until it found its exact shape. And yet, I realized the minute I began that it would never be complete. We are in a continuous process of reclaiming ourselves in ways unique to every situation. So long as we live, we are destined to become entangled or fall apart again. My wish is that you will find the creative inspiration needed to begin the lifelong untangling journey that brings you into vibrant colors of freedom, joy, wisdom, peace, and love.

— Angela McKinney

Introduction

A Primer on Untangling

Many of us organize in a state of unconsciousness. We live in our heads, hide in smallness, and manage symptoms. What we see as the presenting problem is often not an indicator of our real issues. The truth lies buried in time, concealed by shame, fear, or secrecy. We can't solve our problems until we locate our tangled patterns—and accept that we have them in the first place. Denial keeps us stuck, enslaving us to our destructive nature. Meanwhile, most of the solutions are inside us, waiting for our attention and easy to find with proper guidance. Drilling underneath the noise of circumstance shines light onto our hidden, deeper truths, providing us a pathway, at last, to realize our innate nature.

In five sections, The Untangle Method provides a framework to help you see your problems differently: not as failures, but rather as opportunities to realign to your creative nature. In Part I, we will discuss how the Three Parts of the Self—the Tangled Self, Organizer Self, and Creative Self—fit together and provide us with a stable organizing structure to make sense of our inner experiences. These concepts fuse the neuroscience of trauma resolution and the science of integration with a creative application, giving us a blueprint to unwind our tangled states and facilitate our own change.

Once you understand the Three Parts of the Self, Part II will help you locate your own Tangled Self, and reveal how the Tangled Self's authority over our lives is the root cause of our chaotic suffering. The Tangled Self operates in threat responses of "I can't" or "I won't" and distorted perspectives, but this section will help you understand its feral nature and survival purpose.

Next, we will strengthen the Organizer Self in Part III, building resources to separate the Tangled Self from present reality and establish a structure for integration and growth. The Organizer Self creates a "Stabilizing Floor of Okayness" to hold differing feelings and widen our perspective. Once this foundation is complete, we can, at last, reclaim the Creative Self in Part IV. This section will help you discover the part of you that has been there all along but may be lost or forgotten. The Creative Self hungers to be uncaged, and once free, it will help you leverage your skills and imagination in ways that inspire transformation.

Finally, Part V guides us in tying it all together to build a daily Untangle practice. By the end of this journey, I want you to have a three-step process that feels like a waltz: a dance that synchronizes your mind, body, and spirit so that you can untangle anything standing in the way of your freedom. Teaching this method in a classroom is easy. Students perk up, connect dots, breathe deeply, and walk away shifted. Teaching someone how to dance in a written form presents a challenge. But I promise, if you stay with me until the end, you will be amazed at how quickly you can start dressing your old wounds in ways that facilitate meaningful healing and change.

The Untangle Method applies equally for all genders, and individuals as well as groups, both personally and professionally. It offers a creative operational guidebook, a tool that anyone, in any situation, can turn to. My goal is to teach you the same method I have used in my own life and taught my clients who struggle with addictions, life changes, financial collapses, and intimacy issues to help achieve lasting results.

I assume that if you are reading this book, you have a tangled area blocking you from taking flight. You may find it impossible to believe that you can thrive in the face of your current challenges. The idea of confronting uncertainty may fill you with dread, as it did for me. But what is important at this moment is that you have hope. The Untangle Method can and will work. You can emerge from chaos, shame, and invisibility to find your purposeful belonging. You can. You can. You can.

No matter why you picked up this book, you will find creative skills to build a better life. If you read intentionally and engage in the work, you will be inspired to live more boldly. One of the chief principles in The Untangle Method is that change feels good. Working on one's problems doesn't have to be torture; it can be a catharsis. In a short time, you will grow muscles to support new experiences, and eventually, you will build resources to access this part of you anywhere, anytime. The process of untangling begins automatically, for it is the nature of the mind to seek relief from suffering and desire experiences of pleasure, joy, and happiness. Ultimately, this freedom is yours to claim.

PART I

ALL TANGLED UP

a bird
perched on
a branch
is never frightened
of it breaking

her trust
is not with
the branch
but with her wings waiting
to take flight

- Unknown

My Untangle Story:

The Color of Nature

In first grade, we made family trees. I remember trimming the shapes of Mom, Dad, Lee, and Johnny from a cereal box, cutting up multi-colored construction paper for leaves. I hated how mine came out. My mom and brother, Lee, looked orphaned. My father and Johnny took up too much space. I was so small you could mistake me for grass. It was imbalanced and wrong. I felt exposed having the teacher staple it to the bulletin board wall; I wanted to tear it up and burst into pieces.

In reality, my mother was less of a shape and more of a color, sound, sensation. Opera red. Spicy, warm. Bold, curving, sweeping. She bubbled like Coca-Cola with a nervous heartbeat that never let her exhale. My father stretched into the sky like a jagged lightning bolt. He smelled like gun powder. His storms were chaotic. Lee's eyes were turquoise. Costa Rica. Electric eyes that darted behind jet-black bangs like tropical fish. They invited a world of travel, but if you leaned too close, they might bite. Johnny's smile twinkled with Christmas glow. No matter how difficult his circumstances, and believe me, they were difficult, Johnny always giggled and sprouted like dandelion fluff.

Among them, I felt like a smudged watercolor, mixed into a muted, dirty hue. I survived by trying to be white.

Invisible. Everything hurt. People's eyes hurt. The sun's light hurt. A red scream wanted to leap from my throat, but couldn't. I fixated on my thoughts, "What is wrong with me?" Worry expanded inside me like a balloon, and no matter what I did, it was there, pressing against me. My fingers tried to point blame outwards but always found their way back to me, clawing my flesh.

Colors were my way of taking notes. They helped me make sense of things.

On September 10, 2005, nine months pregnant with my first son, navigating a messy separation from my husband, I received the phone call. It was my mother in her high-pitched Southern voice, "Honey, I have some sad news. Your daddy was in a tractor accident, and he needs to have his foot cut off."

"Cut off?"

"Yes, Honey, hmmmm . . . a-m-pu-t-a-t-ed."

She made the word seem like a sing-along. My head spun until the syllables softened their edges and their meaning wrapped around me, transporting me from one shattered world to another.

My voice cracked as I repeated back, "Am-pu-tat-ed?"

"Yes, Honey, that's right, he's at the hospital right now." My parents were divorced, and my mother hated my father with everything in her spine, and though there was concern in her voice, there was a hint of something else. Vindication. God was finally punishing my father. I scrambled to get pertinent details: hospital, doctor's name, anything?

I hung up, only able to repeat three words. Tractor. Amputated. Hospital.

A cloud of debris blanketed me. My heart was drumming; nothing made sense. Sirens. I phoned my midwife to tell her I might be having the baby in Tennessee. She said, go. I called my husband, and he said, don't go. I left.

I followed the yellow lines of the highway as they pulled me through New Jersey, Pennsylvania, Virginia, bending me deeper into memories. Jagged lines stretched across the sky. The clouds cracked. The trees cracked. The highway cracked. It sounded like ice breaking. Bits and pieces of memories swarmed me like bees. I thought about my father's horrible childhood, raised on a poor farm in Kentucky. I had never been there, but I felt like I could smell it, and it smelled like charred skin.

A part of me believed that my father and I were an immortal pattern, that he was, in some sense, eternal. We were entangled in a complicated dance, sealed at birth, stuck in a vinyl record's scratch, where it skips and stays skipping.

I remembered when I was nine years old, and we moved to a new subdivision. Nestled behind our home was a forest. Standing under her trees, the maples' flowing arms, I could take in her world, not just the branches and leaves, but the birds, squirrels, smells, colors, and stars. She had dimensions of sound. It felt like a concerto. I remembered the baby turtles hiding in long wet grass. I had to be careful not to step on them.

I wasn't frightened of the forest like I was of people. I understood her in the way my ballet feet understood Beethoven. My orange hair matched her orange clay. My freckles camouflaged me like her white-tailed deer. Her dark caverns traveled the same textures, coldness, deepness as my interiors. She felt like home. I wanted to weave myself into her root system, climb deep inside her caves to find peace, and feel safe enough to be remade.

Another memory hit.

My father preaching the dangers of riding a tractor, how they killed people, and his demands that I never ride one. And yet here, now. How is it possible that a tractor could take out this larger-than-life man? And why did my father never listen to his own sermons?

I learned that after a fretful two-day search, my father's friend Larry discovered him pinned under a five-thousand-pound tractor in the mountains of his Tennessee property. No road. No electricity. Just one hundred acres of rare land and goats. Dehydrated, my father asked Larry if he had a beer, and Larry said no beer Tom, but I do have Mountain Dew. Larry told me, "Your father raised hell, scolding me for trying to kill him. Didn't I know he had diabetes? Can you imagine being pinned under a tractor in muggy 100-degree heat and refusing to drink a soda? Well, that was your daddy."

My father was helicoptered into the hospital with barely any skin remaining on his arms, hands, and fingers from trying to dig out of the hard earth. He was kept alive on a ventilator, pumped with morphine. His slender, six-foot-five body stretched lifeless, like a stillborn. It wasn't just his foot missing, but most of his leg. A thin sheet softly rounded over the middle section of his thigh, veiling him. He nearly died many times that night, but miraculously, he survived.

I suppose my father had wanted to clear his new land, a pattern that rhymed with his life.

Other memories hit.

The magic of the forest became violently interrupted. Scream. Panic. Chainsaw. My father chopped the forest down, clearing her to make space for a tennis court. He was obsessed with a mission for Johnny to become a tennis star. Buzzing violence sliced the air. An echoing scream wrapped around me. The trees fell too quickly. Pieces of wood shaped like crescent moons smelled like seared flesh. Long, slender trees piled on top of each other like dismembered limbs. I felt deceived and violated. It became my father's forest, and he would do with it whatever he pleased. Was I the only one who could see what was happening? Was I the only one who could hear the trees cry, feel the birds panic, and the frogs in distress?

Our father-daughter dance frightened me. I spent decades trying to fix the unfixable scratch. This dance held tremendous power over me, shaping how I experienced the world and what I thought of myself.

Was I dancing inside the same scratch in my marriage?

At the hospital, I watched his chest, prayed for him to breathe between his shallow breaths. I was over-whelmed by the distance between us, the breach in our relationship extending well over twenty years, and although we made many repairs, the residue of trauma lived on. I awkwardly touched a part of his skin and kissed his forehead. I was preparing to say goodbye, and yet part of me couldn't. At this moment, I realized how much I had been counting on him to be a grandfather to my son, all our difficulties coming to an end, and how deeply I believed in a future where we could be at peace with each other and build meaningful memories.

Days rolled into a week.

Morning light, pale and watery, broke across his room. His condition improved, and the day of his surgery, his fiery fortitude returned. His skin converted from ash to a warm tan. His auburn hair seemed lion orange. He sat up tall and wild like he had risen from the dead, howling at the world: I survived. He was asserting dominance, glory, dignity, and we celebrated him. A glimmer of hope peeked inside the ICU, saying somehow this man, my father, may pull off the impossible. But it would be my father's last declaration. His thirty-minute, exploratory surgery turned into three hours, and just like that—poof—he slipped away.

Chapter 1

Nature

tangled nature: non-committed and rigid, fostering denial.
untangled nature: committed and curious, fostering growth.

In times of challenge, we can draw on different essences of nature to teach us. First, there is "nature," as in the phenomena of the physical world and the creations of Mother Earth. Here there are energies of joy, peace, and love expressed through flowers, trees, and animals, making a home for human beings. Second, there is "nature," as in our human characteristics, which bundle ways of feeling, thinking, and responding that color our view of the world. This nature may make us reactive and destructive or alive and creative. It is shaped in partnership with our genetic makeup and inborn temperament, nudging us into certain directions. Last, there is the "nature" of conscious awareness, which offers wisdom to move through life's challenges, building resilience to claim purposeful belonging. As we embark on this journey of untangling, we must understand all three—their relationships with each other as well as the role of each one in our lives. To understand nature is to understand *our* nature, which, in turn, helps us understand ourselves.

Imagine Flowers

Pink lotus. Floating. White daisies. Swaying. Grey tumbleweeds. Dancing. Beauties of all colors, shapes, and sizes swirling in spectacular fields of forest greens, honey browns, roses, and purples, offering a bridge between our physical reality and the ethereal beingness with life.

Before flowering plants appeared, the world was somber and green, inhabited by fish, turtles, and dragonflies. The arrival of flowers sparked vibrancy and variety, inviting butterflies and honeybees. Today flowering species outnumber by twenty-to-one the ferns and conifers, which thrived 200 million years before the first bloom.[1] From oaks and palms to wildflowers and water lilies to cornfields and citrus orchards, flowers have forever changed how we see the world.

A flower can awaken a presence for the magical nature of living. Flowers sprout confidently through rocky ridges capturing short-lived beauty and inhabit the soil beneath our feet to foster life. They contribute to the fragile, complex living system that houses bacteria, fungi, and all other life forms. They attract a diversity of insects and birds, which help colonize new systems. It is not enough to recognize the mere prettiness of flowers; we must appreciate the deeper joy we humans find within a belonging that is fueled by mystery and wonder. We can feel this sensation come alive every time we step into a forest, where the majesty of nature calls to us in a voice beyond our imagination.

The truth is, we are not separate from nature; we are part of nature. We don't need to merely learn from nature; we need to embody it. Like all systems in nature, if we stagnate, we fossilize. When we are trapped in adverse responses, we become out of touch with the harmonics of life and disconnected from the part of us that can make lasting change. Disconnection fuels feelings of despair, fear, dread, loneliness, and isolation. The further apart we become within ourselves, the more we end up feeling *all* broken, *all* bad, *all* afraid in the roots of our being.

Child psychologist Dr. W. Thomas Boyce identifies two groups of children: "orchids" and "dandelions."[2] Dandelion plants do well in most environments, even thriving in harsh conditions as they travel through the world like little parachutes, landing and sprouting in new fields. Like dandelions, some children overcome challenges quickly, with little to no interruption. They greet adversity with a chuckle, excited to dig and discover how to move through it. They are not burdened with incessant efforts to fix themselves, nor do they complicate their blooms, but they mobilize in service to them. That said, even the strongest of dandelions are not invincible.

Orchids, on the other hand, are sensitive plants with specific needs. High humidity and airflow are required around their root system, or they will rot. Strong light, but not direct sun, or they will wilt. Temperatures above fifty degrees and below eighty-five degrees, or they will die. Like orchids, some children can become ensnared by challenges in ways dandelions don't. They experience more of everything, including threats, fear, and anxiety, as well as beauty, mystery, and awe. According to Boyce, "Orchids can become creatures of rare beauty, complexity, and elegance when met with compassion and kindness."[3]

Many of us expect to be a dandelion, and yet we are orchids. Or we judge the dandelion, thinking it is insensitive. Dandelions can overpower life and become hardened, struggling to experience intimacy. Many dandelions have a part of them that needs more attention, tenderness, and support, while orchids can struggle in the weeds of hiding and emotional disorganization. They need to work on their responses and sensitivities in ways that grow a safe structure to bloom. Whatever the case, none of these responses are set in stone. While our environment is often out of our control, shifting our responses will allow entirely different realities to emerge, helping us build resilience. However, without structure to understand these problems, we may not know where to begin.

We want to understand that our relationship with nature is reciprocal; we call each other into being. Resilience is a capability that can wax and wane. Even the most seemingly resilient people can become drained by relational poverty and stress. The world inside of us and around us isn't fixed. What exists is a state of myriad possibilities. Nature remains a source of essential lessons, each one helping us better understand what we need to thrive. Yes, change requires a willingness to stand inside our lives, look sideways and upside down to open our perceptions and tilt into new experiences, but anyone can accomplish this with gentleness, direction, and subtlety. Whether you are a wounded dandelion, a disorganized orchid, or a bit of both, you can find resources to thrive.

Problems

This section contains mentions of sexual abuse, child abuse, and disordered eating/weight gain.

We each have an innate blueprint unique to who we are, a specific way of meaning-making in our world. As we grow, we gather imprints that influence and shape the expression of our blueprint.[4] Some imprints enhance and activate our unique blueprint, while others distort its expression in ways that disrupt the vital connection. Troubles arise when we get caught in old imprints, remnants of experiences in our past that hijack us and get us stuck. We end up draining energy in the present, managing aches and outcomes leftover from these old imprints.

The imprints we remember with our cognitive mind are examples of what is called *explicit memory*.[5] Other imprints live in our body and unconscious mind, and they are called *implicit memories*.[6] Most of us aren't familiar with implicit memory, and so it seems mysterious that our body might remember something that our mind doesn't.

Instead of tuning into the music of the body, we swirl in head noise, trying to figure out why we are unable to change. We elaborate solely on explicit cognitive memories and miss out on the wisdom that lies in the implicit memory of our bodies.

In 1985, Dr. Vincent Felitti, chief of Kaiser Permanente's Department of Preventive Medicine in San Diego, ran a clinic for those seeking dramatic weight loss. Many of his patients experienced astonishing results, such as one woman losing one hundred pounds in fifty-two weeks. But the rate of the patients' weight regain after release from the clinic was even more surprising.[7]

What had happened? It turned out that having a skinny body was confusing for his patients. Felitti found a pattern: newly slender bodies attracted attention, flirting, and sexual possibility, causing many patients to feel overwhelmed and scared. To cope, they reported that they'd turned back to food to reclaim a sense of safety. Felitti observed that regaining the weight served as a protective shield; it was an attempt to solve complex, hidden problems.

At the time, in 1990, his peer psychiatrists and psychologists told him that he was naïve to believe the rationale his patients gave for relapse. They said these patients' statements were fabrications, excuses for "failure" to keep the weight off. Fortunately, Dr. David Williamson, an epidemiologist from the U.S. Centers for Disease Control and Prevention, was intrigued by Felitti's findings. Their combined efforts resulted in a monumental investigation of Adverse Childhood Experiences, now known as the ACE study, a collaboration between the CDC and Kaiser Permanente.[8]

The ACE Study is probably the most important public health study that many people have never heard of.[9] As with many great discoveries, internist M.D. Felitti came across his findings almost accidentally. However, his findings reshaped our understandings of addiction, chronic disease, destructive patterns, and illness. Felitti and his team found that adverse childhood experiences are interrelated with these issues, even though they're usually studied separately.

Felitti's ACE study group concluded:

" . . . Although widely understood to be harmful to health [addictive/harmful behaviors are] notably difficult to give up. The idea of the problem (example, weight gain) being a solution, while understandably disturbing to many, is undoubtedly in keeping with the fact that opposing forces routinely coexist in our biological system. What one sees, the presenting problem is often buried in time, concealed by patient shame, secrecy, and sometimes amnesia."[10]

One participant in Felitti's study, Ella Herman, owned a successful childcare center in San Diego. Herman told Felitti, "I imagine I've lost one hundred pounds about six times and gained it back."[11] She reported being sexually abused by two uncles and a school bus driver; the first time occurred when she was just four years old. She ended up marrying a man who abused her repeatedly. Then, he tried to kill her. With the help of her family, she fled with her children to San Diego. She shared, "Every time I lost weight, a man commented on my beauty, and I became terrified and started eating."[12] But she never understood the connection until she attended a meeting with Felitti. At the time, Herman was just over five feet tall and weighed nearly 300 pounds. "Dr. Felitti had a room full of people," she said. "The more he talked, the more I cried because he was touching every aspect of my life. Somebody in the world understands, I thought."

When the ACE study data started to appear, it was clear that Felitti and Williamson had stumbled upon the gravest and most costly public health issue in the United States: child abuse.[13] Dr.

Robert Anda from the CDC calculated that the costs of treating the child abuse epidemic exceeded those of cancer or heart disease. From their data, they developed a scoring system from one to ten, which strongly correlates to the risk of disease and social-emotional problems. With an ACE score of four or more, things start getting serious. The likelihood of chronic pulmonary lung disease increases 390%; hepatitis, 240%; depression, 460%; attempted suicide, 1,220%.[14] Eradicating child abuse would reduce the overall rate of depression by more than half, alcoholism by two-thirds, and suicide and I.V. drug use by three-quarters.

While these statistics are staggering, it is essential to note that there are also plenty of complex trauma cases that have only scored one on ACE. The reality is that there are numerous people who cannot point to a specific moment that their life came apart. Many people who suffer from insidious neglect or emotional abuse struggle to recognize any trauma. But that doesn't mean there wasn't trauma. Additionally, the ACE study doesn't consider the outside environment—societal, racial, and gender discrimination, which are additional forms of trauma. I have yet to meet a person who has not experienced some trauma from just being born. At the same time, I think it is crucial to expand our understanding of trauma to include a diverse range of overwhelming experiences that happen to us all in states of relative helplessness.

Most traumatic experiences are not in-your-face obvious but hidden in implicit memory. Many of the more subtle relational traumas can create complex problems, stress, and stuckness, similar to Big-T Traumas like war, rape, or accidents. People think trauma only shows up as flashbacks, nightmares, or severe behaviors, but more often, it manifests as boundary and control issues, unhealthy coping mechanisms, how we eat, handle money, and connect with others. Our perceptions and responses towards trauma are as valid as the trauma itself, especially from childhood when we are most vulnerable. Because, as children, we could not form language nor had the autonomy to leave, we learn intricate ways to disappear, dissociate, avoid, or freeze. And these impulses find their way of reattaching within everyday relational exchanges, recreating patterns of stuckness and disorganization in adulthood.

The Brain

Psychology is, in part, the study of nature; its primary aim is to seek the most effective ways to relieve human suffering through understanding our nature. In *The Body Keeps the Score*, Dr. Bessel van der Kolk, a trauma neuroscientist, masterfully describes how the parts of our brain are interconnected to help us survive and flourish. His findings will help serve as a guideline to understand how the Three Parts of The Untangle Method layer into modern-day neuroscience:

"The most important job of the brain is first and foremost engineered to survive. Everything else is secondary. In order to do that, brains need to 1. generate internal signals that register what our bodies need, such as food, rest, protection, sex, and shelter; 2. create a map of the world to point us where to go to satisfy those needs; 3. generate the necessary energy and actions to get us there; 4. warn us of dangers and opportunities along the way, and; 5. adjust our actions based on the requirements of the moment. And since human beings are mammals, creatures that can only survive and thrive in groups, all of these imperatives require coordination and collaboration."[15]

When we don't know how to read our internal signals, meet our needs in resourceful ways, and mobilize actions that build healthy partnerships, we become demoralized and distrust our instincts. Without understanding how our brains respond to triggers and determine inner safety and collaboration, we are prone to break-downs, numbness, and collapse—or the flip side, scanning the world hyper-vigilantly, evaluating people and our external environment.

Every brain structure has a role to play in these essential functions. He teaches that the brain is built from the bottom up. It develops layer by layer with every child in the womb, just as it did in the course of evolution. The brain can be divided into three interconnected areas: reptilian, limbic, and cortex. The functional complexity increases from the lower, simpler areas of the brainstem up to the cortex.

The most primitive part, the part working when we are born, is called the *reptilian brain*. It is responsible for all the things that newborn babies can do: eat, sleep, cry, breathe, pee, and feel hunger, wetness, and pain. We take these things for granted. However, when trauma interferes—when sleep is disturbed, or touching makes you want to scream, or you are always hungry—the entire organism is thrown out of balance. Since all experience is processed from the bottom up, this region of our brain is the first part to interpret and act on the information coming in from our senses. Developing babies *act* and *feel* their way into thinking, and so do we.

Right above the reptilian brain sits the *limbic system*. The limbic system develops in response to our sensory experience, in partnership with our genetic code and inborn temperament. It is the part of the brain that holds onto our embedded visceral beliefs and memories, which determines our "felt sense." Whatever happens to us as babies and children contributes to our emotional and perceptual map of how we experience the world. If we feel safe and loved, our brain becomes specialized in exploration, play, and cooperation; if we feel frightened and unwanted, our brain specializes in managing feelings of fear and abandonment.

Taken together, the reptilian brain and limbic system make up the *emotional brain*. This part is at the heart of the central nervous system, and its essential task is to look out for our welfare: the moment-by-moment registration and management of our body's physiology and the identification of comfort, safety, threat, hunger, fatigue, desire, longing, excitement, pleasure, and pain. Even at their most subtle, these sensations have a significant influence on the small and large decisions we make throughout our lives: what we choose to eat, where we like to sleep and with whom, what music we prefer, whether we like to garden or sing songs, whom we like and whom we detest, how much money we make or how we struggle to earn money.

At the top layer sits the rational, cognitive brain, the *cortex* area—the youngest part of the brain, which occupies only 30% of the area inside our skulls. In our second year of life, the frontal lobes, which make up the bulk of our neocortex, begin to develop at a rapid pace. As we reach age seven, "the age of reason," we start to become organized around our frontal-lobe capacities; we begin to sit still, use words instead of acting out, and tune into our teachers and classmates. The frontal lobes help us plan and reflect, as well as imagine and play out future scenarios. Its primary concern is with the world outside us, understanding how things work, figuring out ways to accomplish our goals, and managing our time. The cortex mediates the most uniquely "human" functions such as speech and language, abstract cognition, and the capacity to reflect on the past and envision the future. This part of our brain makes a choice possible, underlying our astonishing creativity, as well as granting empathy, our ability to connect with others.

When our stress response activates, however, the brain's higher region, the cortex, can go offline. The emotional brain then takes over and initiates preprogrammed escape plans, like fight-or-flight responses. Sensory inputs arrive through our eyes, ears, nose, skin and are passed into two directions: down to the amygdala, two small almond-shaped structures that lie deeper in the unconscious limbic system, and up to the frontal lobe, cortex, where they reach our conscious awareness. The neuroscientist Joseph LeDoux calls the pathway to the amygdala "the low road," which is extremely fast, and that to the cortex "the high road," which takes longer in overwhelming experiences and triggers.[16] As long as you are not too upset, your frontal lobes can restore balance by helping you realize you are responding to a false alarm and abort the stress response.

The rational brain is systematic and impartial but also slow. Like a muscle, it develops over time if exercised. Without the logical cognition of the cortex, the emotional brain freely jumps to conclusions based on rough similarities. It often entangles past memories with current reality, leaving us reactive, confused, or triggered. Any sensory input, like a sight, sound, smell, taste, or touch, can activate a traumatic memory, keeping us stuck in the past. Complex and confusing associations stored in the lower brain regions with no linear narrative or memory can influence our behavior for years after they're formed. These automatic and visceral responses are set in motion without any thought or planning on our part, leaving our conscious, rational capacities to catch up later.

Just as our brains develop from the bottom up, they are organized to respond and feel before thinking. Cognitive-behavioral therapy and other forms of talk therapy modalities work with the brain from a top-down approach. However, van der Kolk's research demonstrates that systematic repair often needs a bottom-up approach to heal. Simply stated, befriending the body offers a key. Somatic practices are spreading like wildfire to help people rediscover their bodies and increase their ability to heal. Kickboxing, music, theater, and art are valuable avenues to help us come back into aliveness. Our experience of the world is organized through our body's sense of connectedness, affecting the way we feel, think, and behave. The nature of the body needs curious, thoughtful engagement.

Color

The enigma of color has attracted the interests of many gifted thinkers, from visual artists to intellectuals like Newton and Goethe. Scientifically, color can be viewed as a phenomenon arising from the transition between darkness and lightness. But personally, viscerally, color can help us express feelings where words can't. Whether or not we realize or verbalize it, our perception of color elicits emotional responses, offering us a gateway to better understand one feeling, one thought, and one memory.

In the early 1700s, Goethe's theory of colors challenged Newton's view on color, arguing that color was not only a scientific measurement, but a subjective experience perceived differently by each person.[17] Goethe speaks persuasively regarding color harmony, parsing symbols of heaven, hope, and Earthly power in his cultural consciousness. Today, breakthroughs in the use of color as a healing agent for rapid recovery of trauma, depression, physical pain, and spiritual blockages have elevated the power of color for healing.

Dr. Steven Vazquez developed Emotional Transformation Therapy (ETT), a method of color therapy, centering on a triadic relationship between the client, the color, and the facilitator.[18] This overall interaction forms a continuous loop of exchange that bears a strong resemblance to an interpersonal encounter between two people. ETT practitioners use lights and colors to stimulate the brain, reshaping the neural impulses that affect the nervous system. This research-driven approach aims to help the person in treatment move swiftly from a problematic emotional state into a more positive one. Many clients report subjective, personified experiences in this visual interaction with colors like a hug, a look, or annoyance. Some clients even say an ultimate bonding experience, which they describe as feeling "one with this color."[19]

In *Map of Consciousness Explained,* renowned psychiatrist and spiritual teacher Dr. David R. Hawkins lays out an entire spectrum of consciousness and correlated color with each state, from lower emotional levels of Shame, Guilt (red); Apathy, Fear, Anger, (orange) and Pride (yellow); to Courage, Acceptance, and Reason (green); up to the more expanded levels of Love, Ecstasy, Peace (blue), and Enlightenment (violet).[20] As the emotions of the body change, colors change, corresponding to different levels of consciousness.

These are just some modalities of color theory and color therapy, which show promising results, yet the potential of color may still be untapped. The greatest beauty of color perception is, as Goethe observed, its subjectivity. We all see color differently—from a young age, each of us picks a unique favorite. Now, in the context of modern scholarship (including this book), color becomes a portal into higher states of consciousness. At its very essence, color in The Untangle Method is understood as the transmission of energy, an exchange that can help us understand our unique experience of the world.

Interpersonal Neurobiology

Interpersonal neurobiology is an interdisciplinary field that brings together anthropology, biology, linguistics, mathematics, physics, psychology, and more to determine common findings of the human experience from different perspectives. It has defined the human mind as a complex system that is optimally supported through the concept of *integration*,[21] a tool to separate the part of our nature that creates our suffering from the part of our nature that can thrive.

As shells, flowers, and cauliflowers organize within an integrated system to harmonize growth, we humans also thrive under a similar structure; each brain region can create new memories and change its responses. Interpersonal neurobiology asserts that integration is the basis of health, defined quite simply as "the linkage of differentiated parts."[22] As we differentiate the parts of our brain, they don't lose their uniqueness but share space to link, allowing them to sit next to each other. As we touch on different aspects of ourselves, we expand our felt sense, shifting our world-view to access a full range of experiences.

Dr. Daniel Siegel, the founder of interpersonal neurobiology, describes integration as the act of establishing a meaningful link between two different things.[23] He explains that integration is unlike a fruit smoothie in which items are blended to make a new whole; instead, integration is a glass container holding different pieces of fruit, allowing them to remain separate and identifiable, touching each other and creating linkage while remaining unique to one another.

The Untangle Method is aligned with interpersonal neurobiology's premise that integration is the optimal organizing structure for wholeness. It merges our brain-body conversation with an artistic craft by asserting we have Three Parts in our system: The Tangled Self, the Organizer Self, and the Creative Self. When these Three Parts are integrated—differentiated and linked—they provide an internal structure that supports wellness. Our quest is to build an organizing system that allows all Three Parts to sit next to each other and collaborate within one system.

Siegel's and van der Kolk studies on brain plasticity have shown how our brain is shaped and influenced by the musicality of engagement and the quality of our relationships. Our embedded responses and interpersonal relationships, ones with our bodies, color, money, triggers, form a map of who we are. If we want to change this map, we need skills to gather the body's wisdom and emotional insight to self-organize. Untangling builds a predictable and controllable model to grow through a new challenge and develops resilience in the face of it. The work is learning to locate our desynchronized patterns and unwind them into new experiences, realizing, at last, our innate nature.

In the following chapters, we will undertake an intimate reorganizing of the self. We can never undo what happened to us. However, we can create new emotional engagements and scenarios intense and *real enough* to diffuse the old, welcoming us back into the world. We have a tremendous capacity to change. Depending on how we direct our listening and experience our brain-body rhythms, we can create a space to heal through present aliveness, compassion, and joy.

Untangle Exercise: Nature Exploration

Let's return to Dr. W. Thomas Boyce's metaphor of "orchid" and "dandelion." We may not completely understand what it's like to be a flower, but having faith in our ability to imagine is unique to us humans. Dandelion plants do well in most environments, even thriving in harsh conditions, whereas orchids require highly attuned environments to thrive. Is the nature of your temperament more dandelion or orchid? Or maybe a bit of both? Instead of fighting your nature, greet it. The analogy may seem simplistic, but set aside your reservations and imagine:

❖ If you identify more as an orchid, describe your orchid state. Maybe it is an angry orchid that doesn't understand what it needs to bloom? Or an overwhelmed orchid that needs to shut down? Or a joyful orchid that loves finding a more vibrant color? Be specific.

❖ If you identify as an orchid, locate the part of you that might be a dandelion? What if any judgments do you have about dandelions? Identify them. What does resourcefulness look like for you? Often, orchids don't recognize their ability to survive challenges. How does seeing your temperament as a flower help you soften judgment and see your responses differently? Be specific.

❖ If you identify more as a dandelion, describe your dandelion state. Maybe it is a successful dandelion who craves more intimacy and connection? Or an angry dandelion that needs to learn patience and calmness? Or a mighty dandelion that is terrified of being seen? Be specific.

❖ If you identify as a dandelion, locate the part of you that might be an orchid? What if any judgments do you have about being an orchid? Identify them. Many dandelions have a part of them that needs more attention, tenderness, and support. Recognize this part may need a little extra care to thrive and provide that care. What one thing can you do today to help support this part of you? Be specific.

❖ If your nature becomes easily entangled with others or circumstances, explore how you become stuck in the weeds of *if only*. For example, "If only my husband would get his act together." "If only I weren't so heavy." "If only I weren't so old." "If only I had a different childhood." List all of your *if only* weeds.

❖ Imagine a part of you that can root into deeper soil and lift into the blue sky. Make contact with this part of you. Feel it. See it as a flower. Does it have a dandelion spirit or orchid color? Is it a red gladiolus full of determination? Or a playful fuchsia bougainvillea ready to twirl? Locate a part of your nature excited to thrive.

❖ Write a poem to describe your untangling journey.

Here is a prompt:

Just because one part of me is_____
Doesn't mean_____

Here is mine:

Just because one part of me is tangled
Doesn't mean all of me is tangled

Chapter 2

Three Parts Make a Whole

tangled system: hijacked and managed entirely by one part of itself.
untangled system: whole and functioning through all parts.

From great philosophers to the founders of psychology to neuroscientists, countless influential thinkers have concluded that the self has different parts. Carl Jung's theory states that each person's psyche comprises three components: the ego or conscious part, the personal unconscious, and the collective unconscious.[24] The father of psychology, William James, expresses the idea of having three aspects of selfhood: the material self, the social self, and the spiritual self.[25] Interpersonal neurobiologist Dr. Daniel Siegel defines the Self as a complex system having two brains, the "yes brain" and the "no brain."[26] Richard Schwartz, the founder of Internal Family Systems psychotherapy, defines the Self as having multiple parts that split from trauma and need integration for optimal self-organization.[27] In this tradition, I, too, have created an organizing framework based on the concept of integration and have seen the benefits of its results firsthand with my clients. This chapter will be our first look into the Three Parts of the Self, how they differ, and how they impact us. As we move through the steps of The Untangle Method, we'll spend time with each one until we know them and reencounter them as old friends.

Three Parts of the Self

Unaware of our Three Parts, the Tangled Self, the Organizer Self, and the Creative Self, we may lump our various parts into a limited, rigid single-self idea, and the Tangled Self, in particular, tends to become the central, singular focus of that identity. In reality, a "self" isn't a single thing; each of the Three Parts is unique and has its own role to play in our lives. Understanding these Three Parts and how they fit together is the key to beginning the journey of untangling.

Part One: The Tangled Self

I've made several mentions of the Tangled Self so far; now, armed with Dr. van der Kolk's and Dr. Siegel's theories of Self, we can examine the Tangled Self in neurobiological terms and understand its relationship to our other parts.

The Tangled Self is the part of our system that is unconscious and resides in the emotional brain (the reptilian and limbic system). Many assume that thinking happens only in our rational mind. However, the simple belief that the rational parts of thinking control the more primitive, emotional parts is not accurate. Unconscious parts of our brain generate and color most of our thinking.[28] Neurons emerge from the brain stem and spread through our entire body. They travel through our guts, wandering across the heart, lungs, and kidneys.[29] They carry critical information through which the body and brain talk to each other, and the Tangled Self lives in these unconscious conversations.

The Tangled Self's main objective is survival. It acts as our surveillance system, always looking for cues of danger and safety. However, it often misconstrues reality, imagining safe situations to be dangerous or dangerous situations to be safe. When we can't discern between the Tangled Self's perceptions and present reality, we become stuck managing noise and disconnection, feeling power-less to change, grow, and thrive.

Dr. Bruce Lipton, a stem cell and DNA scientist, found that our unconscious beliefs control 95% of what we do in our day-to-day lives.[30] Let that sink in. Most people don't consider how change, even positive change, can threaten their system and impact their identity. They set out to improve their lives by setting goals and mak-ing plans to achieve them without understanding the part of them that created the problem in the first place. In fact, understanding our unconscious systems is the first and most important step in making change stick, which is why getting to know the Tangled Self is a top priority of The Untangle Method.

The Tangled Self is rooted underneath the drama of circum-stances and speaks in the language of "I can't," "I won't," and "it's too much," forming a rigid, limited view of the world. The Tangled Self is mired behind defensiveness and protectionism. It overcompen-sates by exhibiting grandiosity or creating storms of chaos. Or hides by tucking into the blankets of silence, stubbornness, compliance, avoidance, and collapse. However, behind these layers of defenses are pockets of real threats that embody the sentiments of insecurity, terror, shame, despair, and abandonment.

The Tangled Self organizes perceptions based on past experiences, which trigger a deluge of feelings, ultimately driving our behaviors. The Tangled Self is attempting to solve an unconscious problem, but it often creates more harm in the process. Unfortunately, we can spend decades managing the Tangled Self without a flicker of awareness. This is not some failing on our part; it's simply what we humans do. Until we gather skills to strengthen awareness and orga-nize within an integrated system, we default to the Tangled Self's limited structure.

Our visceral lived experiences reside in the Tangled Self, prompting it to respond in ways unique to our circumstances. For the Tangled Self that feels rejected, the world is a chaos of blame, frustration, and outcry, to which it may respond aggressively or hide and disappear. For the Tangled Self that feels it can't say *no*, the world is filled with guilt, temptation, and sin, which cause people-pleasing and resentment. For the Tangled Self that feels it can't fulfill its needs, the world is fraught with danger, and fear, which may have it run away or collapse. No matter what your Tangled Self looks like, we want to understand that it is one part of your system, not all of it. Instead of hating this part of us, let's know that it is, after all, trying to keep us protected and safe.

What enslaves us to the Tangled Self and makes us reenact its painful patterns? Unconscious, punitive self-hate. When we are embedded in the negative self-talk of trying to fix, attack, or perfect this part of us, we get wrapped up in the Tangled Self's war, granting it sole authority over our experiences and creating more fragmentation within our system. We don't want to fight the Tangled Self, but rather, we want to collect its emotional intelligence. The Tangled Self aches to be seen, heard, and validated. As we differentiate present reality from the Tangled Self, we align with greater truth, engaging more actively and empowering new possibilities. Taking this journey with the Tangled Self will be the focus of Chapter 3.

Part Two: The Organizer Self

The Organizer Self wakes up consciousness by rupturing the survival spell of the Tangled Self. It communicates with all parts of our system to establish new rules of engagement. The Organizer Self contacts deeper truths as it detaches from the Tangled Self, providing the structure for integration and growth. It synchronizes with sensations of aliveness and calm that speak the language of "I am becoming." "I am humanizing." "I am arriving."

The Organizer Self links our brain's middle area (the limbic system) with our higher brain (the cortex and executive function). As the Organizer Self becomes engaged, we develop untangling skills to hold conflicting truths and competing opposites, deepening our empathetic, creative nature. The Organizer Self communicates with all parts of our system and straddles paradoxes to access higher states of awareness, offering new perspectives. It engages the emotions of courage, curiosity, acceptance, compassion, willingness, and love to restore a baseline of safety and predictability.

By stretching our internal structure to hold multiple reflections, the Organizer Self hits a pause button. It ruptures denial, taking responsibility for our suffering. As it helps us discern between real and perceived threats, it builds a structure of empowerment. This "Stabilizing Floor of Okayness" anchors us in present reality so that we can monitor the Tangled Self with more clarity and depth. We can then begin to pull out from inner storms of chaos and build new response patterns. As we reconcile the wreckage of the past, we clear the space for a new future.

The Organizer Self is developed through accountability and competency as it investigates the cost of our problems and makes decisions based on evidence. It unlocks the wisdom of emotional learning to move us towards greater connectedness, aliveness, and transformation. What once felt viscerally real in the Tangled Self's experience no longer seems so blinding or perplexing. The Organizer Self lays down a new foundation for growth as it opens the door to a choice—the choice to stand still, look around, and check out all our options. It illuminates the fact that we aren't passive participants in life, but we are the creators of the life we have.

As the Organizer Self questions the myths of the Tangled Self, it finds new levels of love and acceptance through self-forgiveness. It provides us the security to meet needs and restore trust, priming our system for the here and now. The Organizer Self brings all parts home to create pathways for healing, growth, and reclamation. As it separates all parts of our system, it examines all roads to peek around their corners and make better decisions, developing a code of conduct to become better humans, partners, parents, leaders, and organizers. We will learn to strengthen the Organizer Self in Chapter 6.

Part Three: The Creative Self

The Tangled Self, with its visceral, demanding hold on us, is commonly at the forefront of our minds. Meanwhile, the Creative Self may be forgotten or under-utilized. Once the Organizer Self clears the noise of the Tangled Self, we can regain access to this often-neglected part. Like the Tangled Self, the Creative Self also resides in the emotional brain and is rooted in our brain-body conversation. However, the Creative Self is not riddled with a negative bias of "I can't" or concerned with managing underlying experiences of abandonment or fear, but intrinsically understands the interconnected language of engagement, inspiration, joy, pleasure, belonging, and passion. It speaks in the whispers of "I can."

If the Tangled Self embodies our survival system, the Creative Self embodies our thriving system. The Creative Self is rooted in an innate affinity for life and all living systems. It is based on a drive, a thrust that human beings possess to connect and emerge with life. The Creative Self carries inspired images that appear in our unconscious psyche, traveling us into the great mysteries of human experience that we often lack words to describe. It dances within the harmony of life in ways that access our authentic nature and fulfill our purpose.

The Creative Self provides our ability to reintegrate. We are a storytelling, singing, and dancing species. At our roots, we are deeply connected with art, nature, love, and caring. The Creative Self threads past experiences, even suffering ones, in ways that intersect expertise and stir passion. It rewrites our devaluing narratives by leveraging our talents, gifts, and experiences to contribute purposefully. It accesses higher states of value as it interfaces with joy and love. There is a closeness to unity with the discovery of the Creative Self. It embodies compassion for all parts of us, the feeling of oneness with others, and a concern for their well-being.

No matter how much we have been hurt or neglected, this part of us knows how to live vibrantly, love fiercely, and commit wholeheartedly. The Creative Self occupies the pleasurable side of life with a willingness to assert and, at the same time, fully surrender. But to access the Creative Self, we must open towards newness, growth, and variety, which can feel very vulnerable. The Creative Self requires a deep level of connectedness to engage. When we deplete energy fighting the Tangled Self's wars, the Creative Self's impulses get dulled and neglected. As we untangle, we restructure our organizing framework to interrupt the Tangled Self, strengthen the Organizer Self, and finally, reclaim the Creative Self. We will take this journey of reclaiming in Chapter 9.

All Parts Working Together

There is a completeness to the number three, which is used to mediate between two opposing forces or contradictory states. The middle state offers a bridge, an adaptive stabilizing floor to hold oppositional forms, strengthening our capacity for integration, creativity, resilience, and growth. Understanding the role each of the Three Parts plays—and approaching these roles with curiosity, compassion, and love—will allow us to build an integrated whole system. We can learn to embody our experiences more fully, synchronizing with the symphony of our innate nature.

The dynamic interplay between the natural world and the world of the human psyche is articulated throughout this untangling exploration. Nature helps facilitate the most transformative aspect of the work, liberation from an unburdening process and emergent flow with life. Some of us will want to grind into the Earth to make peace with the past. Others will unwind grief by connecting with the wind or visualize color to interpret life. Learning to connect again with ourselves and the Earth, we interrupt the superficial flow of everyday life. Finally, we look into the deeper parts of us, realizing that there is a fundamental ability to love and a yearning to transcend our suffering to care for ourselves and others.

Becoming proficient with The Untangle Method will grant us masterful skills to lead ourselves into wondrous new experiences, rejoining the harmony of ourselves and the world. As you untangle, you will return to a state of vibrancy with all living systems. The sense of emergence feels like a relief, a coming alive. As much as anything, untangling is about coming home. Not to where you grew up, but the deeper home of profound belonging.

Untangle Exercise: Three Parts of the Self

Through The Untangle Method sections, we will spend significant time drilling into the specifics about these Three Parts. For right now, begin to associate words, colors, elements, animals to each one.

❖ The Tangled Self is the part of you engineered for survival and feels powerless to change. If your Tangled Part were a color, what color would it be? What feeling describes this color? If it were an element of nature (earth, fire, wind, air, water, rock, salt), what would it be? If it were an animal, what form would it take?

❖ The Organizer Self is the part of you showing up right now, creating space for the different parts of your emotional brain to connect. Notice the part of you that is engaged in learning. If this part of you were a color, what color would it be? What feelings emerge as you connect with this part right now? What element of nature would it be? If it were an animal, what form would it take?

❖ The Creative Self is the part of you that is hungry for a new experience. It speaks within your nature and is not burdened by threat or fear. If your Creative Part were a color, what color would it be? What feeling describes this color? What element of nature? What animal?

❖ Notice what happens when you separate the different aspects and create an environment for them to engage. What thought or feeling emerges? What parts of nature root you into this synchronized connection? Oceans? Clouds? What word describes the process? It could be home, trees, harmony, curiosity, or anything else.

PART II

STEP ONE:

LOCATE THE TANGLED SELF

"If you want the present to be different from the past, study the past."
- Spinoza

My Untangle Story:

The Color of Memories

This section contains descriptions of sexual abuse and child abuse.

Looking at a dead body makes it real. My father was dead, and the disbelief slowly evaporated as I looked at his face. A pale glow shined on his forehead. My father looked noble, like a warrior. His hair laid loosely around his strong cheekbones, his chiseled face. He looked at peace. His war was over.

Memory can be a cruel thing. It can slice you from the harshest angles, dipping your unconscious into horrible feelings again and again—a moment of humiliation or devastation. When rage rewinds and terror replays, they can spin threads of color that wrap your brain, knotting into a noose.

One memory can become a chokehold, carving out your soul bit by bit.

I was my father's obsession. From the outside, I looked like the luckiest girl alive. I got fancy clothes, toys, anything I ever wanted. Part of me loved this magical power. It filled me with glitter. Hot Air. Taffy pink. But inside, all these gifts had hidden daggers and sharp edges. Something was off, mismatched. After the initial rush of a new present, my body swirled in sensations of dread. What color? Black ink. Impossible to rub away.

We rarely did outings as a family. My father would publicly humiliate my mother for being overweight. Over time, her warm bubbles changed to dark foam. And then my father's eyes turned to focus on me, his perfect image. I smiled and played the part, but his adoration filled my blood with slime. I felt rotten. And I suffocated in guilt, confusion, and self-hate. I longed to combust like a shooting star and be remade into a different life.

When I was thirteen, my boyfriend Jim Ed's smell wafted over me—the sweetness of his deodorant, the smoky floral scent of wood, and underneath it all, freshly cut grass. When his curly locks fell onto my face, I thought I would barrel into the sky and burst into a million colors. I wanted to build a house in this electric charge and never return home. My world tilted; suddenly, I had a reason. I needed to end all the weird stuff with my father. I declared it over. The grossness of his affection. The hand holding at the mall. The late-night visits. The stench of his old man breath. All the ways he demoralized my mother. It disgusted me. And I finally told him so—NO MORE. You have to stop. Stop. Stop.

My father's eyes shifted, cold, snake-like.

I had seen my father's violence acted out on my brothers, but not on me. I never imagined *I* would get choked on the kitchen wall, thrown across the room, or punched in the face. But at that moment, all certainty left me. I had just inflicted harm, and this giant man across from me was capable of killing me. My body was terrified. Bursts of reds—no, purples—no, oranges pulsed through my organs. I wanted to take it all back, weep into my father's knees and promise I would never say any of those things again. He could have my body, have me, have whatever he wanted. I wanted to scream, but my voice was nowhere to be found.

He had a smirk, a puckered expression of disgust mixed with a strange pleasure. Then I heard the word. "Angela Rae, you are just a *whore*, aren't you? You are no longer welcome in my home. You are going to leave, and you are going to take your fat mom with you."

Once he said it, I knew it was final. It was too rehearsed; he was waiting for a chance, and I offered it. He had been feeling rejected by my coldness, and it was now time to inflict his wrath. I had crossed an irreparable line, and I was on my own.

When my father decided to kill you off, you were killed. Instantly. He had done this with his mother, father, brothers, and sisters. And now me. I thought I had an unconditional space with him, but I didn't. I thought I wielded magical power, but I didn't. The terror dropped into the pit of my stomach. I was shit, disposable, worthless. I was a whore. The word kicked my heart out of place. I was without legs, a jellyfish caught in a wave, forced to go wherever the ocean went. What color? Translucent.

Six months later, my mom and I were living in Los Angeles, California, for me to pursue a dance career. The narrative spin made my father look like a hero and my mother sacrificial. Flamingo pink. Gold. Neon purple. Glossy. These colors hurt my eyes. We sold a Hollywood story, and I played the part beautifully. Go, Angie, Go. Become a star. Make us proud.

I was thirteen, and I knew the truth. I was a whore.

———◦◦◦◦———

The skies in Los Angeles were often purple, with splashes of pink hues. Even in the bright morning, the air was heavy and pressed too close. My mother and I moved every six months. We had an old Peugeot that frequently broke down on the 405 Freeway. And we shared a room, moving sloth-like as we floated between the strange realities of Los Angeles and our feelings of homelessness. I bounced between four different high schools in two years. I felt like a piece of furniture, dead, moved around but never able to find its place. What color? Pewter grey.

When I was fifteen, I won the finals of *Star Search*. Performing filled my body with a sense of terror and aliveness—a burst of sparks that let me move out of my head and taste my humanity. But this success stirred rot in my personal life, and what followed sizzled my skin. I was no longer anonymous or invisible. White no longer worked. I felt naked, exposed, hateful as everything clicked toward me. Layers of rage and shame plagued me, making my body feral, animal-like. Everyone tilted towards me, wanting to touch me, draw things from me. My body wanted to scratch their eyes out and hiss down their throats. All colors inverted. Everything went black. I never returned to a dance studio.

Kill. Isolate. Numb. This became my new dance.

For the next ten years, kind people tried to pry inside of me, wanting to help. It was horrible. Everyone needed to stop looking, stop touching, stop trying to get me to talk. I tried bleaching myself white again. But I could never get clean.

I became engulfed in heavy dark ink. My jaws clenched. My limbs were heavy and useless. Overwhelm spewed out of me like a broken sewer line. I felt polluted with aching loneliness. All my comforting friends of food, alcohol, and love had abandoned me. I was shaking, sweating, sick. It was all too much. I needed it to stop. Stop. Stop. The waves were too intense. I wanted to take a knife and plunge it into my skin to stop the anguish. Twisting. Drowning. Screaming. I crashed.

I crawled into therapy when I was nineteen. Spineless, floating, lost, orphaned—no sense of what was up, down, or back. I felt like a zombie. I am not sure how I made it to therapy. It was as if my body had risen in protest and conspired to get help. It was screaming, "No more, no more." I remember the stone-cold therapist looking sideways at me. Her eyes hit me like a splash of cold water. I was in a room being studied, observed through windows at the mental health center at Cedars Sinai. It was a horrible place to have therapy, to lay your soul bare and feel nothing—only cold.

I felt barren, with no songs to sing.

My bedroom shrank to the size of a dollhouse, and the walls pressed up against me so that I couldn't breathe or speak. Then a voice said, "Paint." I picked up oil paints— shades of soot-black, blood reds, muddy browns. I started behind the wall of my bed, circling the entire room with a mural of women's limbs, body parts, heads, eyes. Fingers climbed towards the ceiling, scratching for help. Mouths wide open, voiceless torture. I painted myself into Picasso screams—splashes of cardinal reds, grassy greens, electric blue—until it felt complete. Strangely, I felt stronger, able to tear my fingers out of my flesh and stretch them into the walls to express my truth.

I decided to call my father.

My voice cracked as I confronted him about the harm he did. He laughed as though I had tickled him. And I immediately wanted to puke. He said he had been expecting this call. He had recently read a book, *Fathers and Daughters*, and ordered 500 copies to give to his clients. "I did it all wrong," he said. "At thirteen, you didn't need me to disown you. You needed me to become more dominant. And I failed. I should have walked you into the church and demanded you sit next to me in the front row. But I let you hide out in the back." The more he spoke, the more confused I became. Sickness seeped in. Colors smudged, becoming dirty once again.

I hung up. I spiraled down until my body was silent, but darkness was louder. Numbness entered like a drug. My veins pumped to a violet rhythm. I swirled inside the residue of hopelessness. The spiraling. The circling. The spinning. My eyes squeezed tight. What was wrong with me? What did I do wrong? I waited for a spark or even a faint glow. But nothing. I hovered in the air for what seemed like another decade. And it was.

I wanted to find my way back home, but there was no home. And so begins the journey of untangling.

Chapter 3

Locate the Tangled Self

tangled body: chained to the past, stuck managing pain.
untangled body: unleashed from the past, safe to move.

The Tangled Self narrows our vision, shrinks our capacity, and gets us stuck in "black and white" states, keeping us from seeing the big picture. It carries around a huge reservoir of accumulated negative feelings, attitudes, and beliefs, which become the basis for many of our problems. When the Tangled Self hijacks our entire experience, we feel powerless to change. In this chapter, we will learn how to locate the Tangled Self, understand how it operates, and how it entraps us into one limited experience. Once we have a solid framework to understand the Tangled Self, we can start to make sense of our problems and our part inside them. Like fighting an addiction, untangling requires self-awareness and self-examination to integrate into a more adaptive and flexible system.

Imagine a Fairy Tale

Snow White, Little Red Riding Hood, Hansel and Gretel. Fairy tales can have frightening echoes that linger long after we hear them. Dramatic plots centering around young children abandoned, forced out of their homes, imprisoned against their will, surviving wicked stepmothers, a sleeping coma, or strange requests. Psychoanalyst Bruno Bettelheim regards the cruelty of fairy tales as indicative of psychological conflicts.[31] Their dramatizations can help us symbolically resolve issues. Fairy tales offer a structure to excavate the roots of our stories and illustrate our deepest fears. They teach us valuable skills to overcome difficult times, helping us remember the magic we feel as we reclaim parts of us that we abandoned long ago.

The Tangled Self's power to create emotional reality is a kind of magic spell that swirls unconscious nightmares, bonding with residues of the past. Imagination permeates our entire existence, influencing everything we feel, think, and create. And yet, our imagination can be hijacked by the wars of the past. Survival patterns block our mind's creativity. Instead of creating new stories rooted in safety and aliveness, we end up reliving the same nightmares. Dramatizing our stories in the form of a fairy tale can help create distance from them, making us feel safer to disclose, emote, and release. Rescripting our inner narratives helps us move them into an action-orientated direction, restoring aliveness.

The nature of adversity impacts the body and mind in unpredictable and multidimensional ways. It can be difficult or even impossible to communicate with words. Research has shown that adverse childhood experiences often require approaches that address sensory-based experiences.[32] Expressive arts therapy, music, dance, movement, dramatic enactment, creative writing, and imaginative play are essentially non-verbal ways of expressing feelings and perceptions. Play is a state of mind that fosters flexibility, resilience, and creativity.[33] It engages the imagination in helpful ways that collect potent learnings for transformation.

The body, not the mind, accesses the Tangled Self. When you think about it, our bodies are in a relationship with everything around us. Their interpersonal relationships color our felt experience and shape our neural architecture, forming who we are.[34] Our bodies swirl associations inside all our relationships—even with weight scales, investment accounts, dating sites, sales meetings, credit card debt, scathing emails, or clutter piles—offering us endless possibilities to locate the Tangled Self and untangle its destructive forces. Often, the charge of reactivity, stuckness, shame, disconnection, or whatever issues we have blocking us, resides in our body until it is retrieved and brought into present awareness.

So how do we learn to listen to the body? It is indeed a little mysterious. But we can shake things loose by exploring the interplay between the body and imagination to locate the Tangled Self, allowing us to become nourished by this exploration. As we start metabolizing new information from the body, we begin dissolving things that the mind alone can't. As we become curious about how things move through us and our myriad exchanges, we develop untangling fluency—our body's language to perceive our own experiences.

Tangled Areas of the Body

As we dive in, we want to welcome all of our relationships, even the triggering and confusing ones. We want to press our lips into places that touch our body's experience and say, "Hello." We want to kiss our bodies the way we kiss Mother Earth when we return home. We want to ask often, "How is my heart?" "If my stomach could speak, what would it say?" "If this pile of bills could talk, what do they have to share?" We want to open ourselves to the language of imagination to unearth our stuck states. To invite the body to come powerfully into our practice, we must allow the body to speak, and we need to listen.

To some extent, all knowledge must spring from our interpersonal exchange, as it appears to our bodies and all its senses. How do we take up space, or how do we disappear? How do we engage problems, or how do we avoid them? In these exchanges, we are each a constellation of sounds, signals, images, sensations, and shapes in different configurations. We want to gather insights into how the pieces of the Tangled Self form our worldview. As we connect the dots, we build *coherency*, an ability to see a picture that does make sense, laying down a strong foundation of awareness.

At the beginning of untangling, there can be a period of rebellion and dread about the prospects of confronting your life. Let me assure you that untangling becomes like the sudden relief of inner pressure, the easing of suffering. However, it does require courage to play. As we gather untangling skills, it becomes easier to acknowledge the Tangled Self, reverse inquiry, and let go. Although it can be initially difficult to face uncomfortable truths and experience feelings, there are pathways of engendered hope throughout this experience.

Let's merge our body-brain conversation.

Where do you want to have the most significant impact on your life? Where are you hiding or thinking small? Where do you block yourself from being more seen or from taking brave risks? Is there a room or a pile of clutter that is overwhelming you? Perhaps a neglected instrument or a hobby you abandoned?

If you struggle to locate an area, scan the list below. Check in with your body for thirty seconds to identify if pain or pleasure is associated with a relationship. Circle an area where pain overrides pleasure; or, if you experience deadness or numbness, circle "confused."

Money	Pain	Pleasure	Confused
Sex	Pain	Pleasure	Confused
Dating	Pain	Pleasure	Confused
Opening your heart	Pain	Pleasure	Confused
Commitment	Pain	Pleasure	Confused
Setting boundaries	Pain	Pleasure	Confused

Asking for what you want	Pain	Pleasure	Confused
Bedroom Closet	Pain	Pleasure	Confused
Work	Pain	Pleasure	Confused
Friendships	Pain	Pleasure	Confused
Your age	Pain	Pleasure	Confused
Family	Pain	Pleasure	Confused
Time	Pain	Pleasure	Confused

Add specific areas for you:

When we are shrouded in vagueness, we struggle to know what to do or where to go. Seemingly senseless behaviors become clear once you curiously dive into the body's wisdom. Our bodies have far more knowledge and intelligence than we can imagine. If our bodies are not excited to transform, they will override all self-willed attempts. Healing begins with befriending our bodies. We don't have to love our bodies, at least not at first. That is often too much to ask. But let's get curious about them and start listening to them, if only a little bit.

Once we locate the Tangled Self, we make space for new under-lying impulses and other parts of us to rise to the surface. It is in this collaborative process that the pattern can resolve. Developing bodily awareness and experiencing the world through it becomes a radical act of self-reclamation. When we connect the conversation between our body and imagination, things that used to baffle us start to make sense.

Mismatched Messages

To locate the Tangled Self, we must first understand its *mismatched message*. A mismatched message is a thought pattern that embeds a circuit of memories, triggers, images, sensations, and emotions. Mismatched messages may begin with an impulse to move towards a new direction or goal but are unconsciously coupled with a threat. For example, *If I do this, then bad things may happen.* This belief is reinforced over time, creating a wiring system that holds behavior patterns in place.

Many varieties of common mismatched messages may plague us, such as, "If I let people see me, I will be rejected," "If I become ambitious, I will be hated," or "If I open my heart to love, I will be humiliated," but they may embody any fearful or triggering idea. Mismatched messages may not make logical sense, but they do make biological sense. Retrieved messages are often specific and completely coherent in the context of our experiences and efforts to avoid harm. They program a memorized set of behaviors, habits, feelings, beliefs, and perceptions, like a scripted theater play, seeking protection.

These messages are "mismatched" in that they are ill-fitted for our lives today. Mismatched messages have preconceived biases based on times—potentially years or decades—long past. At one point, they made sense or fit with one experience; often, these formative experiences occurred at a young age when we lacked autonomy and agency to address them in healthy ways. However, many of us, years later, continue to stay enslaved to their emotional power, impairing our ability to grow. Even though reality has changed, our responses to the world remain the same.

Mismatched messages are stored in our body's visceral responses and unconscious mind, organizing our interpersonal exchanges. They wire us into the Tangled Self and produce repetitive experiences that drain our creative resources. Mismatched messages can have us act compulsively, misreading cues that blow up relationships, or they can have us shut down, make ourselves small, and miss opportunities. When our mismatched messages are unexamined, they entrap us in a never-ending spiral of undesirable circumstances, often leaving us demoralized or hopeless.

Instead of training our minds to eradicate the Tangled Self or its negative thoughts, we want to bring these underlying learnings into awareness and make our problems unmistakably apparent. As we do, we begin to understand that the symptoms of our problems exist as part of an adaptive strategy to protect us from harm. Here, we can start to build compassion for the part of us, the Tangled Self, that is acting off embedded memories of the past. Remember, the Tangled Self is only one part of us. As we develop awareness, we can start to separate the Tangled Self's experience from the reality of life today. Locating our mismatched messages is the first step: we must interrupt the pattern by making it visible.

Healing depends on our experiential ability to feel *safe enough* to learn. When we are confused about our reality, we feel helpless to change and capitulate to the emotional power of the Tangled Self. But when we build creative resources to listen and fully inhabit our bodies, we can heal. The good news is that when we can separate the Tangled Self's perceptions (historical imprints) from the Creative Self's perception (innate blueprint), we can stop feeling that there is something wrong with us.

Mismatched messages can circle us back into distressful memories or uncomfortable feelings. Please respect your process. If you start to feel overwhelmed or your emotional reaction is not manageable, please take a break, go for a walk, seek support, or return later. Bite-sizing is critical so that you can digest your experience. Also, untangling desired states of sex, money, or love can trigger more intense responses than a less intense area, such as a pile of bills, a neglected room, a sad purse, or a dirty kitchen. You can always start by untangling an area that is less triggering and work from there when you feel ready.

We all have trauma; we are humans. However, please note that The Untangle Method is not engineered to process traumatic memories or treat PTSD or complex trauma. It is designed to locate unconscious relational bonds that keep us stuck, interrupt their automatic piloting, and gather skills to create a new relational experience.

If at any point you feel triggered by unprocessed traumatic memories, please visit the resources in the back of the book to find trauma-informed therapies and resources to help support you.

Limited Structures

A mismatched message is unique to us based on our experience and can comprise any constrictive belief or thought pattern. However, most mismatched messages will ensnare us in one of four major ways, trapping us in harmful organization systems called *limited structures.* Carol S. Dweck's Ph.D. research on both fixed and growth mindsets has shown that the view you adopt for yourself profoundly affects the way you lead your life.[35] A mindset or a paradigm structure is a filtering framework that makes up a model of how we see the world, shaping our visceral experience of everything we know, think, and believe, determining what we accomplish and value.

The limited structure model we will use here has been influenced by the work of several psychologists, researchers, and coaching specialists and modified to fit The Untangle Method. Tony Kirkland's *Structural Alignment* offers a coaching model of six cluster structures that drill into specific neurological behaviors: ambivalence, alienation, abandonment, abundance, integration, and authority.[36] In a therapeutic context, this *schema* offers a cognitive framework that organizes structures to interpret information. The use of schemas as a basic concept to understand the world was developed by British psychologist Frederic Bartlett, who posited that our perceptions are based on a network of abstract mental structures.[37] Jean Piaget then popularized the definition of a schema as both a category of knowledge and the process of acquiring that knowledge.[38] Piaget believed that people are constantly adapting and updating their schema as they take in new information and learn new things.

The Untangle Method understands limited structures as a thematic function of the Tangled Self; our mismatched messages wire us into the Tangled Self's limited structure, driving perceptions that constrict our ability to grow. We will focus on an in-depth exploration of the most common limited structures: *abandonment, isolation, ambivalence*, and *victim*. Most of us will identify with one of these four schemas, but the Tangled Self usually spends most of its time in one. As we learn to untangle, we begin to dissolve the limited structures that hold us back to build an integrated growth structure, the optimal structure for wholeness and wellbeing. In untangling, we reach integrated alignment when we learn to expand connection, increase awareness, attune needs, and restore trust in ways that gain autonomy and contribute purposefully.

Explore which structure your Tangled Self occupies to shed further light on its story. It may be difficult, but try not to be judgmental or defensive if you identify with a limited structure; simply make a note of your response and move on. Occupying one of these structures does not represent a failure on our part. Just the opposite, recognizing what holds us back is empowering and indicates the beginnings of growth.

1. ABANDONMENT STRUCTURE

When the Tangled Self organizes within an abandonment structure, we manage risk or potential loss, worry, and grief. We become rigid, terrified to try new things because there is always the possibility of hurt, failure, and trauma. We hide behind people-pleasing or fineness. We often struggle to speak up out of fear that we will be rejected or left behind. Needs become neglected in this structure, creating cycles of self-abandonment and sabotage. The Tangled Self believes in mismatched messages, such as, "If I claim my life, I will be hurt," or "My desires are dirty, and I should suffer." "If I ask for help, no one will be there." "If I say no, I will be alone."

2. ISOLATION STRUCTURE

When the Tangled Self organizes within an isolation structure, we manage disconnection and pain because we feel isolated from the world. We can work hard to become better than others, swinging between inadequacy and grandiosity. To overcompensate for deep shame, we sometimes chase external validation, prestige, and social approval but end up feeling exhausted and empty. Many of us don't experience intimacy because we are terrified of being vulnerable and rejected. We manage isolation, alienation, and unworthiness through competitiveness. The Tangled Self believes in mismatched messages such as, "If I am not the best, then I am nobody." "If I let you see me, you will not want me." "If I lighten up, people will take advantage of me."

3. AMBIVALENCE STRUCTURE

When the Tangled Self is organizing within an ambivalent structure, we get stuck managing underlying fears associated with responsibility, trust, and commitment. We spend endless amounts of time self-doubting, second-guessing, and changing our minds. We put life on hold, waiting for the perfect opportunity, perfect partner, perfect job we are not sure even exists. This structure has the least amount of risk short term, but it has a detrimental long-term impact. Without commitment and responsibility, there is no movement towards growth and living. The Tangled Self believes mismatched messages such as, "If I commit 100%, I will be seen as a fraud." "When I finally lose the weight, I will have a life." "If I let go of my fear, I will be hurt or feel out of control." "If I make a decision, I will make the wrong one and be trapped." "If I say yes, I will miss out on something better."

4. VICTIM STRUCTURE

When the Tangled Self is organizing in a victim structure, we become entangled in relational power dynamics with others. The Tangled Self can enter this paradigm with the intent to be a "rescuer" but quickly shifts into a victim and a perpetrator. The victim and the perpetrator share the same structure, with both sides feeling victimized by each other. Control, personalizing, threat, and conflict are all part of this structure. When stuck in this structure, we believe that fate is always determined by someone or something outside of ourselves. It sounds like, "Life is unfair. It doesn't matter what I do." And on the flip side, "I sacrificed my life for you. You owe me." Personalizing thoughts like, "What did I do to deserve this?" There is no winning in this structure, only blame, shame, and bullying. Unfortunately, neither method is conducive to learning, and this structure recreates chaotic and traumatic relationships.

I want to differentiate between victimization and a *victim structure*. Victimization is when bad things happen to us. We are all likely to be victimized in some way by external forces. Victims of trauma need support to own their stories of abuse and violations. The *victim structure* refers to getting stuck in a victim mindset; this comes from the inside. We organize in this mindset not because of what happened to us, but rather because we develop a way of being that is rigid, punitive, and unforgiving. This is a limited structure that captures a part of us into a cycle with charged emotional reactivity and rebellion, unwillingness to learn. And this response is what we want to untangle.

Did any of these messages sound familiar to you? If so, make a note of the structure that spoke to you, and let's move forward to the next part. We will learn how everything fits together, bit by bit.

Untangle Experience: Converse with Tangled Areas

The first step of The Untangle Method is to locate the Tangled Self's mismatched message. To do so, let's turn our stuck area or troubled spot into a real person, a fairy tale spell, an evil stepmother, or a cartoon character. Engage those creative muscles! Let's address it as if it can talk back to us and allow another part of us to register the exchange. The more we theatricalize this process, the more awareness and insight we can collect. I use creativity not to trivialize suffering but as a strategy to air it open. Develop your voice, tone, creativity, and theatrical resonance by doing the exercise out loud. Allow dramatic expression to help you understand your relationship more viscerally.

There are intimate reasons our bodies, minds, hearts, and spirits stay in a certain rhythm. We interrupt our automatic response and investigate our relationship with the opposite rhythm to strengthen awareness and integration. To learn how our Tangled Self operates, we need to explore oppositional dynamics to discover its mismatched message and locate our body's visceral threat. If you typically go slow, what happens when you speed up? If you tend to hide, what happens when you become visible? If you under-earn, what happens when you earn? If you prefer to journal, I encourage you to write your responses with your opposite hand. By exploring contradictory and opposing forces, we gather the "why" behind the stuckness, linking our underground world with our conscious world through reciprocity.

To illustrate the exercise, here are a few example conversations between my clients and their mismatched messages. Try having a theatrical conversation with one of the blocked areas where you circled "Pain" earlier in the chapter or with any other area that speaks to you. Once you have located your relational exchange, consolidate it into one sentence, like in the examples below. Get specific with your blocked area. Bite-size it.

Being Seen

❖ If you struggle to be seen, turn your camera into a silly character with glasses and ask, "Mr. Video camera, what will happen if I become seen and put myself out there?" Allow him to respond. Hear the way he speaks to you, gather the colors and tones of the exchange. Dramatize it. Am I safe to become seen, or does it feel confusing, painful, or dangerous to set into visibility? Explore.

Mr. Video camera said to Kathy, "If you put yourself out in the world, you may be humiliated and come unraveled. It is better to hide."

Managing Time

❖ If you struggle with busyness or a packed calendar, turn time into a wicked, evil stepmother, and ask her, "Miss Calendar, what happens if I slow down and rest?" Allow the wicked stepmother to respond. Hear the way she speaks to you, gather the colors and tones of the exchange. Dramatize it. Am I safe to slow down or speed up, or does it feel confusing, painful, or dangerous? Explore.

Miss Calendar shared with Tina, "If you speed up, things will fall apart, and you will be found out to be a fraud and a loser."

Miss Calendar shared with Nancy, "If you slow down, you will be buried alive. It isn't safe. Something might harm you."

Saying No and Letting Go

❖ If you always say *yes* or can't say *no*, ask, "Mr. No, I feel I always have to say *yes*. What would happen if I started saying *no*?" Allow him to respond. Hear the way he speaks to you, gather the colors and tones of the exchange. Dramatize it. Am I safe to say no, or does it feel confusing, painful, or dangerous to say no? Explore.

Mr. No shared with Peter, "If you say *no*, no one will like you. You will be abandoned and alone. Better keep saying *yes*."

Untangle Exercise: Mismatched Message

After taking some time to process your conversation, consider the following prompts using the message that your tangled area spoke to you.

❖ Write your mismatched message on an index card. Read it twice a day and let it bring you back in touch with how true it feels and what else arises. Don't try to analyze or overcome any part of it. Just be with it for one or two minutes.

❖ When was the first time you remember bonding with your mismatched message? What age? Get specific. The work isn't about going back in time to process traumatic memories but rather differentiating this part of you from your present reality. When we can see the Tangled Self from a distance, we widen our perspective, soften expectations, and build compassion.

❖ What hidden problem is your Tangled Self trying to solve? Is it trying to keep you from being hurt, feeling disappointment, or protecting you from danger? Be specific.

❖ What does your mismatched message have you feel about the world? What limited structure does it organize (abandonment, isolation, ambivalence, victim)? My mismatched message makes me feel the world is ___ (unsafe, unpredictable, boring, painful, empty). Be specific.

Untangle Note:

Many clients roll their eyes when I ask them to dramatize their problems. The idea that our problems are attempts to solve other problems is undoubtedly complex. However, it does keep with the fact that opposing forces routinely coexist in our biological system. Encourage just a little bit of willingness to peek around new doorways and engage your creative brain to gather awareness. Here is a note from Barbara:

"If you think this exercise is silly, I GET IT. I took an Untangle Workshop from Angela three years ago. When Angela asked the group to do this exercise with a cluttered area in our kitchen, I thought, REALLY? I was incredulous. All I can say is that I am so glad I did. I was FLOORED by what my kitchen shelf had to say. I had unknowingly placed all my creative writing materials behind a large photo of my sister. It said to me, "How dare you desire a writing career when it is your job to take care of your sister." And at that moment, something cracked inside of me. My life has never been the same. I have written two books, and I am producing creative work that I never imagined possible. More importantly, my body reconnected with my soul. I feel at peace, in a state of balance and harmony."

Barbara's shelf helped her locate an unconscious reenactment pattern that was sabotaging her writing efforts.

Mismatched Message: "How dare you desire a writing career when it is your job to take care of your sister."

Abandonment Structure: Barbara's mismatched message traveled her back forty years to a challenging time when Barbara had to give up her life and care for her sister. At the time, it was necessary. However, forty years later, it mismatched reality.

Problem: Abandoning writing was her Tangled Self's attempt to solve this complex problem. It triggered Barbara to feel guilty, selfish, bad, or risk being kicked out of her place in the family. She consequently buried her inner fire for writing under safer noise and settled, perpetuating the cycle.

Untangled: Barbara's body was bonding with this unconscious pattern until she untangled her kitchen shelf. To her surprise, as Barbara ruptured her Tangled Self's spell, she unlocked space to reclaim her intimate desires for writing. This was healing. This was transformative. This was joyful.

Untangle Exercise: Write a Fairy Tale

Dramatizing our stories in the form of fairy tales helps to create distance, making us feel safer to disclose. Writing a fairy tale can help us understand our challenges in ways we have not been able to, and foster creativity that builds coherency and resilience. Share how it feels when you are shattered with grief or shame: where do the pieces land? What is your greatest nightmare? We want to understand the Tangled Self's inner workings and how it hijacks our lives. Allow your imagination to take you somewhere new and help you build creative resources to overcome your challenge.

Our fairy tale structure will have three parts: a *nightmare*, an *unexpected twist*, and a *magical ending*. For now, we will focus on exploring the nightmare, the Tangled Self's creation. Imagine your limited structure is a frozen spell that causes you to hide, run, or fight. Explore its visceral wars and internal conflicts—states of helplessness, abandonment, hopelessness, isolation, ambivalence, or victimization. Shape them into goblins, bunny rabbits, witches, giants, or science fiction characters.

You can write it in one sitting, or I suggest you bite-size the three sections to interplay with The Untangle Method's Three Parts. As you move through the fairy tale structure, allow it to help you gather creative resources to overcome the nightmare, capturing a little bit of soul magic.

Please, don't overthink this exercise or get stuck in the weeds of perfection. Seriously, write the worst fairy tale ever. As we embrace the spirit of play, we soften, becoming braver. Set a timer and spend no more than two or three minutes on each section of the fairy tale.

Suggestions for the Three Sections:

Section One – Tangled Self's Visceral Nightmare: Once upon a time, there was a _____ [you] who dealt with _____[visceral description of the monster or fairy tale element]. This experience made them _____ [react], _____ [respond], and _____ [do these things].

Section Two – Organizer Self's Resources: One day, something unusual happened. They came across three items that helped them change their experience: _____, _____, and _____ [rocks, superpowers, or practical things]. As they used each one of their items, they gathered specific resources to overcome the nightmarish tale.

Section Three – Creative Self's Actualization: As they rejoined the world, they were able they were able to do_____(open their heart to love again) or experience_____ (contribution or belonging).

Fairy tales have their root in oral tradition. Feel free to share your fairy tale out loud, or you can simply write it down. When you've finished the exercise, tuck your fairy tale away somewhere safe. We will return to the exercise several times in our untangling journey.

The Untangle Method's Framework

Below is an illustration of The Untangle Method as a technical framework representing the Three Parts of The Untangle Method, which correlate to the Past or Tangled Self, the Present or Organizer Self, and the Future or Creative Self. Regardless of your Tangled Self's specific limited structure (abandonment, isolation, ambivalence, victim), it takes the form of a triangle.

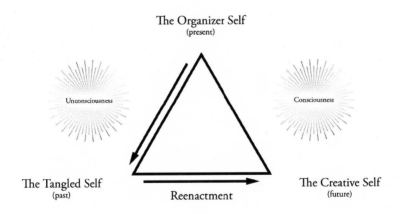

In the triangle formation, the Organizer Self is not aware of the Tangled Self's mismatched message; therefore, we slide down the slippery slope of unconsciousness into painful reenactment patterns over and over again, hijacking our future. Once we discover the Tangled Self's mismatched message, it's possible to interrupt its reenactment cycle and reverse the direction of your patterns from repeating the past to embracing the present.

As we analyze the mismatched message, the Organizer Self is in the control seat, and we have the power to stop reenactment in its tracks. It is not necessary to completely unravel or cease the reenactment cycle at this stage—this will happen gradually—but these first moments of recognition, even if they cause only the slightest hesitation, are crucial to disrupting the pattern. Through the process of untangling, this triangle structure will be deconstructed and redesigned into one of integrated growth.

Untangle Exercise: Reflect on the Tangled Self

Again, we are not looking to attack or fix the Tangled Self. We want to create a space to awaken its unconscious patterning. Take a few minutes to reflect on your mismatched message. Don't try to analyze or overcome any part of it. Just be with it for one or two minutes.

❖ What does the Tangled Self create for you?

❖ How does separating the Tangled Self from the Organizer Self help you see it with more compassion? Be specific.

❖ What one thing would you like to say to the Tangled Self? Be specific. It could be, "I see you." "I am sorry." "I get it now."

Chapter 4

Self-talk

tangled self-talk: a punitive way of speaking to ourselves.
untangled self-talk: a curious way of speaking to ourselves.

What we say to ourselves in the privacy of our minds matters. Our self-talk sets the emotional tone of our inner and outer experiences. When our self-talk is mean, we feel unsafe, responding in ways that foster defensiveness, aggressiveness, and helplessness. This unforgiving language spirals us into an energy-draining mindset that produces overarching sensations of shame and self-hate. It colors our worldview, creating self-fulfilling prophecies. It is the self-talk of "should" and "can't." Without changing our self-talk, we become vulnerable to re-enactment, stuck in the chaotic waters of surviving the past. As we shift our self-talk, we break the Tangled Self's binary hold and start looking closer at the workings of our innate nature. In this chapter, we want to cultivate helpful self-talk. As we continue The Untangle Method's first step, let's work to integrate the Tangled Self through self-talk that is kind, encouraging, and curious.

Imagine a Magnolia Tree

Creamy white blossoms. Glossy green. Intoxicating scents. Something is arresting about a magnolia tree in bloom, bursting with grace and an utter lack of restraint. Magnolia trees have bloomed on Earth for

100 million years. Their flowers opened above the heads of dinosaurs long before humankind occupied the Earth. Imagine strolling up to this massive candelabra of knotted branches stretching forty feet wide, enormous flowers yawning wide open. Crawl under this noble creature, wrapping your body around its strong trunk and savoring its sweet scent.

Now, look closer at the tree. Scan for damaged, crooked branches, injuries from weather or circumstances. Notice that the buds on some branches look weak, impaired, and vulnerable. They may bloom, or they may not bloom. Imagine this glorious tree focusing all its energy on these impaired buds, shouting, "What is wrong with you?" "Why are you so weak, stuck, broken?" "Why can't you bloom like the others?" See an image of a magnolia tree swirling inside of a punitive voice and attacking her vulnerable buds. Feel the cruelty of her harsh tone.

Now, look at the vulnerable buds. Imagine how they must feel, the terror and exhaustion of surviving this incessant attack. Register their visceral defenses, the variety of ways they hide, avoid, or collapse in a search for safety. Hear their screams of outrage. Feel their helplessness as they struggle to belong to the tree. These buds are *not* the problem. They can't help or change what made them this way, nor do they need to be fixed. The tree, in its punitiveness, is the problem.

The tree is creating harm, not safety. It needs to shift its cruel self-talk into one of curiosity and kindness. The tree needs to connect with its inherent value, respecting all its branches—the impaired, vulnerable branches as well as the blossoming ones. When the tree supports the diversity of all its parts, it cultivates wholeness, embodying an integrated growth structure.

The same holds true for us.

As we become fixated on our brokenness, we adopt harsh and unforgiving self-talk. Punitive self-talk is the root of many problems, driving us into addictive cycles of stress, denial, rebellion, and avoidant responses. We are working against ourselves when we attack the Tangled Self, demanding it to get out there and feel *good enough* to join the world. How much time do we spend hating this part of us, wishing it were different? When we look through a harsh, punitive lens, we are bound to see failures and faults. When we scan for all that is wrong and bad, we miss accessing the parts of us hungry to bloom.

Anyone who has suffered from a chaotic life spends endless amounts of time hating themselves. I know I did—the hours of chastising flood our systems with hopelessness, shame, and resentment. It produces unforgiving and terrifying language, which is inflexible and destructive. "What is wrong with me?" "Why am I so broken?" "Why don't I feel *good enough, attractive enough*, or *smart enough*?" We become entangled in the vicious branches of self-hate, recreating loneliness and despair.

To counteract this stress, we become rigid, guarded, and sensitized.. We start managing separateness, shuffling through our experiences with little risk, for we are closed off. Moderating our stress response through kind self-talk helps restore calmness and counteracts the destructive pull of self-hate. Take a moment to track your negative self-talk. If it takes the form of a stone crushing your chest, allow your body to notice it, and let your fingers lift it from you. If it takes the form of noise, notice one instrument you can pull from the noise, maybe a violin? If it takes the form of muddied, confusing colors, notice one color that can convert it to vibrant energy.

There is a deeper underlying intelligence more foundational than your mind, and it resides in your body. Our body-brain exchanges can create new memories and build neural networks. Focusing on nonverbal communication sets the tone for our inner emotional experience, laying down a new path for connectedness. Interrupt your harsh self-talk and say, "Hi there, I am here." It may feel weird at first but allowing your negative self-talk to speak helps you form a new relationship with it and ultimately reshape it. It takes just a little bit of willingness to interrupt the old and turn towards playful connection to rediscover kind self-talk. It is always there, waiting for your undivided attention.

Practicing curious self-talk is a skill that opens the door for more complex human experiences to form. By putting a small moment of space between punitive self-talk and a new response, we allow ourselves to stay present and gain control. Interruption can be its own kind of music, and it is worth taking the time to experience it. We can't change the past, but we can build skills to create new pathways today. As we journey through this book, we will be collecting this language to recalibrate safety and wholeness.

The Language of Untangling

Dr. Stephen Porges' polyvagal theory offers revolutionary insights into the body's stress response.[39] The term polyvagal refers to the vagus nerve, which connects the brain and the gut. The vagus nerve has many branches of sensory fibers that run throughout the body from the brain stem to the heart, lungs, and genitals, connecting every major organ to the brain. The location and function of these nerves help us understand why the body reacts so swiftly when stressed. As challenges and stress increase, our internal state can shift from alert to terror. Being able to hover compassionately with our thoughts and feelings, then take the time to respond, allows the executive brain to modulate the automatic responses of our emotional brain. When we are in a state of homeostasis, the vagus nerve acts as a neutralizer, keeping us calm and open, embodying a felt sense of being safe.

Today our original sense of connectedness has moved dramatically away from our bodies and into our heads. Deprived of safe connectedness, we become marginalized and alienated. Many of us become dependent on regulators such as medication, alcohol, food, and chasing external validation to unhealthy degrees, creating a new set of nightmares. There are multiple forms of harm inflicted when we become disconnected from the body. We lose the ability to detect what is truly dangerous, and similarly, we can no longer discern what is safe or nourishing to us.[40]

Neuroscientist Antoni Damasio has studied emotions for over thirty years and posits that all emotions have evolutionary functions.[41] Similar to how hunger prompts us to eat, emotions motivate us toward goals. Safety is the most important function for our survival, so our fear response, conscious or unconscious, is highly attuned. Safety within ourselves and with other people is the single most crucial aspect of mental and emotional health.[42] Secure connections are fundamental to meaningful, satisfying lives. Without the body feeling safe, our minds cannot heal, attune, or learn.

When we feel safe, it is reflected in our eyes, voice, and body language. We are fully present, calm, and open, embodying a felt sense of safety. Our self-talk is nice and encouraging. Safety isn't a fixed state; all new learning arises from a slightly stressful and anxious experience. Therefore, befriending stress is a critical element in increasing growth, mastering skills, and building resilience. We may never feel completely safe, but we want to cultivate the language of untangling to feel *safe enough*. With a *safe enough* internal environment, we can create flexibility and take significant new risks. We can become a model of kindness to open our hearts and build meaningful experiences with life.

The type of safety I am encouraging travels us into a deeper play within ourselves and the world. It is a dance of crawling back into a kind space to gather resources. We are, by nature, experimental learners and intuitively understand how to engage the world. We were all born with this sense; however, many of us struggle to remember it. When we were children, we were masters of this playful, sensorial language—a way of being we understood before fear, shame, or anxiety got the better of us. It isn't generated from the head but arises from full-body expressiveness. It warms faces, tickles hearts, sparks souls, and springs goosebumps. Here, we are fully present.

Take a moment, feel this language. Its cadence mirrors a tone that engages with puppies, babies, and flowers. It reconnects with the wonders of mystery, the glory of nature. This language remembers the sky we were born under and takes the time to greet trees, oceans, and stars. What color is this language? What instrument does it play? As our internal self-talk changes, our lives change.

Untangle Story: Molly's Sales Meetings

Molly, a forty-year-old real-estate agent with deep-set eyes, attended an Untangle Workshop. She was well-practiced at laughing at herself, but underneath the surface lived rage and frustration, victimizing her. Molly told me that whenever she entered certain groups of people, she couldn't hold her own. Her voice would become faint, and she would disappear. Or she would become a loudmouth, a braggart, and walk away feeling ashamed. She chastised herself for speaking up, and she chastised herself for staying quiet. This ping-ponging experience was impacting all her relationships, and she couldn't make sense of it. She knew she had value to contribute but couldn't seem to connect the dots.

I asked Molly to locate one area, one place that is recreating these sensations. She identified her weekly sales meetings: perfect. To apply The Untangle Method, we need to get specific. As Molly dug into the first step, she located the mismatched message that held her Tangled Self in a painful reenactment:

> "If I assert my voice in the meeting, I will be humiliated and shamed. It is better to be silent."

Speaking up filled Molly's body with pain, threat, and insecurity. No wonder she was frustrated and exhausted—Molly was organizing from an abandonment structure, having to recover after every weekly meeting. I asked Molly, "How did it feel to locate this message?" She shared, "Yucky but real. It is like a thorny pit in my stomach. My arms began to tingle, and my skin burns, like when I was a kid, and I had to compete for my parent's love. My brothers and sisters would often humiliate me. And no one was there to help."

Molly made an association that took her back to her childhood. It was not Molly's job to process her entire traumatic childhood during untangling, merely to notice how a past experience continued to color her present life. I asked her how old she was when she formed this mismatched message? *Eight.* Even though her reality had changed, Molly was still hearing the same punitive voices and operating from the part of her that learned to cower since she was young.

Before Molly could shift to positive self-talk, she needed to identify her negative self-talk. Molly's brutal self-talk rooted her into core shame. It sounded like, "*If only* you weren't so stupid, weak, and needy, maybe then you could have a life," and "Who do you think you are?" Molly shared that her head felt like a pinball machine blasting noise, bells, and dings. I asked her if she could see an image of the part of her holding onto the mismatched message, and what did she see? She said she could see this little girl who looked orphaned, clothes tattered, and shell-shocked. I asked her, "How does it feel to be in contact with this image?" She shared, "Wow. I feel for her. She is so young, frightened, and confused."

I asked Molly to stay with the image. "What do you want to say to her?" Molly struggled through tears but found words. "I see you." "You matter." "I am here." Molly was shifting her self-talk from blame and shame to connection and kindness. I asked Molly, "How does it feel to speak kindly to this part?" She shared, "It feels good. She deserves to be seen and loved. I feel much calmer." Molly was unlearning an old response. Her struggle to speak up wasn't due to some failing on her part, nor did she need to beat herself up over it. Quite the opposite, she needed to separate the Tangled Self and speak to it compassionately. She needed to understand that the Tangled Self is only one part of her, not all of her.

I asked Molly to revisit the sales meeting: "How does this part of you show up there?" Molly laughed, "Oh heavens, she is a mess. Rushing. Disorganized. Dressed inappropriately. Loud. Quiet. Lost. Nervous. Panicked." I asked Molly, "What does it feel like to hold both images, the young, orphaned girl and the disorganized woman?" "Well, I can hear the judgments," she said, "but something feels interrupted. They aren't so loud. When I let myself really see them, I feel compassion. There is warmth around my heart. The woman is a lot like that little girl, frozen and looking to be rescued. Wow, I see it so clearly now. They both need to be seen and loved."

I had Molly write her mismatched message on an index card. "If I assert my voice in the meeting, I will be humiliated and shamed. It is better to be silent." I wanted her to read it twice a day and let it bring her back in touch with how true it really feels *today*. Explore what, if anything, falls away or arises as she connects with it.

The next week, she returned alive with clarity. "I had it all wrong. It is when I don't own my voice that pain and suffering happen. It is better for me to share, connect, and speak. I think I just get in my way and don't trust myself."

Molly was erasing bits and pieces of her mismatched message and becoming available for a new experience. I asked Molly to explore another part of herself, a small part that wants to thrive in the experience of the sales meeting. Travel below the trauma and drama of life circumstances and speak to a part of her that isn't frightened but innately feels *safe enough* to explore a new experience; try using the same words. "I see you." "You matter." "I am here." After a few minutes, Molly shared, "I see this other part of me. She is bold. She has a lot of fire, but she is beautifully dressed and articulate. She has a real sense of her value. My skin feels tingly. I can see her."

I asked, "How does it feel to contact and hold both images, a lost, disorganized woman and a woman knowing her deep value, engaged, and present?" She shared, "It is so strange. I don't have words. It's like they have been here this whole time, and I am just now noticing them. And that becoming a successful woman is available to me now. I have never felt that before."

Untangling was helping Molly establish a new worldview. True behavior change is anchored deeply in the roots of identity change, which I describe as an alignment of your personality with the deepest part of your nature or soul. As Molly reshaped her self-talk, she located her Tangled Self and accessed her Creative Self. She didn't need to fix her Tangled Self; she needed to clear space from the reactive noise to access a part of her that yearned to belong to the world differently.

I was not surprised by the email I received the following week that read:

"It wasn't so much what I shared in the meeting, but it was my experience of 'being' and 'participating' in the meeting. I felt alive, confident, and spontaneous. I created a relationship with the table, the room, and the people that filled my heart with love and joy. After the meeting, I went into the bathroom to weep. My tears felt like medicine, washing over me, and loving me. I felt deep belonging. I feel like I just reconnected with a part of me that I never want to abandon again. There is a love and compassion I can't describe. It was sweet, wordless, and tasted like home. A place I once knew but had long forgotten."

Small interruptions can produce life-transforming changes. It's easy to underestimate the value of untangling one small thing today, one dirty purse, one tangled need, one conflicting feeling, or one cluttered bookshelf. Too often, we convince ourselves that massive success requires massive changes. We set impossible standards, then turn on ourselves for not measuring up. Bite-sizing allows us to build an activating practice that enhances our capacities for new experiences. One small victory can lead to another, then another, getting a little easier each time.

By greeting one tangled area with compassionate self-talk, Molly took the first step that would lead to many more. Did she still struggle to assert her voice in other situations? Yes. But now, she had an orientation to untangle each one and start practicing. Rewiring ourselves requires specificity, vision, and repetition. Breaking down the mismatched message allows us to bring *more* of ourselves into a relationship. It trains us to welcome new experiences, which leads us to developing the confidence we need to restore trust.

Untangle Exercise: Self-talk and Responses

Untangling targets the deepest level of change, a change within your worldview. The relationship we have to our mismatched message acts as a guidance system that enables us to determine our state of being. By focusing on one mismatched message, we create space to dissolve old worldviews and engineer new ones. To do that, we must shift our self-talk.

Many of us become enslaved to punitive self-talk because we try to change our habits or patterns in unhelpful ways. Or we are too frightened to try something new or let go of an old coping mechanism. Our current behaviors are not necessarily the best ways to solve our problems today; they are just methods we learned to use and still resort to. But this is no reason to hate or punish ourselves. Instead of shaming ourselves to death for our old responses, let's be with them differently.

Kind self-talk implements new responses, which in turn shifts the way we see. It isn't knowing all the answers or thinking you're perfect; it is simply reframing how you view setbacks, removing negative bias, and approaching life with the idea that you can handle things—even if they don't go right. We want to work in ways that interrupt old responses and cultivate new ones. I suggest expressing your answers aloud or writing them down. If you provide a space of encouragement for your voice, it will illuminate clarity. The more you theatricalize and play, the more you deepen awareness and understanding.

Explore your sensations as you consider the following inquiries:

❖ Locate Your Punitive Self-talk:

What do you secretly say to yourself? Create space to hear it and say it out loud.

Negative self-talk falls into four categories: *personalizing, polarizing, magnifying,* and *catastrophizing.* You may identify with one of these categories, or multiple. Explore which form your negative self-takes.

Personalizing – blaming yourself for things out of your control. Ex. "We didn't close on the deal; it must be because they didn't like me, or my presentation wasn't good enough."

Polarizing – seeing things in black and white; good or bad, right or wrong, all or nothing, with no grey areas. Ex. "I made a mistake during the presentation, so it was a failure."

Magnifying – only focusing on the bad or negative in every scenario and dismissing the positive. Ex. "I got plenty of compliments on the presentation, but only that one harsh critique matters."

Catastrophizing - expecting the worst. Ex. "If this presentation doesn't go perfectly, it will ruin my relationship with my coworkers, and I'll eventually get fired."

❖ Identify Self-talk Traps:

Locate specific situations where you may indulge in more negative self-talk, like social events, networking, or asking for help. Identifying these traps can help you put in more preparation for mindfulness and working to shift it actively.

❖ Physicalize Your Response to Negative Self-talk:

When your body bonds with punitive self-talk, what posture does it take? Do your hands cover your face, does your chest squeeze tight, does your jaw clench? What behaviors do you engage in? Do you lash out, bite your nails, reach for a drink, go to sleep, run away? Be specific.

❖ Understand Your Response:

Instead of judging your responses, know that there is a good reason you keep doing the same thing. We want to befriend our responses. What is your response trying to do? Calm you down? Avoid pain? Get a sense of worthiness that you matter? Be specific.

To your response pattern that isn't working, say: *"Good, vital response of mine crying out for my attention, I am here for you! What do you need more of from me?"* Listen. Let it speak back.

❖ Shift Negative Self-talk to Positive:

Again, this isn't about feeling perfect or reciting heady affirmations. It is about reframing your experience intimately within yourself. For Molly, it was "I see you," "You matter," "I am here."

For someone who might be triggered by speaking to someone new, negative self-talk could be, "They think I am weird and don't want to talk to me." Positive self-talk could then become, "I am interesting. This person seems interesting. Maybe I will make a new friend."

Untangle Experience: Your Integrated Magnolia Tree

The term "felt sense" was first coined by a young researcher named Eugene T. Gendlin, who worked under psychologist Carl Rogers.[43] Our felt sense locates us both with our body and the environment, having three distinctive perspective elements. One is to feel firmly rooted inside yourself, another is to know where you are in any given setting, and the last is to feel the relationship between your parts to one another as well as your whole-body relationship to the space around you.[44]

Take a moment to ground your feet into the Earth, stand tall.

Feel the Earth's magnetic energy holding you. What is the language of this space? How does the Earth support you? Notice your feet. Do they walk you, or do you walk them? Notice the natural sway within your body. Are you swaying your body, or is your body swaying you? Feeling alive is not a matter of learning new movements but of rediscovering your own.

Imagine your body is a tree.

Feel into its rootedness and its natural sway. Both exist. Feel the rhythm of your body's circles, movements, dances. Feel into all the different parts of yourself and their branches that extend back in time, present in time, and forward into the future. Notice the part of you scared, small, constricted. Notice the parts of you hungry, strong, dying to bloom.

Greet them all with a warm "hello."

Locate breath. Locate presence. Locate stillness. Now, explore your left hand. In your left hand, place your Tangled Self, the part of you that holds onto your mismatched message. It may hide you or collapse your spine. It may have you feel like you are floating in space, trembling in fear, or spiraling in buckets of overwhelm. Listen for thoughts such as, "I can't handle it, I will never be good enough," or "I am not safe. I have to disappear."

Make contact with this part of you.

The Tangled Self is only one part of you. Notice how your punitive self-talk attacks and blames this part of you. Feel it. It may feel like a localized tension in the chest, a knot in the throat, butterflies in the belly, or heat up the back. Notice. The Tangled Self doesn't need to get with the program, *we* do!

Now interrupt it. Shift your self-talk.

Shake like a wet dog and pound your feet on the ground. Let the noise dissolve and become aware of your sturdy trunk, the Organizer Self. The Organizer Self does not need to merge with the Tangled Self or collapse into its feelings. Instead, it wants to stand next to the Tangled Self. Root into the deep, stabilizing force of the Organizer Self. Register its vertical axis, the line between your feet and the tip of your head. This level of practice requires no judgments or critique, distractions or words, no excuses or qualifications. It just is—a state of embodying like meditation.

Greet your Organizer Self with a warm "hello."

Explore the Organizer Self's stance, sway, movement, and posture. It sees life from a different perspective. Find the little nuance of a swirling movement around this internal axis—subtle variations of swaying aliveness and circling swings. Give your body a chance to recalibrate the sway. It is a different rhythm than the Tangled Self. The Organizer Self stands inside the assertiveness of "I am here. I am becoming. I am available." Don't force it. Provide space for the Organizer Self to find its own movement. The Organizer Self creates an embodied space for all parts to come home.

Now, explore your right hand. The right hand holds the Creative Self. Feel into your right arm to access the Creative Self, a part of you hungry to bloom. The Creative Self feels like energy circling through your body to tickle your skin and dance with particles of light. The Creative Self syncs us into the rhythms of birds, flowers, and stars. Allow the Creative Self to circle, move, and sway your body.

Greet the Creative Self with a warm "hello."

What part of your body lifts and wiggles? Register a tiny part of you that wants to claim space vibrantly, if only a little bit. Allow this part to occupy space. Notice a pattern of images, splashes of inspiration for this part of you to open its blooms. Speak to it and encourage it. As much as you may have a shy part, explore the part of you that is gutsy. Sway between these parts. As much as you may have a terrified part, explore the part that is hungry to be uncaged and love fiercely. Sway between these parts.

As the magnolia tree has its injured branches and resourceful branches, so do we. In our left hand, we have the Tangled Self. In the right hand, the Creative Self. And holding space for all is the Organizer Self. It is amazing to wake up and realize change can feel good. So often, we think that change must be painful. Shifting within the body is natural, fluent, and graceful. We are building awareness of something emerging, another part of us capable of coming alive. Movement is at the heart of being alive.

And being alive is something we are all the time. Sway between fear and excitement. Sway between stuckness and movement. Sway between the Tangled Self and the Creative Self. Register your capacity to stand between these worlds. Notice how strong and capable you are. Notice how you can travel deeper. Notice how you can convert punitive self-talk into focused curiosity, traveling deeper within yourself to find your way back home.

Chapter 5

Attunement

tangled needs: neglected or over-prioritized needs, breaking trust.
untangled needs: able to identify and fulfill needs, restoring trust.

ttunement is an intuitive understanding of our needs—
physical needs as well as needs for relational safety,
connection, and love—and the secure belief that we can
sustainably meet them. Without attunement, our creative natures
are drowned out by the cries of our unmet needs. As plants move
towards sunlight, humans ache to move towards our needs. How we
feel about ourselves, the joy we receive from living, depends directly
on how we meet needs and express our feelings. In this chapter, we'll
discuss our *four principal needs* and explore the landscape of the
Tangled Self's unmet needs to gather clarity and insight. Attuning to
these needs will, at last, free us from the Tangled Self's reenactment
experience as we complete Step One of The Untangle Method.

Imagine Penguins

Waddles. Splashes of yellow. Barrel-chested. Zavodovski Island, surrounded by the stormiest seas in the Southern Ocean, is uninhabited
by humans but home to an abundance of chinstrap penguins. Parent
penguins take turns gathering food and guarding their chicks against
the violent struggles of survival. To forage for food, the parents of
a chinstrap chick must brave treacherous waters, thirty-foot cliffs,

freezing temperatures, and hungry predators. If the parents are lucky enough to survive, they return to land with a forty-mile commute to the nursery. With bloated bellies, they are greeted by 500,000 screeching chicks.[45] Unbothered by this chaotic noise, they walk calmly, steadily, and deliberately through the screeches until they locate the calling of their one hungry chick.

Imagine having this level of tenacity and attunement within your life, a bond within your body that isn't bothered by reactive chaos but can laser-focus to create order and purpose. No one told the penguins how to cut through the noise, how to brave the distance and cold, or gave them the strength to do so. Their deep attunement is simply part of their nature. And just as they access an innate sense of clarity, so can we. At one time, we did know how to read our bodies and meet our needs. We intuitively knew when we were hungry and when we were full or when something felt right or wrong. We want to build an untangling practice that drills into organic intelligence. It isn't so much learning a new technique as it is rediscovering it.

When we were young, we were incessant learners, not because we had to be but because we loved to be. We thrived by feeling, touching, sensing, and moving our way into learning. If you have ever watched a baby, you've seen them travel through a complete needs cycle in three steps: locate, mobilize, satiate. When they are thirsty, they attune with their thirst, gathering energy to grab a nearby sippy cup, drink from it, and satiate. They satisfy the needs within this simple three-step process. Locate. Mobilize. Satiate. We want to remember this innate rhythm, for it is inside all of us. As we attune with more precision, we restore trust by developing skills to move in healthy directions.

When we fail to meet our needs, chaos and rigidity ensue. We act impulsively and manage behaviors that send us in the wrong direction. Or we become so needy, not able to tolerate being alone for even a moment, that we fill our time with frantic activities: endless socializing, people-pleasing, talking, working, overeating, gambling, pill-taking. We become stuck in self-doubt and overthinking. When we fail to meet needs in healthy ways, we minimize how we genuinely feel. We can become cold and lack empathy for others, masking our pain in various destructive ways. We may find ourselves blaming others. Or decide it is better *not* to have needs. We shut down, growing more isolated from ourselves, others, and the world.

The simple truth is that meeting needs in healthy ways determines our quality of life. This has been known for as long as human records exist, and yet it is complicated for many. The oracle's advice in ancient Delphi, "Know thyself," implied it.[46] But if it's true, why are we so helpless to understand what our bodies and hearts are longing for? The answer many of us search our lives for is far simpler than we think. Just like the chinstrap penguins, we can embody needs in ways that connect us with our innate nature and access its wisdom.

Needs

While each of us is unique, humans share some fundamental needs which offer a map to the way we make decisions. Maslow's hierarchy of needs is a motivational theory in psychology, comprising a model of human needs.[47] Maslow asserts that needs lower down in the hierarchy must be satisfied before we can attend to needs higher up. From the bottom of the hierarchy upwards, the needs are physiological (food, shelter, survival), safety (order, predictability, control), love (social engagement, belonging, interpersonal relationships), esteem (achievement, mastery, dignity), and self-actualization (highest level, personal realization).

Maslow's hierarchy is logical in that it prioritizes our most basic requirements for survival, on the grounds that we can't be socially or existentially fulfilled if we're starving and cold. For The Untangle Method's purposes, we will focus on an area near the top of Maslow's pyramid, the requirements for personal and emotional fulfillment. The *four principal needs* of interest to us are *certainty* (safety and assuredness), *significance* (esteem and dignity), *love* (interpersonal relationships and belonging), and *variety* (growth and contribution). Everyone prioritizes these needs differently, and the way we rank them as individuals helps explain why we act and respond the way we do.[48] The Tangled Self usually spends most of its time chasing one or two needs at the expense of all others, leaving some over-prioritized and others unmet.

Before you read the needs overview below, make a brief note of your personal ranking of the four needs. Don't overthink this or try to anticipate what the ranking might indicate; simply answer on your first impulse and move on to the reading. We will return to your ranking in the following exercise.

THE FOUR PRINCIPAL NEEDS

Certainty

Certainty is critical for wellbeing, for it is the need for assurance that you can avoid pain and gain pleasure. Certainty pertains to our physical safety, but also our emotional, spiritual, and financial health and well-being.

Tangled **Certainty:** We need to feel safe and secure, or we may become anxious and overwhelmed. The Tangled Self attempts to end all uncertainty by sheer force. When our inner life feels fragile, we can become enslaved to methods of control and resistance. We try to control others or our external environments. However, this exercise is doomed to fail and will consistently leave us feeling powerless, overwhelmed, helpless, and ashamed. To compensate, we may engage in excessive behaviors: compulsive cleaning routines, exercising, and over-working. Or we learn to cut off cravings and desires, which kills motivation.

Untangled **Certainty**: When we meet certainty in healthy ways, we understand we can't control people, places, or things, but we can control our responses. We can dig into uncomfortable truths to gather clarity on how to expand connection and reclaim desires. Here, we collect assuredness that we can meet our needs and, at the same time, motivation to develop our ability to take risks and grow. This certainty is not rigid but flexible. Resourceful certainty secures a steady, calm footing to gather an organizing structure to activate with life, meeting all our other needs.

Significance

Significance is the need to feel valuable. Having our worth validated is critical to our purposeful belonging. Understanding why we are driven to feel significance allows us to utilize this need to help us achieve our goals and find a meaningful contribution.

Tangled **Significance**: When our egos are fragile, we chase external validation, trying to be liked, desired, or accepted. We camouflage deep insecurity with grandiosity, money, power, elitism, or work addiction, yet we struggle to receive healthy praise. We act out in ways that make us feel bad, or we constantly measure success by comparing ourselves to everyone else, which fuels competition and aggression. The truth is that we are neither as small and powerless as we secretly feel, nor or we as powerful and marvelous as we try to appear.

Untangled **Significance:** The most crucial step in emancipating the need to chase external validation is finding more personal rewards in the events of moment-to-moment life. That is not to say we should abandon goals endorsed by society, but rather develop our own mastery and set of goals that embody a richer experience. As we expand our capacity to be seen as the authentic person we are, we will restore our inherent value to meet our need for significance in surprising new ways.

Love

Connection with love is our deepest desire and, at the same time, our deepest fear. If love is your most important need, you have a rich understanding that love does awaken you with the gifts of life. While this can lead to fulfilling relationships, it can also cause you to sacrifice your self-care and over-attune to others' needs, causing you to feel victimized and resentful.

Tangled **Love:** When this need overrides all other needs, we suffer. We can hide in fantasy or find ourselves over-giving to people who do not appreciate our value. To cope, we develop responses of avoidance, addiction, and dependency. Or we spend our lives waiting— waiting to be chosen, waiting to be rescued, waiting for others to change. Fearing abandonment, we may stay in painful relationships. When love is fraught with pain, we shut down, ultimately abandoning ourselves by becoming entangled in negative responses. We manage isolation, loneliness, and anxiety, eroding our self-respect.

Untangled **Love:** Resourceful love expresses itself in many ways. Love facilitates healing and transforms life. When we have an untangled relationship with love, resistance dissolves, and our radiance is no longer hidden. It is a love that encourages trying new things, stretching, growing, and messing our way into the richness of life.

Love emanates from the heart, for it is not a passive love or a wishful love but an embodied strength. And mind you, this need not be romantic love—any important connection, with friends, family, a pet, or even with yourself, can be a healthy source to fulfill this need.

Variety

Variety is the need for change, a critical need that embraces uncertainty to fuel growth. Variety organizes desired states, which stir appetites for novelty and excitement. While we need variety to fuel motivation, over-prioritizing variety can perpetuate a cycle where nothing ever feels like enough.

Tangled **Variety:** Tangled variety builds a consumption mechanism that is faulty, stressful, and ineffective. Although our life may seem full of adventure, we may secretly fear commitment and rejection. These fears contribute to deep feelings of emptiness, where "filling up" with constant activity creates a progressive loss of awareness. There is an arrest of growth and a loss of genuine interest in others, resulting in social problems and increased selfishness. Most of all, we may lose the ability to truly love and trust another person, which results in isolation and self-hate.

Untangled **Variety:** When we meet variety in healthy ways, we shake out of "black and white" states. Variety increases our risk appetite and opens doors to massive growth. Meeting this need helps us explore the world outside our comfort zone. An essential part of knowing ourselves must also be recognizing the limits of our own wisdom and understanding—knowing what we genuinely know and knowing what we have yet to learn. Embracing variety allows us to engage creatively, valuing new experiences for their own sake.

Untangle Exercise: Needs Inventory

In every relationship we untangle, we want to get curious about meeting all four needs in new ways. What need is the Tangled Self chasing? Which need is it neglecting or abandoning? What needs cause you confusion or pain? Which ones cause you pleasure or joy?

As you gather a deeper understanding of how your Tangled Self is meeting or not meeting needs, another part may emerge to give insight into meeting them in healthy ways. Remember, the Tangled Self is only one part of you, engineered to survive. You also have other parts that organically understand how to meet needs and claim new experiences.

Respect your process of inquiry. Baby steps matter. Your needs matter. Consult your prioritized list of needs from the last section or make one now. Number the four needs according to their importance in your daily life, with number one being the most important, four being least important. Then answer the questions for each need, considering the implications of your priorities.

Tangled Self's Number 1 Need:

When the Tangled Self is chasing this need, what patterns of feelings, thoughts, and behaviors does it engage? Has this need been over-prioritized? How could you start to meet this need differently today?

Tangled Self's Number 2 Need:

When the Tangled Self is chasing this need, what patterns of feelings, thoughts, and behaviors does it engage? Has this need been over-prioritized? How could you start to meet this need differently today?

Tangled Self's Number 3 Need:

When the Tangled Self is chasing this need, what patterns of feelings, thoughts, and behaviors does it engage? Has this need been neglected? How could you start to meet this need differently today?

Tangled Self's Number 4 Need:

When the Tangled Self is chasing this need, what patterns of feelings, thoughts, and behaviors does it engage? Has this need been neglected? How could you start to meet this need differently today?

Often, our Tangled Self's Number 1 Need is something close to our heart, strongly valued, while our Tangled Self's Number 4 Need may be something we rarely think about. It may seem counterintuitive to say we are "overvaluing" something positive like Significance or Love, but know that we need not forgo these needs, simply give them space to breathe. Likewise, an overlooked need may hold the key we've been missing to spark joy in our lives.

Feelings

As we seek to meet our needs resourcefully, it may help to appreciate the vital role feelings play in our lives. Feelings are so integral to our day-to-day experience that we take them for granted and underestimate their power. Many of us spend decades pursuing intellectual knowledge, subjugating our needs, and trying to rationalize feelings away. Even saying the word "feelings" can conjure dread, a push-pull dance between the part of us that longs to feel alive and the part of us that is scared.

Emotional maturity has nothing to do with age but revolves around the ability to tolerate feelings. Some become flooded with intense feelings—slamming doors, screaming, throwing things. Others point their emotions inward, resulting in withdrawal, shutdown, or passiveness—less dramatic but also destructive. When we can't tolerate or trust our feelings, we become vulnerable to numbing, overeating, drinking, blaming, and avoiding.

Difficult feelings are not "bad" but are often a sign we're on the right track; some emotions that make our knees weak or stomach queasy are signals of aliveness and potential growth. The capacity to express feelings is essential to living a fully human life. Feelings motivate us to take action, either impulsively or selectively, and learning to regulate them is an essential skill. Emotional regulation lets us build a relationship with our feelings, allowing the sensation to pass through the body rather than distracting or numbing it.[49] This helps us to stay grounded in our present experience and better attune to our needs.

Feelings first evolved in humans to alert us to danger and threats of survival.[50] As we have explored in this book, we receive a constant stream of mind-body reports about the state of the world through our feelings and perceptions, providing us a quick assessment of whether something is safe or dangerous. But what about the ocean of subtle sensations that we are not aware of?

The mind is driven by feelings. Each feeling is the accumulation of many thousands of thoughts. In our adamant avoidance of feeling, many of us have become cold, emotionally insensitive, overly aggressive, or numb. We indulge intense emotions but fail to recognize or value more subtle ones. When we numb uncomfortable feelings, we also numb joy and aliveness. And this leads to deadness. Amid painful feelings, we start to believe it would be better off *not* to feel.

Because many of us attempt to avoid or escape feelings, they become suppressed in the body, creating all sorts of disordered behaviors in our interpersonal relationships. Our attempt to feel or not feel determines our choices and is at the heart of many struggles. When we deny our feelings or repress a feeling out of guilt, we miss the opportunity to learn, heal, and grow. We may try to push these feelings out of our awareness, but they are still there, influencing and shaping our life's decisions. Learning to recognize and surrender to negative feelings leads us to a progressive increase of positive feelings, while resistance to a feeling keeps that feeling going.[51] As we increase our capacity to feel, conflicts with others decrease, career goals are more easily accomplished, and self-sabotaging behaviors based on guilt diminish. Negative feelings become replaced by feelings of acceptance, gratitude, and love towards ourselves and others.

The first step is to allow yourself to have the feeling without resisting or judging it. It is, after all, just a natural and temporary state. As we start expressing ourselves, we can feel more of everything—more love, more joy, more inspiration. We can also experience more sadness, more grief, and more pain. And that is OK. As we explore the diverse variety of our feelings, not repress them or deny them, they open space for new feelings to emerge. Learning to respect feelings for what they are and greeting them will enable them to pass like clouds in the sky and for others to arise.

Untangle Experience: A Feeling Chart

The Feeling Chart is a tool that circles you through a variety of feelings. The idea is to notice, reflect, and surrender to the array of sensations and emotions that live inside one experience. Often, we become stuck between one or two feelings, failing to notice the symphony of other emotions. When letting go of a feeling, focus on the feeling, not on the thoughts.

There is a "ninety-second rule" of emotions as physiological events, for they typically last just a minute and a half.[52] Feelings pass and come to an end. Your body always wants to return to homeostasis. Take the time to understand that your body is an instrument of feelings, with a wide variety of intense sensations, as well as subtle nuance. As you become more adept at expressing your emotions, you will gather skills to select the feelings you want to create.

A Feeling Chart helps to build emotional compositions.

As one feeling or sensation arises, you want to discover where it lives in your body. Does it tickle your skin, tighten your chest, or flush your face? What color does it radiate? What texture? Dark, warm, heavy, slippery? Or smooth, prickly, or fuzzy? As you savor the experience, allow it to pass and another one to arise. Register the space in between the sensations. Spend one minute with each sensation to compile your unique Feeling Chart.

Here is an example of Stacy's Feeling Chart.

Stacy was frustrated with many areas of her life. Her romantic life was dead. Friendships were anemic. Work was just OK. She didn't know where to focus her attention but decided on her closet, which was messy and neglected. I asked Stacy to imagine the closet was organized, closing her eyes to feel into the experience of its completion. Stacy grew clarity and connectedness with each feeling, ultimately fueling energy that moved her in new ways.

Here is a glimpse into her journey:

The first feeling to arise was calmness. As Stacy explored calmness, she felt initial relief. It felt like a weight had been lifted from her chest, more ease in her body, energy to move. Her breath was deeper, calmer. As she stayed with the sensation, she embraced it and allowed it to pass.

As calmness passed, she was greeted by excitement. There was a warm tingle in her arms, making them want to swing—excitement to look better, feel better, live better. As she stayed with the sensation, she embraced it and allowed it to pass.

As excitement passed, she was greeted by overwhelm. Overwhelm felt like pressure. Her shoulders started to tighten, and her breathing became shallow. Thoughts began to intrude. Punitive noise swirled. "I'll have to date, put myself out there." Yuckiness filled her stomach. She noticed her urge to shut down. However, as she stayed with the sensation, she embraced it and allowed it to pass.

As overwhelm passed, she was greeted by nervousness. Nervousness felt tingly in her fingers. She noticed anxiety as she engaged the idea of putting herself out in the dating world. As she stayed with the sensation, she embraced it and allowed it to pass.

As nervousness passed, she was greeted by sadness. The sadness felt like a huge bubble stuck in her chest and that if she popped it, she might not ever stop crying. She allowed herself space to cry, and as she did, she allowed sadness to pass.

As sadness passed, she was greeted by shame. The shame felt like molasses, sticky, slow. It stirred thoughts that made her feel guilty. She heard, "How dare you want anything more from life. You should stop and settle for crumbs." As she stayed with the sensation, she embraced it and allowed it then to pass.

As shame passed, she was greeted by love. Love felt like a renewal. She felt a glimpse of sunshine kissing her face. Her tears changed, and her body softened. She shared, "It seems like such a little thing, but my heart wants a life partner, and I know I would be a good one." As she stayed with the sensation, she embraced it and allowed it to pass.

As love passed, she was greeted by gratitude. Gratitude settled like clarity, like a blue sky. She shared, "It fills my body with warmth, like a bubble bath. Gratitude synchronized Stacy's heart, building a partnership within her. As she stayed with the sensation, she embraced it and allowed it to pass.

As gratitude passed, she was greeted by peace. Peace felt like a warm mist, an inner stillness of calm and confidence. She shared, "Peace to realize I want to love, and I want to be loved. Peace to realize I am alive." As she stayed with the sensation, she embraced it and allowed it to pass.

Untangle Note:

A month later, Stacy reported:

"Well, I did it! It took twenty hours, and I wept, cried, and laughed through the process. But I have a new relationship with my closet. I feel so proud of it. I didn't realize how much shame I had with it until I untangled it. Every day I open my closet, I receive all this aliveness. It sounds silly, but there is a universe inside there, stirring my heart. Last week, I pulled out a beautiful dress that I had never worn and took a friend for a special dinner. Every part of my body felt alive, happy, excited inside this dress. I could feel I was becoming a better friend. I realize I have ways right now to expand love and connection. I am done waiting. I can have intimacy, romance, joy in my life NOW."

By the very act of doing a Feeling Chart, Stacy primed herself for emotional learning. As she expanded her curiosity, she began connecting more fully to her experience. New motivating impulses and decisions ignited. Clarity formed. As she moved through her feelings, pieces of her old world began to fall away, and other feelings began to poke through, opening a new world for Stacy to claim. She wanted more from her life. Stacy's cluttered closet opened a portal for her to rejoin this deeper knowingness and access direction to mobilize towards them with commitment, creativity, and pleasure.

Feeling Chart Prompts:

As birds know flight, when to leave, and when to return, we humans have feelings. The Feeling Chart is a tool to process moving through a stuck area emotionally. Remember, these are 5-minute exercises. We want to locate our feelings and surrender them one by one, not become trapped. We want to allow them to arise and pass like clouds.

Close your eyes.

Focus your attention on the experience inside your body as you travel through seven to nine feelings. Imagine you are on the other side of your tangled area—whether it is decluttering a closet, addressing a neglected email inbox, asking for a raise, or clearing a crowded calendar.

Through this experience, we can acquire new information that helps us connect dots to make sense of our behaviors. If you become overwhelmed by a triggering feeling, please interrupt the exercise. Go for a walk, talk to a therapist, or process it later with a mentor.

Complicated feelings often need additional support.

As one feeling arises, notice where it lands in your body. Feel its descriptive colors, sensations, textures, and tickles. Allow yourself to explore it fully for one minute, and then allow it to pass like a cloud—circling through emptiness and arising of a new sensation.

The first feeling to arise is_____.

Now that this feeling passes, the next feeling to arise is_____.

Now that this feeling passes, the next feeling to arise is_____.

Now that this feeling passes, the next feeling to arise is_____.

Now that this feeling passes, the next feeling to arise is_____.

Now that this feeling passes, the next feeling to arise is_____.

Now that this feeling passes, the next feeling to arise is_____.

The Untangle Method's Framework

It may not look like much, but it is an enormous feat to break open the triangle's top point. Fulfillment of Step One—locating and understanding the Tangled Self—requires you to break the addictive hold of normality and take responsibility for your needs, feelings, and problems.

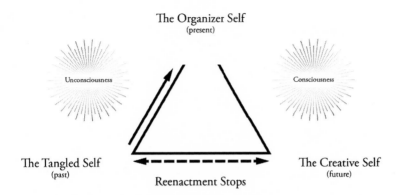

Many of us have lived life on a pin top. At the first sign of stress or confrontation, we lose all footing and slide down into the Tangled Self's nightmarish world. Breaking the spell of the Tangled Self helps us gain awareness for the part of our nature that holds onto the past. By shifting our response to the Tangled Self, we lay down a powerful foundation to activate the Organizer Self.

We exit the wars of punitive self-talk as we develop an encouraging way of relating to and understanding the Tangled Self. The technique needed to perform this shift is inside us, and it is our job to learn how to use it. As we continue forward into Step Two, we strengthen the part of us—the Organizer Self—that dismantles our limited structure to rebuild it in ways we can thrive in.

Untangle Exercise: Needs

Let's take a moment to revisit the Needs work.

❖ Locate, Mobilize, Satiate. There is a rhythm to fulfilling needs. Take the time to practice this three-step rhythm. We want to remember its organic flow with everyday routines: making the bed, satisfying our thirst or hunger, paying bills, etc.

Locate. I am thirsty. Stay with the impulse and mobilize to get a drink. Satiate it. Allow yourself the moment of enjoying the fulfillment. Practice. Practice. Practice. Feel the joy of connecting, mobilizing, and satiating a complete needs cycle.

❖ Return to your Tangled Self's prioritization of needs (certainty, significance, love, variety). What were your Tangled Self's Number 3 and 4 need? Be specific.

❖ Now pick one need, Number 3 or 4, and explore how you could make this need your top priority. If it is variety, how do you increase variety today with cooking, exercising, spending time with a loved one, or playing with your kids? Be specific. Practice locating, mobilizing, and satiating with meeting this need in new ways.

PART III

STEP TWO:

STRENGTHEN THE ORGANIZER SELF

"And the day came when the risk to remain tight in a bud was more painful than the risk it took to blossom."
- Anaïs Nin

My Untangle Story:

The Color of Awakening

This section contains descriptions of sexual abuse and child abuse.

There is no hierarchy in death, only bones. My father's body burned. His rib cage was flapping inside the flames. Arms looked like branches turning inside out to wilderness, ash, dust. The sacred workings of cremating. The beauty and horror of it. The vaporizing of a human body from flesh to spirit—a holy act. A ritual performed with great dignity, rarely seen by anyone. I felt the last heat of my father. Or so I thought.

I'd had little contact with my father during my twenties. Every year for my birthday, I would receive a Holly Hobby card, something appropriate for a five-year-old. America's most beloved character would fall into my mailbox on February 7th with a crisp $100 bill. Dragon fire would shoot down my arms. My eyes would sting. Its wholesomeness always made me want to puke.

Meanwhile, little by little, I pieced together the wreckage of my small life. In my women's groups, I became a little braver, climbing out of my long orange bangs. I was finally able to share my name without crying. The act of becoming visible and taking up space was exhausting. Over time, kind eyes no longer felt violating. As I shared, I softened my feral howl. I was learning to become more human.

I continued to check off the boxes. I got married, returned to school to become a therapist, bought a house, and rescued two dogs. I worked hard, but in my pelvis, guts, stomach, heart, and throat, I was empty. I had accumulated knowledge, but I was fragmented and overwhelmed. For the next decade, I survived barely. Dead. Hollowed. Colorless.

As all things unresolved do, life rhymed, repeated, recreated.

In 2007, two years after my father died, my second son was born, and four months later, my brother Lee tragically died from a heart attack. He was forty-five. Heartbreak. Heart attack. Heart pain. Decades of shame polluted his colors. His turquoise eyes no longer burned. Life caught me in a historical scratch that immobilized me. I couldn't see clearly, or even know what direction I was moving.

Early motherhood tore me into pieces. I couldn't sleep, spell, think, love. I was a walking zombie. Deadness. Spit-up. Vomit. I circled into the hole of darkness, despair, ruin. The war of staying sober had never been so brutal. I was hanging on by a thread. And I was frustrated. What was wrong with me? I'd done everything right. And yet, I was drowning.

In 2008, nothing felt quite right; there were twitches, anxieties, terrors, and pains that seemed constant, ping-ponging between melancholia and hypochondria. My depressive disorder was relentless. There was no pretending it away. It chewed me up, gnawed me to bits. I crawled into trauma therapy, EMDR. I was surprised by how similar

EMDR treatment was to the sensorial exercises I did in act-ing school. Locating memories through bodily sensations was familiar, like drinking water.

My first session explored horrible choking sensations pressed around my neck. It took me back to my child-hood bedroom. I stood there with my feet rooted into the memory, watching until my ribs crunched together and pulverized my heart. I felt intense excitement and terror. It started as a fun game with my father, but then his weight and rhythm changed. Intensity grew in his eyes, tucking his chin into his chest and pushing his elbow against my throat. His pulses became more intense. I was choking, terrified, scared, couldn't breathe. A pillow blanketed my screams.

As I opened this memory, weird images hit me. The col-ors of my room deepened. Red tulip. Cracked pear-green walls. Burnt orange shag carpet. Scents invaded me. Bounce dryer sheet. Old spice. Aged breath. My bones felt like egg-shells. The grief was spilling out of me, sepia dark. I watched as the memory version re-enacted the experience. Flash. I flew out of my body, watching from the ceiling. Blackness fell over me. Ink spilled. Where was my mom? Mom. That one syllable triggered a wave of panic, confusion, rage.

Colors out. Colors in.

Then the thought hit. I had broken something. What if I wasn't meant to unlock all those memories? What if they were supposed to stay tucked away, hidden forever? I felt like I was blindfolded and spinning. I realized I took in thou-sands of drinks not to remember. I puked a million times to get rid of the disgust. I don't think this ever happened again, but moving forward, every form of mild affection, from handholding to kissing my neck, always made me green with nausea. All forms of touch became contaminated. Shame wrapped around my belly like Velcro. Prickly. Painful. Raw. Was I raped? No. Not exactly. Everything became dim and muted in the hues of uncertainty.

I asked her, my mom, about it. "Oh yes, sweetie, I had to leave the house. All that howling made my skin crawl." For a moment, she tried to drink in the memory. Her expression softened as she settled into the heavy air. A whisper of anxiety swirled around me. How old was I? "I don't know, maybe three or four or five." She scrunched her nose like she'd caught a foul scent. "P-H-E-W. I was so happy when it all stopped." Her features sunk deeper into her wrinkles, looking fragile.

"So you left, Mom?"

"Well, yes, Honey, I couldn't do anything. You know your father would have killed me if I had tried to interfere." After a long silence, she said, "Do you know how happy I was when we went to Los Angeles? I was so relieved to get Y-O-U away from him. The way he treated you was so nasty. P-H-E-W."

The cadence of her voice made my temples throb. My father was dead, and all that was left were my fragmented memories. The outside air was thick and muggy. The fluorescent streetlights cast their ghostly beams on this uncomfortable in-between space. I settled into its emptiness. There was no breeze. I caught myself running my thumb in circles, trying to send the thoughts away.

And then something happened.

Pale, watery light broke through. I heard another voice emerge. It circled up my spine and warmed my heart. I could feel a different rhythm. I took a breath. New questions hit. Where was I closing my eyes, pretending things would magically get better? Instead of being angry at my mom, where was I *being* my mom? Cymbals hit. Another question emerged. Where was I pressing too hard against my soul and suffocating its life force? Instead of being enslaved by my father, how was I *being* my father? Vibrations broke something free.

Shortly after, my husband and I divorced. We restructured our relationship in a healthy way that matched truth and integrity. And it continues to this day. Divorce aligned my spine to see him more clearly, and my part in all the drama. I was no longer a victim but a creator of my wreckage. It was both. And as I remember it in this way, I continue to heal. We both remarried, embracing the diversity and joy of our larger family. I am now called "mommy Ang" to his two-year-old adorable son, who greets me with delicious eyes of awe and wonder.

Things were improving, but two years later, guilt curled its fingers around my gut, kicking me out of sync once again. I had just remarried and returned from my honeymoon in a miserable state. My new husband loved spending money, and it made me incensed. My blood bubbled—every shade of red in the universe. I climbed out of the car and went into my office to surgically untangle money. The anguish was too much. I was willing to open my soul and see what was hidden under its triggering flame. And then, I retrieved the memory. It was a word spoken to me thirty years ago. A word that I had worked hard to forget, but there it was, still coloring, influencing, shaping my life.

I asked money if I allow myself to desire you, what will happen?

It whispered, "Who are you to want anything nice. You are a *whore*. You should suffer for all the filth you brought onto your family."

Rage ruptured my denial. I had to hold my jaw back from biting something. The word burnt holes in my spirit. It circled like a raging fire, disorienting me, searing my skin, and branding me unworthy. I tried to rub the sting from my eyes and the disgust from my body. Black ash. Smoke. I could taste it on my tongue. I was finally registering its poisonous gas. This memory had been invisible for decades, carving out my insides piece by piece.

This one word echoed on and on. *Whore. Whore. Whore.* It was like a wild hyena, laughing as it devoured the remnants of my value. As soon as I retrieved it, the story poured back to me. Other memories flooded my mind—memories of begging my father for money. My mom was out of work and depressed, with a body heavy as lead. Knotted, I was in a trap. No matter where my mom and I lived, we were financially tied to him. I had to transact with my father, making sure he felt loved and appreciated. I was alone. I had given up my voice, my truth, my story. And this made me feel filthy. It colored my life like a dirty rag, affecting how I felt about myself, impairing my aiblity to earn, ask for and receive money.

And then I recognized this tangled part, like seeing a shape form in the clouds. I stared back at it, studying its face. Suddenly, the wildness fell away like a costume as it became more exposed. Its snarling, disfigured fury folded in on itself. It looked scared, confused, frozen, young. I witnessed it. I saw all its faces. My belly filled with a warm, iridescent glow as I separated this part of me, my Tangled Self, from the rest of me. I realized this part wasn't bad. It was frozen, holding onto the past.

A web of new colors spun inside me, wrapping me in self-compassion, acceptance, and love. It felt like silk trimmed in gold fringe. As I took in this experience, the echoes changed. I could hear a whisper vibrating through my heart, saying, "You are not bad." "Your desires were not dirty." "You did nothing wrong." As shame ruptured, creative possibility found its way back to my spirit. It was as if I could see color for the first time. I was lighter, more accessible, electric blue. Like a visceral line, my life grew new branches of color, influencing everything I saw, touched, smelled, tasted, felt, and created.

I was forty-two years old when I discovered I was not a whore.

Chapter 6

Strengthen the Organizer Self

tangled mind: burdened by mismatched messages.
untangled mind: converts suffering into inspired learning.

Many of us are suffering from amnesia. We've forgotten who we are and lost track of what we are meant to do. We are wearing cracked glasses that show us our lives through limited structures of isolation, ambivalence, abandonment, and victimization. While the Tangled Self's nature seeks safety and survival, it also fragments truth and reality. The Organizer Self interrupts the Tangled Self by taking off its cracked glasses and adjusting the lenses to help us see clearly. Step Two of The Untangle Method begins with the Organizer Self: what is it, and how does it work to dismantle our mismatched message? This step strengthens the Organizer Self by monitoring the Tangled Self with more compassion. It forges new grounds to travel with our mismatched messages, pulling apart their signals and reclaiming an understanding that matches the reality of our lives today. When all of our parts can agree on what is important, what else might we achieve? This is always the next question when we awaken to the Organizer Self, our source of empowerment.

Imagine Zebra Finches

White freckles. Red rouge cheeks. Tiny zebra stripes. Magnificent birds dance with joy as they sing their love songs with their whole hearts. In nature, young zebra finches instinctively adapt their love songs to those of adult birds. Adolescent male finches spend several months learning complex songs from their fathers. They will practice their songs several hundred thousand times before harmonizing and matching them perfectly.[53] Several *hundred thousand* times! The resulting songs vary widely from bird to bird, but they reproduce a similar process each time. They optimize their learning from interpersonal engagement and repetitive practice.

Researchers have noted that zebra finches look for tiny social cues from their mother or father when learning songs rather than learning through rote memorization.[54] Every day, the zebra finches break down their love song into easy-to-manage parts. As they tear down a mismatched version, they continuously dissolve and rebuild it until they achieve a harmonious match. This is called *reconciliation*. Reconciliation allows zebra finches to expand their repertoire with minimal effort. Richard Hahnloser, a professor at the Institute of Neuroinformatics, researched zebra finches to show that even as they sleep, their brains are spending time reconciling the patterns.[55] Once they have integrated their music, they claim their love song as their own, flying away to find a mate and belonging to their larger life.

Like the zebra finch, we must reiterate, retraining ourselves until our old patterns of thinking and being are untangled, uprooted, and transformed. As we engage our mismatched messages in the present, we strengthen awareness to collect contradictory evidence. The Organizer Self circles back to ask, "Is this really true *today?*" challenging our mismatched message. This jolts *contradictory learning*, a process of exploring what is true about the message and what is not true, which helps make room for creativity, intuition, and growth.[56]

Contradiction is vital to create higher levels of learning. It clears space to retrieve positive memories and responses that question our mismatched message, finally giving it a chance to be rewritten as our love song. These explorations may look like asking, "If I commit 100%, do I *really* know something bad will happen?" "If I claim my desires, will I *really* be hurt?" "What is more true, fear of being rejected or abandoning my desires?" Each time we discover conflicting evidence, we encounter contradiction, helping us "dissolve" a bit of the old message and make space for a new perspective.

If, however, we identify our mismatched message but do not engage the contradiction and rewrite new information, the old mismatched message will automatically re-lock. Why? The Tangled Self's mismatched message has often been around for decades and is part of a complex hardwired system. Like the zebra finch, we want to return to our mismatched message regularly, breaking down its pieces and becoming remade by it.

Bryon Katie asks an excellent question in her book *The Four Questions* to challenge attachment: Do I know this thought to be 100% true?[57] We can't ever know anything to be 100% true, yet the Tangled Self automatically believes every anxiety is 100% true. It may still feel real, but we need to evaluate if our mismatched message is true and real for us today. The Organizer Self stays with the mismatched message until it discovers the 1% "No, I can't know it to be true for sure." Even if we can move the needle down just one point, from 100% to 99% true, this admission ruptures the Tangled Self's emotional spell, opening a pathway for new life to emerge.

As the Organizer Self touches every part of the mismatched message, it rattles the Tangled Self's certainty and builds emotional learning. Emotional learning creates new neural circuits in the brain to build connectedness that wasn't previously working.[58] The Organizer Self dismantles, investigates, and reorganizes within a deeply felt sense; it tears apart our mismatched message, breaking it down to its purest essences, and puts it back together like a collage, in a shape that makes sense for life today. Each time your brain strengthens a connection to advance mastery of a skill, it also weakens connections that weren't used at that precise moment.[59] New learning always creates new neural circuits, but it is only when this new learning also unwires old learning that transformation occurs.[60]

Breaking down and rebuilding our messages allows us to see these same pieces of ourselves differently, unlocking the chains of the past and opening to a new future. Research has shown that our brains have a powerful capacity to change.[61] In the past, scientists thought that our brains are essentially static after we become adults. However, we now know that the brain can change dynamically over time. This capacity to change is called *neuroplasticity*.[62] The more actively we direct the mind into new learning, the stronger our brains and attention grow. This is the precise reason we need to build a repetitive practice; repetition is a key principle in neuroplasticity.[63]

We want to strengthen focused effort and attention by engaging questions and by listening to our responses. The more we cultivate this listening, the more we will become present and aware. And the stronger our ability to distinguish between the past and the present, the greater our awareness grows to make better decisions. We can argue that the only physical reality is the *now*. The past is a memory, and the future is only our imagination. However, how we view our history and our futures influences how we feel and what we do in the present. When we understand that our Organizer Self's focused attention can change the mind, we become empowered to transform our lives.

The Stabilizing Floor of Okayness

The Organizer Self lives in conscious awareness, offering another perspective. It pops its head up above the Tangled Self to see things differently. It establishes a new baseline of inner security by greeting reality in all its visceral dimensions—the experiences flying inside us and all around us, a searing sense of beauty, love, grief, pain, wonder, mystery, and awe. In this way, the Organizer Self understands that we need to become OK with the blood and grit of being human. It builds the Stabilizing Floor of Okayness to handle the rawness of reality. And in doing so, it grants us strength and access to power that is not easily intimidated, ushering in a new landscape of confidence.

The Organizer Self advocates more from life and integrates a vast amount of information to build resilience. Resilience is not an automatic property, but rather it is the learned ability to tolerate negative sensations and create a reservoir of pleasurable ones. Research shows that resilience is not about being positive; instead, it is learning to integrate opposing states and building skills to return to strenuous work and not give up.[64] Clinical psychologist Dr. Christina G. Hibbert compares resilience to learning how to play the guitar.

"When you first try to play, your fingers get sore, and you get frustrated. Some may even quit after the second or third lesson. A resilient person pushes past that initial discomfort and soon begins to realize that there are greater joy and satisfaction ahead. As part of this process, your fingers get tougher and stronger the more you practice. Pretty soon, the process becomes effortless and even enjoyable. The more you play, the more your fingers can tolerate the string tension, strengthening their abilities required to play well."[65]

More than anything, developing resilience relies on practice—after all, it is a learned ability. Untangling provides the Organizer Self with endless opportunities to practice. And though it may be difficult at first, there is no reason a sensitive orchid temperament cannot develop resilience just as well as a dandelion. It takes practice and commitment. The Organizer Self realizes that a thriving life doesn't happen magically but requires *more* from us—more heart, more skills, more bravery, more intimacy, more stamina.

The Organizer Self expands our ability to see life more broadly and deeply. It understands that our lives have worth and realizes that every new piece of information can either create disorder or create harmony. Therefore, it demands articulation and discipline to claim life. If we strip it all away, our deepest hunger is to know ourselves more fully and strengthen our relationships—whether with nature, a partner, individuals, or groups, the Organizer Self discovers joy with living.

Above all, the Organizer Self understands we have conflicting wants; the Tangled Self wants to hide, and the Creative Self wants to blossom. It reconciles both, and in doing so, builds the necessary structure for all parts to collaborate. The Organizer Self operates in the realm of integration by differentiating the Tangled Self from the present and the Creative Self. In this way, the Organizer Self shifts reality.

Untangle Story: John's Relapse

Alcoholism and addiction are complicated, usually requiring a multipronged approach. Neuroscience and trauma resolution have radically shifted the landscape of addiction treatment. If you are struggling with addictive issues, know that you are not alone; please consult the resources at the back of this book to support your healing. You deserve it.

When I first met John, he lived with his father, who kept him under 24-hour lock and key to protect him from relapsing. John didn't want to drink; however, after his seventh failed rehab attempt, the family, in a last-ditch effort, wanted to see if I could help him achieve a new outcome. The following conversations occurred over six weeks as I worked with John three-five times a week.

On our first day, John, a forty-five-year-old man, dressed in a wrinkly, untucked Oxford shirt, long cargo shorts, and a strange 80's bomber jacket, hung his head down heavy with shame. He said, "Sobriety is just not for me, I guess. I muster all this willpower to get sober, and then something happens. I feel this screeching noise inside me. I can't describe it. And then I always do the same thing. I play the role of the 'good student' at rehab. I pretend to be doing the work, but I am not. I count days, hours, minutes until I get out, run away, and drink. Once I start drinking, I just hate myself. So, I need to drink more and more to shut up the noise. It is a horrible cycle. I don't know what is wrong with me."

After hearing John's story, I knew that if John wanted to break this vicious pattern, he would need to locate his mismatched message with rehab. The best way to find these tangled, mismatched messages is through creative engagement. I encouraged him to turn his screeching anxiety into a cartoon character. Shape it, color it, form it, act it out. Initially, he rolled his eyes, but as I challenged him, a little willingness cracked through the surface, and John started playing around with a silly voice. The more extreme and theatrical, the more alive and present John became.

Mr. Anxiety whispered to him in an evil voice, "If you go to rehab, John, you are going to be hurt, manipulated, and abused. You may even be killed. You better run for your life, John!"

I asked John, "How real does this mismatched message feel now that you located it?"

He said, "My body is buzzing with how real it feels. No wonder I run away and get drunk. I feel like I am going to die. But when I sit here and feel it rather than run from it, something crystallizes. I can't explain it. It melts or gets diffused. It becomes separate and much smaller, way less scary. I can still feel it, but it feels more manageable."

I had John write his mismatched message on an index card. I wanted him to read it twice a day and let it bring him back in touch with how true this feels, just the way he was feeling right then, and what else arises as he connects with it. I didn't want him to try to overcome it all at once, just sit with it.

The following day, I asked John about the exercise. He said that, to his surprise, he'd started recalling glimmers of his experiences at rehab that were positive, like working with a kind therapist. He said, "She made me feel safe, but I couldn't put words on it. And I didn't open up to her."

I observed that previously, John had been 100% certain that rehab was a bad and terrifying place, so I asked him how it felt to recognize both messages—that rehab was terrifying and dangerous, and that rehab could offer safety and support. He told me, "It is kind of surreal. It's like there is part of the world that I didn't notice before, even though it was there. It feels like a huge relief."

I was excited to hear this revelation and asked John to continue to anchor himself to this experience and keep letting both exist. The danger and terror of rehab were part of John's reality, but they weren't the *only* part; today, John could also acknowledge hope, support, and safety there.

John's mismatched message provided him a specific task to focus his emotional brain. Was it a mirage, or was it true? If John went to rehab, would he really be hurt, abused, and harmed? Or, if he continued to drink, would that hurt him? Which one was actually more true or dangerous for him *today*? As he explored, the inflamed experiences he had at previous rehab facilities began to dissolve, and John began to reject his mismatched message.

As John circled back to his mismatched message, he gathered contradictory learning. He needed to pull out the pieces of his own experiences and rearrange them within a larger context of his experience. Once John retrieved other memories and associations, he opened a new door to access other forms of relief. Here, things started happening, stirring, and falling away independently.

At the start of our next session, John's energy was different.

"I have been moving around the different words," he said. "The three descriptive words I used—*hurt, manipulate,* and *abused* don't describe rehab, but they definitely describe me. Rehab will not kill me, but my drinking will. I am the one hurting, not rehab—I hurt myself, I hurt my family, I hurt people's time, I hurt my future. I am also the one who manipulates, not rehab. I pretend to be a good student, but I am not. I fool people and use people. And ultimately, I am the abuser. Mostly with myself but also with others. What I thought was happening to me, I see it is actually *in* me, and I am doing it."

John systematically reframed each descriptive word associated with rehab and gave it a new meaning. As he metabolized these different perspectives, he ruptured denial. And as uncomfortable as this was, owning these truths was a huge step for his liberation. John dismantled his victim structure as he took responsibility for his part of the problem. Once John recognized he was the one creating his situation, he simultaneously realized he was the one who could change it. Confidence emerged as he rejoined with a part of him that saw receiving treatment could be safe, healing, and meaningful. It wasn't about self-willing a new change. It was about becoming available for a new experience.

Willpower spreads us thin, draining our energy, and is insufficient to create lasting change on its own. An overreliance on willpower often results in demoralization and perceived failure. True behavior change is anchored deeply in the roots of identity change and experiencing a systematic shift. As John reorganized his relationship with rehab, he created space in his system to align with the aspect of him that wanted to get sober and stay sober. All his decisions and efforts stacked on top of this deep knowingness. Did it diffuse all his anxiety? No. But it diffused enough anxiety for him to create a new step forward in the road of recovery.

John decided to go back to rehab. He picked a small place that was suited for complex cases and people his age. He engaged the process wholeheartedly, collaborating with his treatment team, making meaningful friendships, repairing family relationships, and discovering he could get sober and stay sober. As a result, he left rehab, this time for good.

Interventions look different for everyone. Many interventions are punitive and increase distress, enslaving the cycle. Others are met with kindness to help people restore their sense of dignity. For John, he needed help showing up to receive the treatment he deserved; otherwise, nothing stuck. Wherever you are in your healing, I hope John's story helps you see the tremendous resilience we can garner when we feel *safe enough* to explore our inner and outer landscapes.

Untangle Exercise: Deconstruct Your Mismatched Message

To deconstruct something, we have to understand it well.

The Organizer Self builds a repertoire of experiences that can hold the Tangled Self's perception and simultaneously access a new worldview. As we actively engage our mismatched messages, we start rearranging them in ways that widen our perspective. This is not a one-time deal but a process of reiterating, returning, tweaking, learning, and refining.

Take a moment, locate your fingers, greet them, and say, "hello."

Most of us take our fingers for granted. Please register all that they do and all that they have accomplished. Structurally, the fingers and the hand are among the most intricate parts of the human body. Our fingers will flex at least 25 million times in a lifetime! Many of us have resilience tucked inside our fingers. They have helped us write difficult papers, master an instrument, create beautiful gardens, craft a piece of art. Fingers can cut things apart and place them back together in ways that help the brain make sense of them.

Use the prompt questions below to help you deconstruct your mismatched message. Write it out, pull it apart, and travel with it. Start finding sparks of inspiration or contradictory evidence to rearrange it in a new way. There is no right way in this work. Only you determine how to engage the process.

1. I know your mismatched message feels true, but is it 100% true today?

   Peek around your life, investigate it. Explore worst-case scenarios. Maybe in the past, the Tangled Self couldn't handle the experience, but can you handle it *today*? Test it. Challenge it. If we lock into 100% certainty, there is no space for another perspective to emerge. Find the 1% that is uncertain or a time when you remember an experience that contradicts it. Explore. Allow the process to surprise you.

2. Move the Pieces Around

   Pull the words apart and rearrange them. Organize new pieces from them that match other truths of your life today. What words highlight different parts of your experiences? Often what we project out is what we are doing. Ask new questions. Look at all the angles and sides. Peek around the corners.

3. Move Needs Around

What need am I really trying to meet (Certainty, Love, Significance, Variety)? Locate it. And give it air by saying out loud, "I require a much more interesting and satisfying way of meeting this need." Experiment with how to meet the need in a new way.

4. Strengthen New Responses

What would allow you to let go of the mismatched message and be available to rewrite a new message (more courage, permission, commitment, support, safety, encouragement, trust, love, clarity, certainty, joy, fun, compassion)? Be specific.

Write a new response. A format for building a new response is: *If X arises, I do Y.*

For example, if I get anxious, instead of eating, I'll call a friend or go for a walk. Instead of lashing out when I'm angry, I'll write an angry email and save it in draft form. If a colleague triggers me at work, I'll imagine wearing a raincoat, and nothing they say or do penetrates me.

5. Safety and Danger

Am I safer *today* to hold onto this mismatched message, or am I safer to write myself into a new experience? What is true today? Is it possible this message is hurting me, not keeping me safe?

Determine today which pathway restores your life force and which one blocks it.

Can I be with both? A part of me that holds the danger and a part of me that sees it differently? Explore how it feels to have both perspectives. And at the same time make new determinations.

6. Dissolve:

If your mismatched message were no longer in your life, what three things would you be doing that you are not doing right now? Explore. Color it. Feel it. Allow a new shape to form.

Explore, what would it look like to mess your way into success here? What if mistakes were welcomed, even encouraged, with no one way or right way. What other aspect of yourself emerges and wants a new experience?

Untangle Experience: Walk

If we wait for the perfect time to begin learning, our life will never be perfect enough. We must not wait to begin but understand how to begin again and again. If we train ourselves in the middle of challenging times, our circumstances can help fertilize massive growth. Habit formations accelerate in times of crisis, both in destructive and positive ways. The Organizer Self helps us to embody present life to its fullest no matter what our circumstances. In doing so, it reclaims life force energy to mobilize us in new directions. As penguins have their march of resilience and life force, so do we.

Take a moment to say hello to your feet. Yes, I want you to remember your feet and their ability to walk you into new experiences! Admire their exquisite design, how they make it possible to walk upright effortlessly. Acknowledge how your toes enable you to run, and your arches allow you to push off without falling over. Our feet help us balance in the world and move in ways our minds cannot. The bones in our feet represent a quarter of the human skeleton, and yet we rarely give our feet any attention unless they hurt. Move out of your head and let your feet spring in new ways.

Walk outside five minutes a day.

This walk is not about exercising or listening to the latest podcast. It is about creating space to inhabit your body and restore rhythm. It is about opening and attuning with the part of you that can handle more and receive beauty from the world. Let your body stir with awareness of nature. Like learning ballet, piano, or playing tennis, we must finely tune this skill. Be aware of how your body moves and makes contact with the world. If we want to strengthen our ability to receive aliveness, we must become attuned to our intricate rhythms of exchange, within our body and the world around us.

As you walk, place the Tangled Self in your left hand. Register the way this part of you walks. What curves in your spine? Does it create backward circles, a chaotic pace, or hunching shoulders? Register its rhythm and speed. Feel the harsh language that wraps around it. It spirals in the "I can't. I can't. I can't." Now stop. Break the cycle. Turn your body in a new direction—land in the here and now. Say hi.

Yes, wiggle back into yourself. Welcome the here and now. Welcome aliveness.

Keep walking. Notice how you become captured by the Tangled Self, and at the same time, how quickly you can stop. Interrupt. Move into a new direction. Make circles and zigzags. Notice the choice you have in your feet. Notice the mobility you can create. Notice the aliveness you feel when you shake things up. Notice. Notice. Notice.

Turn, spiral, and swirl in a new direction. Feel the circuits, harmony, and balance. Notice all the directions inside your body, not just the linear ones of forward and back. Allow your body to move in widening circles—your body thirsts for pause, lateral movements, circles, reflections, and diagonals. Instead of obsessing about the right next step, expand your circle and travel into new terrains. Feeling your aliveness is not a matter of learning new movements but of rediscovering your own. It is not just arm and leg movements that need rediscovery, but the movement of the whole body. Register its playful skips and rolling hips. Allow it to take you somewhere new.

Enlarge the movements of your walk. Swing your arms. Indulge the movement. Notice the simple shift in your response. How does your body feel about moving with more energy? As you walk, allow your feet to experience your freedom march of zigzags and circles. Notice the language that wraps around this walk. It is "I am here." "I can handle it." Feel the colors of energy, movement, connection.

Notice how the light hits a leaf.

Keep walking.

Notice how Mother Earth holds you.

Keep walking.

Notice how the air gathers around your cheeks.

Keep walking.

Embrace mystery at every corner and feel the miracle of the blue sky. Keep walking. Take in the purrings of nature and hear all their conversations. Keep walking. Open your heart and hear the singing of birds. Register that your life matters. And you are the creator of your experiences. Let your feet help interrupt, stop, and wake you up. Keep walking. Find swirls, movements, twirls throughout the day as you move from the car to outside, from the sofa to the kitchen, and wiggle yourself into present connectedness.

Keep welcoming yourself home.

The Untangle Method's Framework

The Organizer Self builds the Stabilizing Floor of Okayness to expand our capacity to handle all of life.

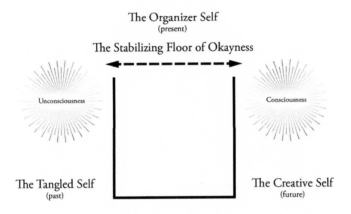

In this step, the Organizer Self comes online, expanding the Stabilizing Floor of Okayness to provide us with a new footing, a new flooring, a new perspective. We don't get there in one day. We get there brick by brick, plank by plank, board by board. The Organizer Self stretches our ability to hold contradictory forces. It acts as a neutralizing force for a new life to emerge. The more we separate the past from the reality of life today, the more we build creative resonance to connect here and now. As we spend less time being hijacked by the Tangled Self, the Organizer Self creates a safe space for all parts to emerge and unite meaningfully, ultimately creating an embodiment of love.

Chapter 7

Hard Truths

tangled reality: mired in defensiveness and denial of truth.
untangled reality: alchemizes truth with accountability.

Many of us need an intervention that breaks the addictive hold of "normality" to open ourselves to a new way of living. To create something new, we must make peace with where we are, our current reality. Ignorance dissipates in the light, and nothing dissolves dishonesty faster than the simple act of revealing the truth. The Organizer Self grinds into the gritty minerals of our deeper truth and welcomes all of it. There is no room for denial, which erodes our ability to reconcile our suffering. This chapter aims to continue Step Two of The Untangle Method by breaking down obstacles that keep us from fully integrating the Tangled Self. To do this, we need to register the cost of *not* claiming the life we are meant to live. Many people I work with find this step challenging, but without confronting reality, we cannot succeed in clearing the path to freedom.

Imagine a Ballerina

Pink slippers. Pirouettes. Magic lifts. We may think of ballerinas as delicate fairies, breezing in gold dust leotards and twirling on satin pink pointed shoes. However, dancers have a resilient capacity that pushes their artistic craft to near perfection. Misty Copeland,

American Ballet Theater principal dancer, has shared that dancers live inside the reality of their bodies every day.[66] Each morning, dancers wake up with an intimate understanding of their body's current state. Today, their body may be able to do a triple pirouette. Or today, their bodies may lose a triple pirouette. Some would find this process intolerable, but Copeland finds it exhilarating. As she says, "It is a chance to be reborn every day."[67]

Copeland was born with hyper-mobility, or extreme flexibility of her joints. The condition is often seen as advantageous for dancers, literally giving them a "leg up" on their competition, and this was the case for Copeland in her early life. However, this initial advantage became harmful in her adulthood, leading to disruption, fractures, and lengthy recoveries. Copeland claims that the injuries happened because she didn't know how to work correctly with her body. She was trapped in a cycle of managing aches and pains until one day she woke up and decided, "No more!"

At age thirty-five, Copeland became unavailable for her old way and available to learn a new one, requiring a different part of her to show up—one that, in my work, I call the Organizer Self. She retrained herself, dissolving old, unwanted muscle memory and rebuilding herself into a different approach to ballet, one that was very simple. For the first time, Copeland developed muscles around her knees to make her legs straighter. She became willing to strip away the hyper-mobility that provided a previous advantage and learn a new form of ballet. This was not lighthearted work but deeply committed work. But as she integrated within this structure, she optimized healing and wellbeing.

We need to do the same.

Though we may not all be world-class ballerinas, part of Copeland's story is alive in each of us. Based on our past realities, the Tangled Self developed coping methods that granted us an advantage, or may even have been necessary to survive, at one time. We don't need to pathologize the Tangled Self or its symptoms, for it is a proper function of our emotional brain that generates learning across decades of life. However, like Copeland's hyper-mobility, these apparent advantages may have done more harm than good for us over the course of our lives. In today's reality, the Tangled Self is often creating harm, injury, and pain.

Like Copeland, most of us need a visceral experience of defeat to become willing to say, "No more!" Admitting defeat is not a sign of weakness but signals courage, a willingness to face fear and grow. To emerge stronger, we need to take responsibility for the problems in our lives and develop a friendly relationship with reality. Taking responsibility is characterized by living harmoniously, making the necessary adjustments needed to thrive. Here, obstacles of the past can now act as stimulants to achieve higher levels of performance. This is where creativity, strength, and productivity begin. Just like a ballerina, we can unlearn old postures and train ourselves into new dances of aliveness. As Copeland shared, "It seems simple, but I do have the ability to strengthen my body and have it do whatever I want it to."

And so do we.

As we dismantle our mismatched messages, we become grounded in the reality of our life today. It may be disorienting to interrupt your Tangled Self and start looking around your life honestly. It may come as a shock that your childhood home was not as safe as you had thought, or maybe you are stunned to realize you had more love than you ever noticed. The gap of reality starts small but can grow for an entire lifetime. And there is nothing you can do until you confront it, look bravely into its eyes, and decide the next right thing.

Rock Bottom Pain

All of us would like an easier, softer way: to never look back or experience grief, rage, or regret. But we must if we are ever to grow. Learning how to metabolize negative emotions is critical for our liberation. This takes a steady, calm approach and plenty of patience, but we are all capable of it.

The main function of denial is to deflect personal responsibility. If you popped denial and stopped the cycle of hiding, what would you be doing in your life? What relationships would you reconcile? Notice what actions you need to take, what feelings you need to express, and what damage you need to repair. Notice what swells in your chest, cracks in your heart, and collapses your spine. Yes, it can be painful to wake up and confront the wreckage of the past. However, pain resisted creates suffering, and pain, when greeted, is liberating. Instead of repeating cycles of denial and surviving demoralization, let's build a spine of courage to handle the truth in all its visceral dimensions.

Say hello to your spine.

Our spine stacks up like a tower of Legos. The spinal column is made of thirty-three vertebrae, divided into five sections. Our spine allows us to stand upright, bend, and twist. A healthy spine has strong muscles and bones, flexible joints, ligaments, tendons, and sensitive nerves. We also associate a healthy spine with a sense of courage or willingness to take action. Becoming reality-based demands such action—making amends, getting sober, asking for a raise, owning up to lies, leaving a bad relationship, sharing our pain, starting to date, or calling an old friend. As we gather reality-based confrontation, we build spines that can handle our uncomfortable feelings.

Many of us have survived a painful loss, and this is what gives us a voice. Often, what we experience as heartbreak—the loss of a job, a marriage, or the plans for our life—may be our liberation, a door to growth that we can't see at the time. Though these experiences are unpleasant, they weave together the tapestry of our humanity. We need to embrace our pain, touch it, and feel it. We need to turn towards our suffering, not hide from it.

Unfortunately, many of us are entrenched in a harsher, dirtier type of pain—the pain of not living—the pain of keeping secrets, living small, giving up. This pain collapses our spines, exiles courage, and spirals us into shame. However, this pain is not to be avoided. It is a pain that needs our attention, for it helps us discover the roots of what matters to us deeply. This pain aches to transform suffering, for it rattles us to the bone and activates urgency to make changes. Just a glimpse of this pain opens the road for meaningful change.

We don't need to solve all our problems today, but we need to grow spines that can confront reality. The Organizer Self creates the space to hit rock bottom with pain. A pain that honors a deeper truth that we are unique and have inherent value to contribute. A pain that says, "No more" to under-earning, over-working, and hiding. "No more" to being overwhelmed, "No more" to enabling abusive systems. We need to register pain to break free of these negative patterns. And we can do it bit by bit.

Taking Inventory

We humans are prone to fall for exaggerated versions of reality. Junk food, pornography, TV, and video games drive our reward systems into a frenzy. For example, when nature's strawberries are converted into concentrated pop tarts, we trigger a larger-than-life biological response. In *Atomic Habits*, James Clear documents scientists who refer to these exaggerated cues as *supernormal stimuli*—heightened versions of reality that produce a stronger response than usual.[68] As we become reliant on heightened pleasure-seeking behaviors, we dull the joy of meaningful everyday connections. Real sex becomes dissatisfying. Strawberries taste bland. Nature seems boring. What many don't realize is that short-term pleasure-seeking is not true pleasure; thankfully, the true pleasure of everyday life will return as you interrupt addictive cycles.

By taking inventory, the Organizer Self wakes up to this deception. We now have the power to turn the tables for the Organizer Self sits in the middle of motivation. It rewires impulses by reconciling how the Tangled Self chases short-term pleasure to escape pain and how the Creative Self embodies true pleasure through purposeful living. The idea of pain and pleasure as basic human motivators was first made famous by Sigmund Freud in 1895.[69] However, it was philosopher Jeremy Bentham who first commented on the role of these principles in human life, stating that "nature has balanced mankind under the governance of two sovereign masters, pain and pleasure. It is for them alone to point out what we ought to do, as well as to determine what we shall do."[70] If we don't take the time to work with pain and pleasure in healthy ways, they both have the power to control us.

Most people don't make changes unless they connect to pain. To some degree, we must feel uncomfortable with the status quo before we consider a new approach. The closer something is to us in time, the more we register the pain associated; it's harder to ignore. The further into the past we go, the less we feel or register consequences and the more denial we can create. Denial pushes everything away, whereas the Organizer Self brings everything close.

You may initially resist a self-inventory, but over time, you will appreciate the clarity it brings. The following exercises will guide you through the process of accessing the Organizer Self's inventory ability. In confronting its actual harmful behaviors, lost time, neglected relationships, and hidden costs, the true impact of our continued living in a tangled reality is laid bare.

Untangle Exercise: Register Costs

Below is a formula I designed to calculate material, financial, psychological, emotional, and spiritual costs associated with the Tangled Self's mismatched message. If you need to review mismatched messages, visit page 61. We want to explore both sides of pain and pleasure as we stir into our experiences to locate these costs.

(Cost of Energy + Cost of Time + Cost of Damage/Harm + Cost of Missed Opportunities + Cost of Stress + Cost of Health + Cost of Money + Cost of Relationships + Cost of Adventure = Cost of Life)

Let's not get stuck on doing this perfectly; many of the factors above are hard to put a price on, but this is ultimately an imaginative exercise. We want to dissolve any illusion that this part of us can build a thriving life. To do this, we must find out just how much our mismatched messages have warped and taken from us, and will continue to take if we don't change. We need to look directly into the eyes of the unhappiness we have caused ourselves and others. As we register painful costs, we become clear with what we don't want and more willing to create what we do want. Be brave and curious.

As you engage in the responses below, quantify the cost into a dollar amount. Yes, really! We need clarity, and dollar amounts help us register pain and absorb costs. If you're not sure what dollar amount to use, try using your hourly pay. The questions below are prompts, but feel free to create your inventory based on your unique mismatched message.

❖ How much *time* has been wasted managing your mismatched message? Scan your life. Locate all the ways you avoid confronting your challenges and the habits you have formed in response. What are they? How much time do you spend each day battling your old habits? Calculate the hidden cost.

Pleasure: Describe in detail if you had all that time back, what could you have accomplished? Would your body be stronger? Would your bank account be more robust? What traveling and activities would you be doing? Use descriptive emotions and list benefits. Close your eyes and bring the image close. Notice the pleasure that arises seeing yourself live like this. Notice the pain that arises by not realizing it. Calculate the missed opportunity cost.

❖ How much has your mismatched message cost you *financially*? Do you overvalue yourself, play the big shot, and waste money? Do you ignore budgets? Do you accumulate debt and long-term financial insecurity? Do you recklessly borrow money, caring little whether it will be repaid? Or do you penny-pinch, refusing to help others or care for yourself? Imagine not fixing this area in your life. Register all the pain, frustrations, stress, anxiety, including all the emotional and spiritual costs. Give it a dollar amount.

Pleasure: Imagine your life is free from money drama and money stress. Describe in detail what would change. What would fall away, and what snaps into focus? What would you be doing? How would you invest it or share it? What activities would you engage in? Be specific. Notice the pleasure that arises seeing yourself live like this. Notice the pain that arises by not realizing it. Calculate the missed opportunity cost.

❖ How much *energy* have you drained, wondering what is wrong with yourself and trying to fix your problems? How tired are you from blaming others or waiting for others to change instead of changing yourself? How much do you exhaust yourself trying to control others instead of building your own resources to thrive? Or by living in fear, worry, self-pity, and depression? Register. Add up all the emotional, financial, spiritual, and mental costs. Give it a dollar amount.

Pleasure: Describe in detail if you had all that energy back, what could you have created? How would these creations change your life? What would you automatically let go of? What feeling would you have? Use descriptive colors and imagery to see the benefits. Close your eyes. See it. Feel it. Notice the pleasure that arises seeing yourself live like this. Notice the pain that arises by not realizing it. Calculate the missed opportunity cost.

❖ How much *harm* has your mismatched message created for yourself and others? Who was hurt, and how badly? Did you injure your marriage or children? Did you underperform at work? Did you lie, cheat, or steal? Did you turn on yourself? Feel it. Add up all the emotional, mental, and spiritual costs of carrying around the added stress, pressures, lies, betrayals, resentments, pity parties, blame and shame, regrets, silent treatments. Give it a dollar amount.

Pleasure: Describe in detail what happens if you convert harm into love. What changes? What tenderness emerges? If your resentment were blown away, what would shift? How does your life look in service of love towards yourself and others? Use descriptive images to capture the details. Close your eyes. See it. Feel it. Notice the pleasure that arises seeing yourself live like this. Notice the pain that arises by not realizing it. Calculate the missed opportunity cost.

Untangle Note:

List Yours:

(Cost of Energy + Cost of Time + Cost of Damage/Harm + Cost of Missed Opportunities + Cost of Stress + Cost of Health + Cost of Money + Cost of Relationships + Cost of Adventure = Cost of Life)

John's example:

John's cost from his mismatched message, "If I go to rehab, I will be hurt, abused, and manipulated." Included: cost of rehabs and treatment $450,000 + cost of harm $2,000,000 + missed work opportunities $500,000 + missed experiences with friends and family $500,000 + missed marriage and baby $500,000 + missed creative experiences $1,000,000 + missed travel and adventure $500,000 + missed time $1,000,000 = $6,450,000 lost.

John needed to register the cost. He needed to make it ugly, harsh, real, and true. He was a talented artist who desired more from his life. He missed out on tremendous opportunities by managing alcoholism. He needed a lot of help, but his mismatched message interfered with his ability to receive it. John didn't need to beat himself up over these losses, but he did need to wake up and understand their cost. Instead of enduring pain, John needed to shatter any illusion the Tangled Self was securing his wellbeing. It wasn't. He needed to poke through the pain and reunite with another part of him that wanted to become someone new. As he alchemized all his truths, he strengthened his commitment to his sobriety. He was alive after all, and there was still time to make a meaningful difference.

Declarations

Yes, it is difficult to zoom into these costs and feel their pain, but it must be. Without registering consequences, we fail to break the Tangled Self's vicious cycles. And when we push the pain away, we push away the motivation for change. Often, the pain of not allowing ourselves to claim life is more excruciating than the pain we avoid by living cautiously, merely trying to survive.

When we look at the hard truths, we realize our actions matter, and we have the power to decide how. Confidence, resilience, and courage are inside us. We build these attributes by digging into rigorous honesty and vulnerability. Once the old ways are relinquished, our hearts and souls have space to then access a deeper part of us, an essence of our innate nature. The dignity of this part doesn't increase or decrease with age or money. It has inherent worthiness and bears moral responsibility.

The Organizer Self strengthens resolve through commitment. When we waver on little decisions (Can I eat this today? Should I take just one drink? Is a little debt so bad?), we deplete our ability to make the big ones. The Organizer Self interrupts uncommitted noise by declaring, "No More!" It stops the behaviors that take us into unhealthy patterns and moves us into the committed bravery of "Yes!" As much as there is a part of you that has reached down into negative behaviors, you have a part hungry to live on purpose. The Organizer Self hears it all and decides the right next step.

Declare your "No more!"s and declare your "Yes!"s.

Feel your spine strengthen as you gather assertiveness with your declarations. Speak them freely. Speak them out loud. Speak them from your heart and howl them from your spirit.

I say NO MORE to_____
(Ex. shrinking away, playing small, undercharging, drinking alone, accumulating debt, holding onto the past, hiding my value, not getting help, abandoning my talents, binging on food, calling my ex, controlling others)

I say YES MORE to_____
(Ex. asserting my value, going to therapy, engaging my talent, helping others, getting sober, loving my life, living on a budget, making my time matter, getting in shape, eating well, appreciating all that I have)

If I die tomorrow, I will regret_____
(Ex. not being fully known in my relationships, that I didn't commit harder, that I shrunk from my challenges, that I stopped myself from loving fiercely, that I didn't take the leap)

Notice the part of you that wants to lead a good and meaningful life. The part of you that wants to convert your pain into meaning.

The part of you that wants to transform your liabilities into assets. Allow this part of you to come out, if only a little bit more.

Untangle Story: Lucy "Go, Go, Go!" Executive

Lucy, a energetic woman in her early fifties, worked as a high-powered executive. One day, she called me in a state of anxiety that overwhelmed her. She was in trouble at work for butting heads with peers and stirring conflicts. When I visited her worksite, Lucy's office screamed in a cluttered rage: papers everywhere, overstuffed filing cabinets, a broken lamp, and unhung pictures. Her office was a small, dark cave with no windows, not at all reflective of Lucy's professional stature. It was confusing.

On one level, Lucy had garnered a sense of pride, even identity, around her hectic work schedule. Even though she worked at a prestigious firm and was well respected, her ego-driven, competitive system also produced crappy results. Lucy was exhausted, and her internal language was punitive and unforgiving. Her schedule was overcrowded with work, leaving barely any time for friends, travel, self-care, or romance. Her energy was unharnessed and wildly aggressive. Lucy's current system was creating sickness, fits of rage, and accidents.

Lucy needed a reality check. She needed to register the cost of her overworking cycle and learn from her pain. Lucy used The Untangle Method to investigate slowing down, the opposite of "Go, Go, Go!" She asked herself, "Does it feel threatening or safe to slow down?"

After a few minutes, she arrived at the thought: "If I slow down, I feel like I will be buried alive. It becomes dark, painful; something bad will happen."

Lucy's mismatched message took her back in time. She recalled being six years old and taking care of her mentally ill mother and younger brother. As she rooted inside this memory, she felt anxiety pinch her chest. Overworking was a similar impulse that mirrored her childhood response. Busy. Busy. Busy. If she didn't stay busy, something bad might happen. While this response was necessary to safeguard her as a child, in today's reality, it was creating stress, accidents, and problems. As Lucy engaged her mismatched message, she connected the dots, and things that used to baffle her started to make sense. She shared of this realization, "No wonder I am always busy. I have been operating this way for so long. But something is unloading."

Survival systems are our default, dominant system. If Lucy was going to thrive with slowing down, she needed to access another part of her that values other experiences, such as love, joy, peace, growth, well-being. I had Lucy write her mismatched message on an index card and look at it two times a day. Just to be with it. Allow it to shapeshift or change on its own. Lucy returned to our next session and shared this immediately:

"Slowing down is not going to kill me. Slowing down is going to restore me to safety and happiness. Going "Go, go, go!" will kill me. I had it completely backward." Lucy did a cost inventory to banish any remaining doubt.

Cost (missed experiences with family $1,000,000 + missed time with friends $1,000,000 + missed marriages and babies $5,000,000 + missed travel experiences $1,000,000 + missed kisses with new lovers $1,000,000 + missed intimate time for self-care and health $1,000,000) = $10,000,000 lost.

The costs were enormous and painful. Lucy also did a breakdown of her annual salary into an hourly rate. When you are working seventy-eighty hours a week, even a large salary can have one under-earning. Numbers don't lie, and they tell their own stories.

Lucy was horrified by her hourly rate. The numbers rattled her to the core, forcing her to confront facets of her life that were not working and feel the brutal tides of sadness, emptiness, and grief. The pain that she wasn't married or a mother. The pain that she neglected friendships and abandoned her desires. The pain that she was over-working and under-earning. Lucy didn't need to beat herself up over the past, but she needed to contact this pain to motivate change.

Lucy continued to wake up, integrating resources to slow down, such as breathing, meditating, and somatic experiencing. As she regulated stillness, she discovered a body that could receive more from life. She confronted her work addiction and enforced accountability by leaving the office at seven o'clock each night. Was it scary for her to leave? Yes. Did she fear she would miss out on an opportunity? Yes. But this is where she became stronger. She trained herself into a new calendar system, using bright color-coding to excite her brain with social activities after work and on the weekends. She took contrary actions to build new connections, and consequently, her life and business skyrocketed.

Three months later, the entire landscape of Lucy's life had shifted. Lucy asked for a 30% raise and corner office, which were both granted and joyfully received. The dark chaos of her previous office was transformed into calm elegance. Lucy was working 20% less and earning 30% more. She rebuilt friendships, discovered romance, and organized wondrous travel adventures. Instead of resenting everyone around her, she became the embodiment of freedom.

Lucy shared, "For so long, I felt like I didn't have a choice. Slowing down forced me to feel things that were hard and look at things that were painful. I always thought I had to work harder, but now I am working differently. I feel like I reclaimed my life. I was so lost and disconnected from who I wanted to become. I don't have words to describe it. Other than peace, love, acceptance. I am not chasing my significance. I am allowing it to shine through me. And I am so grateful."

Untangle Exercise: Boot Camp Life

The Organizer Self redesigns our internal and external environment to rewrite our stories. The work is not solely mental or emotional but all-encompassing. To thrive, we need a foundational self-care system to support our whole self. We need good hygiene with our calendar, time, sleep, money, food, and exercise habits. We can do all sorts of work on our mismatched messages, but if our organizing system is weak, stressed, or disorganized, our resources will be limited and frayed.

We need to think of ourselves as athletes and see wellness as our training. Yes, even if you have never stepped foot in a gym, confront the part of you that wants to get your life in shape. Being the best version of yourself requires healthy routines that strengthen your mental and emotional capacity. Become an athlete with your wellness systems. Below are three critical relationships to consider untangling during your journey.

Time:

Time is the organizing structure that holds our lives together. It is one of the most important relationships we have, and yet, most of us are unsure of how it makes us feel. We fill our calendars up with a busy *To-Do List* that produces tedious experiences instead of a *Vibrant Being List*. Others of us avoid lists altogether, managing chaos or lostness. What is your relationship with time? Notice it. Does it cause pain or confusion? If so, untangle it.

Imagine time is organized by color, emotion, activities, connections. The more attractive and vibrant our relationship with time, the more pleasure we create. Color-coding a calendar system helps restore creativity, variety, and intention. Get an old-fashioned paper schedule. Use colored markers or crayons. For example, when I see blue, I get excited to spend time with my sons. Red for client calls. Green for exercise. Yellow for meditation. Brown for learning. Orange for creative writing. Purple for husband time. Pink for girl-friend time. I use grey for my To-Do List. White for open restorative space. We all need to unplug, recharge, read a book, get lost.

Explore what happens when you see your calendar in color. What color do you need to add more of? Where can you add splashes of new colors? What excites you to see? Play. Explore.

If managing your time is a challenge, inventory it. Where do you waste time, and what more could you do to enhance time in meaningful ways? On average most Americans spend five hours a day between social media and television. Imagine twenty-five hours a week, one hundred hours a month, and 1,200 hours a year. Inventory your "wasting time" habits. What could you create with all that time? Get specific. Maybe you build a vegetable garden, redesign your office space, write a book, or return to school?

Exercise:

You may be surprised to see physical exercise here in this metaphorical boot camp program. But exercise has been shown time and again to be a pillar of good mental health. Exercise stimulates the body to produce endorphins and enkephalin, the body's natural feel-good hormones.[71] These hormones make problems in life seem more manageable. The simple act of adding exercise to your daily routine can add a significant interruption from the damages of stress and survival states. Exercise helps to ground presence, build strength, and accesses confidence.

Many of us have lost connective tissue to do difficult things. Instead of committing to exercise, we make excuses. No matter how out of shape we may feel, if we can move our bodies, we can exercise. Choose something you know you are 100% guaranteed to succeed at. Once clarity is established, you don't have to wait around for motivation; just follow your predetermined plan. The simplest way is to write it down.

I will (Exercise) at (Time) in (Location)

Even if it is a five-minute walk, declare it. Write it down. Give it a color. Put it into your new calendar.

Resistance comes in many forms and responses. What is your relationship to exercise? Are you rigid about your pilates class or overwhelmed by the idea of running? Notice any dreaded eye-rolls, reactions, or noise. Are you willing to try a new gym or a different type of exercise? If you always do yoga, what happens if you decide to go to a boot camp class? Or if all you do is lift weights, try running outside. Notice any resistance. Hear it. Feel it. And tilt into new directions.

Again, we want to stretch into oppositional experience, even with exercise, to access strength and integrate balance. New environments force us to be more present, allowing us to become surprised. We may have forgotten the gymnastics training we had in our bodies until a split movement brings us back to it. Or the joyful 80's dance we have in our hips until we move our body in a new way. Shaking up our exercise routines can help us find resources to thrive. Even if you just start with one little movement. One push-up. One sit-up. One downward dog. One class. One walk. One dance. Start. And keep moving into it again and again. It is incredible how strong our bodies can become when we stick with a new pattern of exercise. However, before beginning a strenuous exercise, please engage your doctor's recommendation.

Sleep:

Our body is naturally designed to go to bed at a certain time. Most of us have a sleep pattern that makes us "a night owl" or "an early bird" or somewhere in the middle. These sleep patterns are called a chronotype and are under strong genetic control. No matter your preference, if you are a "night owl," it is gifted to you at birth, and you carry that throughout your life.[72] Although this pattern moves forward and back at different times in our life span, we usually fall into one category.

When you are mismatched between your biological chronotype and your sleep schedule, you struggle to get deep quality sleep. When you work against your chronotype, there are real consequences—higher risks of anxiety, depression, diabetes, cardiovascular disease, shorter life spans, and immune issues. No matter your chronotype, you need quality sleep to feel good and be healthy. Piece together patterns of activity that help you sleep. It could be walking, listening to music, dancing, drumming. Pay attention and structure a schedule of rhythmic activities that help you sleep.

REM sleep provides a collection of complimentary benefits. Let's call it overnight therapy. REM sleep acts like a nocturnal soothing balm, taking the sharp edges off our difficult emotional experiences and helping us heal. We absorb the information we have been learning all day and integrate it. REM sleep tests specific connections between the recent information and the back catalog you have developed across your life span. So, when you wake up the next day, you have a revised web of associations within the brain. Match your sleep schedule with your chronotype and biological needs. Get help if you need it. Pay attention to that sweet spot where you access the best sleep. Finally, we don't build Rome in a day.

Untangling is a process of repetition. What is most important is noticing. Yes, see the little interruptions, breakthroughs, and decisions you are making along the way. The discerning moments that peek through the clouds and say, "Oh, hi, there you are." The moment you decide to walk in a new direction or say "No more!" to an old habit. The courage you mustered doing a more strenuous activity.

Notice all these little moments and celebrate them. We are so quick to rush to the finish line that we forget our deep, innate rhythm of "locate, mobilize, satiate." Make sure to satiate any new awareness, activity, or interruption you achieve. **Give yourself a little wiggle.**

Untangle Note:

Resistance is a Buddha slap for awareness. Greet resistance.

Two years ago, I decided to write this book. However, I was struggling to find the time. I heard my inner victim's language tell me, "I am too busy." "I have too many clients." "My kids will hate me." "My husband will hate me." "I can't write for shit."

I received a coaching session, and it was suggested I join a workout class. My immediate response: *ridiculous*. Didn't she know anything about me? I go to yoga. I run. I help people reconnect with their bodies. I was a competitive gymnast. I won *Star Search* as a dancer. I spent my childhood in a gym. What the heck? I haven't been inside a gym in over twenty years! Why boot camp? Why a gym? I *hate* gyms.

Wow. I needed to untangle.

I startled myself with the strength of this reaction. So naturally, I signed up for boot camp; I had to explore the resistance I was feeling.

As soon as I entered the class, the "gym smell" made me nauseous. The metal, the chalk, the rubber assaulted me. My mouth watered. I ran into the bathroom and splashed cold water on my face. I wanted to run away, but I dug into my legs and returned to class. It was brutal.

As I stayed with the interval training, I felt my muscles warming. Twenty minutes into the class, all the horrible sensations passed. I felt new ones. Relief. Stillness. Alertness. *And*—pleasure? It swelled inside my body. Muscles began talking with other body parts. The 20,000 hours of childhood training awakened a symphony of connection. My body was strong—it was performing. Confidence shook me and shouted at me. Are you *kidding?* Look what you're doing! You don't think you can handle writing a *book?* Please, you can write a book.

Other thoughts drummed in. Do you not remember the six hours of daily training, the screaming coaches, and the grueling travel? Do you not remember working three jobs and going to school full time? Do you not remember being pregnant, divorcing your husband, and paying all the bills? You can handle difficult things. You can. You can. You can.

Do you not remember?

No, I hadn't remembered my history in this way. I needed my body to rupture my victim self-talk.

After one boot camp class, unstoppable energy emerged. As soon as I was committed inside my body, I found the time automatically. I started waking up at 4 am every morning to write. It was never a time issue; it was a commitment issue. My Tangled Self thought I couldn't handle it, but another part of me, my Organizer Self, proved myself wrong, and in doing so, reclaimed a part of me that aligns to my deeper soul.

The Untangle Method's Framework

The Organizer Self pops denial and right-sizes us into reality. As it does, the sides of the rectangle grind into a more condensed structure of a square, symbolizing trust, honesty, solidity, and stability.

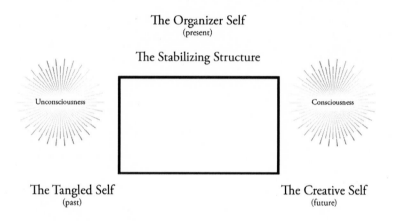

The Organizer Self
(present)

The Stabilizing Structure

Unconsciousness

Consciousness

The Tangled Self
(past)

The Creative Self
(future)

This step requires us to take absolute responsibility. Until we pop denial, many of us will not let go, recover, or build the necessary capacity to transform our lives. At this level of connecting, one can cope with disappointment and effectively handle life's opportunities. As we reconcile our truths, we invite a variety of insights to arise, some painful and uncomfortable. We start honoring a more complex experience to establish inner unity. At this level of acceptance, we become dedicated to resolving issues and finding out what *more* is needed to solve problems.

Untangle Exercise: Accountability

Let's take action towards accountability *today*:

❖ What is one opposition action you can take immediately? For example, if you have difficulty spending money on yourself, what one thing can you treat yourself to? If you need more energy, what new exercise can you try? Be specific.

❖ How can you create more pleasure with your time management? Be specific. How can you add variety to your day, even if it is just a five-minute walk, sitting on the grass, or enjoying a sparkling glass of water? Be specific.

❖ What is one hard thing you would *regret* if you didn't do? Be specific. What would stop you from accomplishing this goal? Be specific. Say your declarations out loud. I am willing to to tell my truth. I am willing to get help. I am willing to commit 100 percent. I am willing.

❖ Do you need more support, help, energy, commitment, skill, confidence? Be specific. What one action can you take to help support yourself today? Be specific.

Chapter 8

Love

tangled heart: closed off and bonded with pain.
untangled heart: safe, open, and bonded with joy.

Confronting reality can make us feel uprooted, off-balance, disoriented. That is OK. We are creating conditions to support a greater life, and this takes time. The Organizer Self is working to become a radical truth-teller as we shift our focus away from the Tangled Self into the center of our being. We are becoming more robust as we rub up against toxic emotions and convert their sufferings into our medicine of healing. The Organizer Self plants us into love, even while acknowledging pain. It remembers our capacity to love and be loved is unique to our innate nature. Love dissovles negativity by washing away our regrets to noursih gorwth. In this chapter, the Organizer Self digs into the soil of love to embrace all parts of ourselves, our bodies, and our stories. This will allow us to complete Step Two of The Untangle Method, strengthening the Organizer Self.

Imagine Recovery

Catastrophic crisis. Smoking explosions. Nuclear fallout. In Russia, on April 26, 1986, a nuclear power plant exploded in Chernobyl. An eerie scene still exists at that ill-fated site, which remains the largest nuclear accident in history and one of the most polluted places on

Earth.[73] More than fifty emergency workers were killed in the immediate aftermath, and hundreds of firefighters left to tackle a blaze
that burned for ten days, sending a plume of radiation around the
world. A 1,000 square mile exclusion zone was enforced, and more
than 350,000 people evacuated. Plant life collapsed, and few animals
survived. Chernobyl's nuclear zone continues to radiate high levels
of toxicity, stopping people from resettling the land. It was assumed
that the area would become a desert forever, devoid of plant and animal life for centuries. However, something unusual happened.

Over the past three decades, Chernobyl has recolonized its plant
life to reseed an abundant forest. Even in the most radioactive areas
of the zone, vegetation began recovering within three years. Because
plants can't move, they have no choice but to adapt to the circumstances they find themselves in, layer on top of the old, and rebuild
anew. As the forest returned, it opened its arms to provide new
homes for all types of animal life. Today, moose, deer, beavers, brown
bears, wolves, lynx, bison, badgers, raccoon dogs, birds, and red foxes
populate and thrive in this once toxic wasteland. Chernobyl, an area
known for the deadliest nuclear accident in history, has become a
refuge for all kinds of animal and plant life to reemerge, finding new
resources to support life.[74]

As Chernobyl has found its way back, we can find ours.

Biologist Janine Benyus suggests shifting one's perspective from
learning about nature to learning from nature.[75] For billions of years,
animals and plants have been solving many of the problems we deal
with today. Each one has found what works, what is appropriate, and
what lasts. All animals and plants are held in a delicate balance, and
every entity has its purpose and role in its ecosystem. Nature has a
resilient capacity to recover from horrible events, and so do we. We
don't need to purify ourselves into pristine conditions to thrive. We
need to become more resourceful and flexible like nature, building

ways to fortify a structure for integration and growth. This way of organizing gives us a clear view of the world, and thus a sense of security.

Under the right conditions, our bodies will heal and transform. The human body is an incredible organism of change. The natural state within our body is engineered to let go, regenerate, and rebuild. Our bodies create a new liver every six weeks, a new stomach lining every four days, and stomach cells every five minutes. By the time you have finished reading this sentence, 50 million cells will have died and been replaced by others.[76] Your heart beats without your directing it. Seeds turn into flowers, embryos into babies, and buds into blooms. When we lose touch with these organic forces, we start pushing against life, losing our ability to trust the process.

When we manage broken hearts, it is easy to forget how resourceful and capable we are. At the center of all personal traps is our inability to love and be loved. The Organizer Self breaks down barriers around our hearts to open new pathways for emergent life. The gateway to engaging from a place of recovery is the ability to open the heart and become touched by love. The more attuned we become to love, the more we root into a rhythm with life itself. When we trust within a process of love, we become more free-flowing, and risk-taking becomes less frightening. As we reclaim love, we shift the rules of engagement and fall back in love with the world, growing us a deeper capacity to embrace the wonders of change.

The Muscle of Love

There is a boldness in not editing one's story. To not rip one part out and replace it with another page but sit inside of it. By telling our stories and accepting the nature that weaves through them, we can reconnect to love and forgiveness. We want to honor our pain and, at the same time, listen underneath its noise to hear the birds singing, see the sky clearing, and feel the drumming of our hearts.

Let's put down our weapons and pick up our hearts. Decide to love the life you have, not the one you dream about having. Build strength right now to love. Love all of it. Love your clutter piles, your credit card debt, your sex life or lack of one, your lousy profit margins, your fat, your wrinkly body, your ex-husband, your age, your screwed-up family, your traumatized past, your political opponents, your horrible compulsions. Decide to choose love right now.

Yes, it is difficult. Hating is easy. Love requires us to give up attachments; it requires we give up the fear, the scorecards, the hurts, the disappointments, the resentments, and expectations. It requires us to give up certainty and living from our heads. It requires us to love the parts of us we wish we didn't have. It requires that we take responsibility for the life we have and the one we want to create.

Many of us see the problem of love primarily as that of *being loved,* rather than that of *loving.* We dress ourselves up or accumulate success to become *loveable*—a mixture of being popular and having sex appeal. Untangling works to grow capacity to love by learning to open our heart to love again, and again. So long as we do not know how to love, we cannot believe that others love us.

The Organizer Self embodies authentic love, a love that is free from fear and characterized by non-attachment. It is a love that is consistent, safe, and predictable. It's rooted in an ever-present capacity to love all parts of our being. You do not need to perform a certain way or hide certain parts of yourself to receive this love. You don't have to "do" anything, for it is always there, always present. No matter how far off the road you have traveled, love is there waiting for you.

Let's attune and hear the whispers of our hearts. With love, our mouths find language to express our pain as well as our joy. If opening your heart doesn't feel safe or isn't enjoyable, you will automatically close it. Tune into your heart's intelligence, welcome it, and say, "Hello." Ask it, "What do you need to love fiercely with no attachments?" Is there constriction or expansion? Notice the rhythm that dances between the two, opening and closing. It isn't about getting somewhere but discovering where you are. As we commit to love again, life becomes a steady, calm process of awakening.

If your heart could speak, what would it say? Listen.

Inhale, and exhale.

The heart rediscovers the language of "I am enough and worthy of belonging." Love allows beauty to be grown from imperfection. As we grow resources to love within life and our relationships, we create spaciousness for growth and healing. Lovingness is a way of being that transforms everything around you. It happens on its own.

Untangle Experience: Three Things that Shift a Fairy Tale

Return to your Fairy tale. The Organizer Self embodies the bridge between the nightmare and the world of enchantment. It utilizes cognitive effort to locate three items that will become resources for overcoming our obstacles. To do this, it uses a dynamic interplay between the brain's memory and control systems. Without memory and imagination, our minds would be static—not conducive to creativity or solutions.

> **Organizer Self's Resources:** One day, something unusual happened. They came across three items that helped them change their experience: _____, _____, and _____ [rocks, superpowers, or practical things]. As they used each one of their items, they gathered specific resources to overcome the nightmarish tale.

When Heather came to see me, she was collapsed in her marriage. She loved her husband, but he acted out with money, violating her trust. Heather was tired of feeling resentful and managing deadness. Though her husband was taking responsibility for his behavior, she didn't feel love, only cold. As she picked up untangling skills, she curiously explored what would happen if she opened her heart. Heather's heart whispered, "If you open your heart to love again, you will be hurt and may die." She dramatized her mismatched message into this short version of a fairy tale:

> "**Once upon a time,** a little girl was afraid to feel love. Love felt like a scary dragon who wanted to devour her body, choking her to death.

> One day, she discovered a special door where she could barricade herself inside a closet. She was safe from the dragon and felt relieved. The closet was dark, cluttered, and musty. She looked around and found **three things,** clown glasses, ballet shoes, and a ball.

> As she put on the **clown glasses**, she peeked through a tiny crack and could see the dragon. It was terrifying to see this giant monster sitting on her bed, but she kept staring. Suddenly, the dragon shape-shifted. Its long, slithering tongue dissolved. Its spotted, oily skin became human skin. The moans became soft cries. The dragon became an older man. He seemed sad, collapsed on her bed. She felt sorry for him but was still afraid to move.

> As she put on her **ballet shoes**, she continued to watch the older man, and suddenly he became a seven-year-old boy,

exactly her age. His clothes were farm dirty, and he seemed lost, anxious, and scared. She thought maybe she could go out and talk with him. But no, she wasn't ready.

As she continued to watch, the boy shifted into a two-year-old baby, bubbling with joy and happiness. She then picked up her **ball**, opened the closet, and went to play with the baby. As she did, she reunited with her heart. Her body felt warm, happy, and alive.

As she loved the baby, she looked into his face and saw the images of the scared boy, the sad man, and the dragon. In a moment, she realized she was capable and safe to love all of them."

Untangle Note:

Heather never thought clown glasses, ballet shoes, or a ball would unlock her heart, but her imagination did. She shared, "I never understood how scary it felt in my body to open my heart and love. It is humbling to know that I need to crawl and play in such a young way. My journey is so much bigger than the issue I have with my husband. In a way, his issue is helping me heal. It felt so unsafe to love in my childhood. I do need to bite-size it. For when I do, I get to open my heart again with a man I love. I feel more empowered and confident. Together, my husband and I are creating a space of healing."

Fairy tales stir our emotional brain to access new learnings. The result is a fundamental change in our perception of the world. A fairy tale structure provides the Organizer Self with a targeted guide for learning. It helps this part of us engage and solve a complex problem. Although the "three things" may seem innocuous, they link particles of history and insight to help us overcome difficulties and envision a new possibility.

Get specific with your fairy tale. Study the three things your imagination automatically pulled together to help you shift your outcome. How can these things help you today? Be specific.

Untangle Story: Lory's Abandonment Structure

This section includes descriptions of sexual abuse and child abuse.

Lory, a forty-year-old business owner, was struggling in her relationship. She was jealous, distrusting, and insecure, and at the same time, intimacy was complicated. She felt caught in a vice where nothing worked. Lory was sick of feeling triggered and surviving overwhelming sensations. In her head, she knew her boyfriend loved her, so what was the problem? Her body didn't share the same certainty. It felt like it was constantly under attack by dark forces.

Lory panicked when she ventured into the world with her boyfriend. Whether it was out to a park, a restaurant, or a movie, everything felt dangerous. Suppose her boyfriend's eyes veered off to a pretty woman. She had no resources to manage her response. She felt like she was in quicksand. Obsessive thoughts ensnared her and stirred distrust, insecurity, and suspension. She didn't understand why she became so needy and insecure. "Why? Why? Why?" she wanted to scream.

Lory hadn't been in a sexual relationship for over ten years, and she was wondering if she should stay out of them altogether. Her anorexic lifestyle was an attempt to protect her from these chaotic triggers but ultimately created more loneliness and unhappiness in the process. How could she support her needs for love, intimacy, and sexual connection without all the emotional mess? As Lory worked the first step of The Untangle Method, she located this whisper:

"If my boyfriend doesn't desire me *all* the time, I feel like I will die. I will be abandoned and thrown out. I can't handle it."

I asked Lory how it felt to make contact with this part of her. She shared, "Weird. I didn't realize it felt so dangerous in my body. Now that I said it out loud, however, it does make sense."

For the next two weeks, Lory explored her mismatched message. Then she returned and shared, "When I was twelve, two horrible things happened. My mother died, and my brother molested me. And I worked on both in therapy for years. But what I am sensing now is another piece of that experience. I remember my brother hunting my friends and having sex with them. I was alone, angry, and feeling left out. When I asked him to stop, he just laughed at me and told me I was jealous. I felt so ashamed because I *was* jealous. I didn't want him to take my friends. I wanted him to make me feel special."

As Lory gathered reflective intelligence, she discovered more complex truths. She was rearranging the pieces and unlocking emotional learning. *Please note*, Lory wasn't reliving or surviving the horrible feelings or sensations of past violations; she was anchored in the present, pulling the pieces apart and arranging them into compositions that made sense for her today.

Regarding this experience, Lory said, "I had no one back then, and I didn't feel loved. My brother's attention was all I had. I never realized how much I wanted him. And part of me feels bad, like I did something wrong and dirty. I think I have secretly shamed myself for decades." I asked Lory to visually locate this twelve-year-old part that needed her brother. Once she clicked an image in her brain, I asked what, if anything, she wanted to say to her directly. Lory slowly formed these statements: "I am sorry you had to go through this." "You are not bad or dirty." "You needed more help, love, and support."

After communicating with affirmative love and embodying kind self-talk, Lory realized that she had spent all her time in therapy learning to forgive her brother, but she never really forgave herself. And this was coloring her current relationship. She shared, "I have a lot of compassion for this part of me now. I can see it so clearly. It isn't so much about my boyfriend. It's really *me* who needs to show up differently and not abandon myself."

I asked Lory how she felt holding both worlds—the old world that needed her boyfriend's desire 24/7, and a new world that had love inside of her, making her feel seen, worthy, and whole. Lory said a knot in her heart was loosening. Her initial mismatched message was, "If my boyfriend doesn't desire me all the time, I feel like I will die." And it changed into this one: "If I abandon this part of me, I feel like I will die. My boyfriend is not responsible for [this part of me]. I am. I need to partner with both of them well." And she did.

What Lory experienced could take a lifetime to fully process, but by shifting her mindset towards love and forgiveness, even a little bit, she accessed the ability to move forward with her life. Forgiveness can be difficult, especially when you have been abused. Lory did not need to forgive her brother's unforgivable acts; that was not what was being asked. She needed to understand the part of her that was tangled and buried inside her triggers today and show that part of herself love.

As she nudged closer within her inner landscape, obstacles fell away, and her experience with the external world shifted.

Consequently, as she began trusting herself, she was able to trust her boyfriend and the world more freely. As she expanded her ability to love, she found meaning and purpose more significant than her boyfriend. Her journey was no longer about "making it work" with her boyfriend but anchored in committed freedom to healing herself as she traveled with him. She developed agreements and systems with her boyfriend to regulate her responses and partner within herself and him in meaningful ways. She began belonging to her whole self.

Lory visited with me a few months later and shared, "I can't believe I haven't had any more triggers. Those horrible triggers were a wake-up call. They really did invite me into a deep place of healing with myself. And now I have a feeling of peace that I never imagined possible. I have a Stabilizing Floor! I can't believe I lived so long the other way."

Sexual abuse toward children and adolescents is a stark reality worldwide. A common misconception about child sexual abuse is that it is a rare event perpetrated against girls by male strangers. To the contrary, it is a much-too-common occurrence that results in harm to millions of children of all genders, in large and small communities, and across a range of cultures and socioeconomic backgrounds. Survivors of abuse need to be supported and helped in every way possible. If you have been mistreated or abused, you are not alone. You deserve love, support, and validation. And if you suspect that someone is being abused, please step in, investigate, and serve the situation in the highest good.

Untangle Exercise: Forgiveness

Can you be with your grief, or mine, without trying to fix it? Can you forgive the part of you that acts in ways you hate or has in the past? Can you hold space for all aspects of you to emerge safely and be greeted kindly? Love collects the language of compassion and for-giveness. You don't have to walk on your knees through the desert to repent and receive forgiveness. You have only to allow the soft part of your body to open towards love, and you will find forgiveness.

Forgiveness is an experience that must be felt, not thought. It is an expression to be spoken, not buried in silence, and a choice that must be encouraged, not forced. Become willing to touch a part of yourself that can embrace self-compassion and wash away regret. We must strengthen our Stabilizing Floor of Okayness and open our bodies to rupture shame and receive love, if only a little bit. The heart is one of the beautiful jewels of wisdom for its presence transcends thought.

Take the time to touch your skin. Remember its regenerative powers.

Our skin is the interface of the body between our external and internal worlds. It is our largest organ, giving us boundaries to locate where we are. Breathe into your skin and feel into its unconditional love. Notice how your skin provides a container, holding your bones, blood, breath, and cells together. Through your skin, you can regrow and heal in ways you can't within the mind alone. Let's remember our skin before shame, fear, or uncertainty. Feel how your skin can receive tenderness, care, and love.

Spend five minutes enhancing touch with your skin.

Imagine you have a smooth cream infused with pinecones and lavender in your hands. I want you to smell this cream and feel its silkiness. I want you to crack open just a little bit and rub this cream into every crevice of your body. Touch into the part of you that knows how to love freely and fiercely. Allow yourself to remember that you can love and receive love.

Stretch its ability to forgive yourself.

Forgive the part of you that chose the bad relationship or made the wrong decision. Forgive the part that is terrified of becoming seen. Forgive the part of you that couldn't find the resources to let go or get help. Forgive the under-earning and under-living. Forgive the suffering, collapses, and confusion. Forgive the blaming, withholding, and punishing. Forgive the lies and the hurts. Forgive the angry outburst and the defensive worry. Forgive the loss of life, the missed opportunities, and failed experiences. Forgive the regrets, the resentments, the disappointments. Forgive the past and all the wreckage. Forgive the people who hurt you and whom you have hurt.

Allow your skin to help you. Imagine forgiveness comes in the form of a cool mist against your skin. Or a kiss from the sun. You may find it in the rivers of water or in the veins that flow into your heart. Allow your cells, particles, and atoms to activate forgiveness. As we forgive, we rupture barriers that stand in the way of our hearts.

Many of us have tiny muscles here. That is OK. We want to work with where we are and grow from there. We don't need to force it but rather dip our toes into its waters. Here is the rich cadence of the language of self-forgiveness. I am sorry I abandoned you. I am sorry I checked out. I am sorry I didn't advocate. I am sorry I underestimated your value. I am sorry I have punished you. I am sorry I forgot how to love you. Please forgive me. Hear these pleas, then heed them.

Forgive now. Forgive fully. And know that you may have to do it often!

The Untangled Method's Framework

By the end of Step Two, the square acts as a springboard, opening all corners of its structure to make room for another part of us to emerge, the Creative Self.

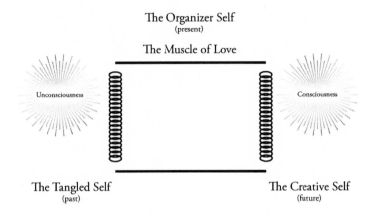

For so long, we have been rigid in our thinking. We thought we needed to get it right, be pure, or have pristine conditions to transform. However, like nature, we can build on top of old patterns and toxic emotions to integrate them within a new design. We can convert our suffering into healing as we dig into the rich soils of love and forgiveness. As we fill in the ugly holes of the past with love and understanding, we convert them into beauty. Here, we discover our songs of belonging. There is a restoration of serenity, joy, and peace. Learning to love and forgive all parts of our experiences allows us to complete Step Two of The Untangle Method.

Untangle Exercise: Greet your Creative Self

Let's get ready to greet the Creative Self by opening our hearts:

❖ What color is associated with opening your heart? What feelings are associated with this color? What new impulses are sparked? Be specific.

❖ How can you connect with this color actively? It could be that you find clothing that matches into it, paint your office with its color, or buy a journal in this hue. How can you embody this color to remember your capacity to love and forgive? Be specific.

❖ Once you have embraced forgiveness, what colors, images, visions appear? What new life wants to emerge? Be specific.

PART IV

STEP THREE:

RECLAIM THE CREATIVE SELF

"Information is just bits of data.
Knowledge is putting them together.
Wisdom is transcending them."
- Ram Dass

My Untangle Story:

The Color of Healing

Grief is a physical landscape where nothing feels safe. It is a state of being where sorrow holds the eyes steady. I stare at the sea. I stare into darkness. I wake up and stare in pain. I scribble into a notebook. My father is dead. I am not a whore. My brother is dead. I should have helped more. And I am alive. My mother will never be the same. Our family knows death. All families know death. Death has teeth; when it bites, it won't let go. And sometimes, there are no answers, no words.

The air was humid on the morning of my father's funeral. I stood in front of a full-length mirror, dripping with sweat. I have edges of my father's face—his small head, deep-set eyes, auburn coloring. But I am more delicate, cat-like. I tried to pull a black shirt over my pregnant belly. The weight pressed my ribs into my lungs, so I could barely breathe. My eyes were stinging, and everything around me felt greenish-brown. The last thing I wanted was to interact with another human being.

Like gathering a torn-up map, I'd strung together fragmented pieces of my father's story over the decades. He was eight years old when his mother abandoned the family, shackling him with the responsibility of taking care of his three brothers and three sisters and managing his poverty-ridden, raging, alcoholic father. His father was on trial, accused of murdering the man who had driven his wife to Chicago. The defense attorney who represented my grandfather was the only person my father would ever speak about, saying, "I could not believe someone like him was willing to help. We were poor. My father was an educated, alcoholic farmer."

Although his father was convicted of murder, this nameless defense attorney who served with care and dignity provided my father a life raft—a vision of what he could become.

Right then, at age eight, my father decided to become a defense attorney. He wasn't in school at the time, but his vision influenced all his choices and helped him overcome adversity at every turn. It helped him survive his uncle's farm labor nightmare before the state intervened to place him in an orphanage. It helped him overcome the humiliation of not knowing how to read when he entered school as a third grader. It pushed him to earn a college scholarship and become an All-American Basketball player. It helped him turn down three professional basketball offers, choosing to go to law school. Vision fueled my father's commitment, providing clarity, purpose, and tenacity.

New pieces of my father's history knitted together during the funeral.

I was confronted with the scale of his legal work. Hundreds of impoverished Appalachian people attended. They were toothless, stuttering, traumatized, circling the streets to pay their respects. They were crying, at a loss for what to do without my father. In story after story, I heard how my father had helped their brothers, sons, and daughters. My father had never shared this meaningful work, he only boasted and obssessed over his "big insurance cases." I wept with confusion, joy, love over this man, my father, who became the man from his childhood story—a man I would have liked to have better understood.

I was struck by rugged beauty. How one person, a nameless man, inspired my father's life. His hands were stretching through my father's body. I could feel all their layered textures, colors, and sensations. Goosebumps. Mint. Green mist entered my pores as I looked into the eyes of these people and wept.

I met uncles and aunts from Kentucky, who validated the horrors of his childhood: how my father was sexually abused by my grandmother, how my grandfather would line up his seven children and threaten to shoot them if his wife left, and how he would come home drunk with his brother and rape his wife, how my grandmother went on to have seven more children in Chicago and not one of her fourteen children attended her funeral, how my father had to usher his drunk father back and forth to the courthouse. All this was swirling and flying inside my father's body, nowhere to discharge, no place for my father to find a home.

How could I not be traumatized? It was inescapable. Trauma is scribbled into our blood.

During a eulogy, I learned that my father did corporate legal work for free to provide furniture for his clients when released from prison. My father would say, "How can you move your life forward if you get released from jail, and you don't have a bed to sleep on, or a kitchen table to eat from? You need practical things to rebuild your life."

As I heard these stories, I resonated: I am my father's daughter. We are both answering the same call, mission, impulse—trapped inside a historical scratch, victims of male dominance, violence, toxic sexual abuse, trying to claw our way out. Waves poured through my body as I better understood my father. Did it excuse his behavior? No. But did seeing it in this way provide me a larger lens to process it? Yes.

The aches are still there, but their colors have changed.

Somewhere in the twisted branches, I am here now. When I resist my colors, I get stuck in splintered connection and miss the creativity embedded there. I needed to get close to my suffering, to ask, "Why are you here? Why have you come? What happened to you?" There is richness in the darkening. I wait. I soften. I talk to it. As I touch down there, I discover images that swell me into heart-soaking tenderness. And belong only to me. Maybe the world without suffering is the real poem?

As awareness grows, some memories soften, and others click into focus. Memories are fickle, but they speak. Our stories are constantly revised. Over time, many horrible events are bleached of their intense horror. However, memories that have been traumatized are preserved essentially intact thirty, forty, fifty years later. Bad memories cover up the good, crowding space for any new ones to form. As we process these unresolved memories, they become integrated, allowing us a chance to own our story and write ourselves into a new one, if we so choose.

The memories of my father's death haunted me. The little decisions I made in the hospital. My brother's death haunted me. I heard his pain but didn't do more. The memories of blaming my mother haunted me when all the while, she was terrified and doing her best. I was captured in my own spell of unworthiness, too busy nursing on all the wrongs that had been done to me, not the ones I was creating. What color? Permanent red—the color of an angry pen, keeping score. I needed to soften its hue and forgive it *all*. And from its ashes, find a way to stand and help others.

There is no scientific evidence on how to deal with loneliness, alienation, death, or leaving a marriage. The unconscious is much too slippery. We must borrow from writers, artists, poets, nature, and spiritual practices to unravel suffering and greet inspiration. Healing requires a response that can only emerge from an appreciation of the depth of the soul. And healing is a continuum. It has layers, peaks, crevices, and waves of its own. Forgiveness requires humility and strength. And forgiveness is difficult.

Energy larger than myself had to break down inner rocks of self-hate to unburden my suffering. Rainfall washed away separateness and let loose my war cries safely. Wild winds spun me into thunderous dances of joy. As love swelled, the pain became interrupted. And I am returned to presence and awe.

The outside world is always changing. Every day I place my feet on tender grass. I lay down on Mother Earth and feel her hold me. I look around and notice: yellow dandelions dancing across a field, the glitter of a rainbow fish, the hollyhock, the mockingbird, the sun climbing out of the blackness every morning, like a flower, and falling into a thousand colors every night. These drops of beauty fill my heart, and something happens. As I find forgiveness, I rejoin my spirit.

Beneath the Earth is a sphere of geological forces strong enough to rupture its surface. We, too, are forces of consciousness capable of shifting fixed patterns and bursting free. We are all conjoined to the undulating web of life. We want to recognize the dignity of each living thing: mobile, fixed, insect, animal, tree, and octopus. The world offers herself to your imagination and bathes us in her regulating rhythm. It calls to you like a wilderness announcing your place in the family of things. We are not alone or separate but an active part of an expanding and contracting force that celebrates and collaborates within all living systems.

As I walked out of my father's funeral, hot air hit my face. The sky painted itself a brilliant blue. Swirls of white blossoms expanded like an exhale. Breath returned to me. Drifting through the sky, I saw the palest bit of rose seep in the touch of sunset. Something settled between my ribs. I lifted my arms out to the sky and stood inside my spine more fully. What color? Blue. Green. Orange. I squinted. I could see new colors—a streak of lilac, butterscotch yellow, pumpkin orange—all of them swirling together.

As I untangle, it untangles me.

Chapter 9

Reclaim the Creative Self

tangled vision: clouded by shame, confusion, and disconnection.
untangled vision: activated by clarity, purpose, and meaning.

At last, we have primed the doors to welcome the Creative Self. As we travel deeper into our inner landscapes, we discover a sacred space—a space without language, without noise. A space of emptiness. Often, when we think of emptiness, two parts emerge: the part of us that is afraid of emptiness, and the part of us that is excited to embrace its creative potential. In Step Three of The Untangle Method, we invite the Creative Self to step into this space. As much as we have a Tangled Self, protective and scared, we also have a Creative Self, brave and excited for a new experience. As much as survival is part of human nature, so too are creativity, joy, and pleasure. Stepping out of the familiar, punishing states where we've lived for so long, we step into the unknown, where the Creative Self is waiting for our attention, waiting to be greeted, waiting to midwife our new life.

Imagine Arrival

Welcoming a baby into the world is one of life's most rewarding events. Who does not relate to the image of birth? Birth is perhaps our most primal experience of love and, at the same time, release. When we birth a baby, a part of ourselves, or a creation, there is a space, a pause button of relaxing into its arrival. And then, with a breath and release, we meet it. It's bliss and awe. Giving birth to something fills us with gratitude. We are always birthing ourselves, always birthing something new, and it takes time. We are not racing towards liberation, for its arrival is a meaningful journey of twists, turns, and swirls that travel us into mystery, beauty, and bewilderment.

The Creative Self embodies the larger dimension of life in all its dazzling, spectacular ways. It rattles us awake and celebrates, "Yes, you are finally here!" The Organizer Self embraces contact with all our parts, realized and unrealized. In The Untangle Method, we seek to understand not just the part of us that is entangled in the past but the part of us that has *never* been realized or perhaps even recognized. For many of us, the Creative Self has been kept under lock and key, buried far deeper than any pain or trauma. The Organizer Self midwifes the Creative Self into life—for the first time, or again and again, as many times as needed, healing us in ways that no other part can.

When we allow ourselves to strengthen a relationship with the Creative Self, our perspective of the world shifts. Untangling becomes like a force. Like wind. Like love. Like spring. Like birth through our bodies that unleashes grace, stabilizing inside our deepest core. The Creative Self remembers this rhythm. Its movements are built into a natural life system, and we are part of it. Instead of managing our life by sheer force and self-will, let's allow the Creative Self to take us in a new direction.

Every transformative shift requires a similar process: a dismantling of the old, and a foundational restructuring, and a mobilizing of a new. It is a dance with life that synchronizes us. The Organizer Self is not about finding "the answers." It is about undoing the basis of the problems, clearing space to make contact with the Creative Self. The Organizer Self establishes the structure for integration;

however, it is the Creative Self that transforms this structure into oneness. When the Tangled Self's responses are removed, the Creative Self shines through. It pulses with inspiration, inviting us to surrender even more into the mystery of the world. Something that was closed finds an opening. Air hits and expression forms. Envision sinking in, feeling welcomed into this organic flow of exchange even for just a few seconds.

Enchanted Space

Those of us who are struggling to elevate our consciousness and access the Creative Self can turn to an enchanted space. Enchanted spaces are not necessarily religious, but they are sacred. We touch their grounds differently, in ways that feel holy. They provide a vehicle for something new to come through. This is where new ideas are formed, and dedication arises.

For many of us, nature is an enchanted space. We need to go outside and sit on a patch of grass. We need to wake up to the intelligence of shrubs, the soil beneath our feet, and the sky above our heads. As we marvel at Earth's mysteries, we want to remember that the atoms of our body are traceable to stars that have exploded in the galaxy. We want to be brought to our knees by wonder. In nature, we can be totally absorbed in what we are doing and experiencing, scarcely noticing the passage of time.

For others, experiencing great art or making art can bring us closer to enchantment. Art can be created from scraps of steel pipe welded together to create objects of wholeness. Whether it's music, food, literature, architecture, poetry, or a flower arrangement, art inspires us. It viscerally explores all facets of love, capturing complexity and grace. Beauty can express itself in so many ways that we have good reason to say it's in the eye of the beholder. The Creative Self sees beauty in all forms.

Enchanted spaces are everywhere. Classrooms, dance floors, museums, playgrounds, art studios, journals, and gardens can all become enchanted spaces. Self-help groups, for example, offer a space that touches and expands our being. In these anonymous rooms, no one is interested in what others are doing in the outside world, what they have, or who they know. They are only interested in whether they have acquired inner goals, such as honesty, openness, willingness to help, humility, and awareness. Enchanted spaces demand us to pull authenticity from them, where something unexpected starts to work.

Enchanted spaces cultivate a quality of being that resonates within a structure of engaged support, community, and belonging. No matter what this space looks like for you, it is a place that you want to return to over and over again. Enchanted spaces nudge us closer to the Creative Self, shifting and changing us, never to be the same. In these spaces, everything is stripped away, leaving only what we need. This kind of space requires a different kind of intelligence, one we may not fully grasp, but one that leads us into more wholeness, to a greater understanding of our innate nature and our place in the world.

Artistic craft uses creativity to comprehend the difference between chaos and meaning. One can simply understand this as the difference between noise and music. We untangle chaos to pull music from it. Like music, this process moves through you. It's circular, not linear. Craft provides instrumentation to author your life. You can take any mismatched message, and the more you deconstruct it, the more available you become to be taken somewhere new. And there is no art or transformation without love.

The great psychoanalyst Carl Jung emphasized the vital relationship between art and soul, for art is the pathway to human dignity and spirit.[77] The Creative Self makes a piece of art within our lives.

It understands the artist's infrastructure of harmony, balance, and rhythm and gets inspired by feelings, insights, or contours of an image. The Creative Self embodies the highest expression of the human spirit, as it becomes the way we communicate with ourselves and each other.

Estonian composer Arvo Pärt, who is often described as "transcendental" or "mystical," provides a description of a creative process like this:

> "In my life, my music, my work, in the dark hours, I have the certain feeling that everything outside this one thing has no meaning. What is it, this one thing, and how do I find my way to it? Traces of this thing appear in many guises, and everything that is unimportant falls away . . . Here I am alone with silence. I have discovered that it is enough when a single note is beautifully played . . . That is my goal. Time and timelessness are connected. This instant and eternity are struggling within us."[78]

Right now, you may feel like this part of you is gone or that you never had it. But you don't need to be particularly "creative" in the literal, artistic sense to access a wealth of inspiration from within the Creative Self. Our creative instinct is natural and resides in all of us. Across a lifetime, each of us adds countless pieces of knowledge and perspective to our senses of self—who we used to be but, more importantly, who we are inspired to become. The ability to be nudged closer to the Creative Self, learning not with intellect but with wonder, is still in your reach. As we remix deeper truths and string together new expressions, inspiration emerges, and with it, the power of transformation.

Visit an enchanted space—or if you can't visit, close your eyes and envision yourself there—and you may begin to feel it stirring.

Untangle Experience: Theater Play

It takes craft to excavate your soul, mold it within your own hands, and offer it to the world. For untangling purposes, Theater Play will be our enchanted space. Throughout Step Three, we will return to this space several times to layer insights and capture inspiring details, strengthening our connection with the Creative Self.

Actors construct a character's inner life through a process called sensory endowment. They clear space from their own identity to locate the cadence the character breathes, the rhythm the character walks, and the emotional pulses the character feels. Through this creative engagement, actors embody the skin of their character, which brings a visceral experience to their performance. Actors are no longer in their heads, focusing on memorized lines, but instead, they are living and breathing within the character's point of view of the world.

Theater dressing rooms are enchanted spaces for actors to engage in the musicality of character. Here, actors build the intimate organizing essences of what motivates their character to be, move, feel, hide, and express. They sit in these spaces to enhance the parts of them that unleash their character. They dress in a wig or unique scarf. They form the character's walk and select special shoes. They add makeup or strip it off. Through their imagination, they open themselves to creative presence.

We want to do the same.

Theater Play creates a space to capture vision. It allows us space to try on new identities as garments and muster the strength to realize them. It is a place to help us locate imagery, sensation, inklings, and attributes to collect elements of the Creative Self that move our spirits. Theater Play creates a space of *permission*. Permission to see all parts of ourselves from a different lens—parts of us that may have been too terrified or nervous about being seen until now. Or parts starving to claim life.

Recall your mismatched message. For example, "If I take up space, I will be hurt or rejected."

Imagine you are sitting in a theater space as an audience member.

Look at the dark, empty stage. When you are hijacked by your mismatched message, what does it look like? Witness your Tangled Self arriving on stage. What appears? How do they walk and talk? What colors do they wear, or how do they hide in black or costume-like clothes? Be specific. How do they hold their shoulders, and in what direction does their face tilt? What is their energy? And tempo? How old do they seem? Do they hide behind a fake smile, or martyr, or good girl, or an angry rebel?

Dramatize it.

Watch them. See them. Understand them.

As you experience your Tangled Self, what feelings and sensations arise? Be specific. Does it feel uncomfortable to see them struggle, or wear dull colors, or collapse? Does it pain you to see them blow up relationships and live an isolated life? Does it make you sad to watch them try to hide? What problems are they trying to solve? What do they need from you or want you to understand? Explore.

Meanwhile, the Organizer Self watches from the theater seat, within or beside you. As it watches, it develops skills of observation, anchoring neutrality and curiosity. The Organizer Self harnesses our cognitive capacity to monitor the Tangled Self with kindness, love, and support. The Tangled Self and the Creative Self create emotional experiences, whereas the Organizer Self creates inner leadership. The Organizer Self acts as the director to arrange the different parts of our experience to come together and create new music.

Once you have realized your Tangled Self, dissolve the image. Hold space for the emptiness.

Take a deep breath. Register the emptiness, the dissolving, eroding, and washing away. Notice what it feels like to hold unknown space. Does it fill your body with relief, or do you start to tighten? Notice. Emptiness is a sacred space of in-between that creates space for inspiration. Notice tiny sparks that move you from nothingness to creativity, chaos to beauty, noise to music, darkness to vibrant color.

Now, imagine the mismatched message is gone.

Look at the stage. Witness a part of you, the Creative Self, arriving. The Creative Self speaks in the language of "I can," "I will," and "I am." It is the part of you excited to rewrite you into a new story. Allow yourself to collect an image of this part of you emerging from the darkness. What appears? How do they occupy space? How do they hold their head and place their shoulders? What is the energy of their movement? What clothes do they wear? If music accompanied their arrival, what would it be? A violin or flute? What color resonates with them? How do they assert themselves and belong to the world? What heroic action do they accomplish? Allow them to get bigger, more colorful. As you watch them, what do they do that gives you spine-tingling joy?

See them. Witness them. Study their expressions.

Root for them. How do they express their desires in ways that excite you? What action do they take that inspires bravery? Is it a weird sense of humor, wild passion, sensitivity, powerful ambition, vulnerability, sex drive, longing? Encourage them to go bigger. What ruptures your heart and has you cheering? Be specific.

Greet their arrival.

What do they do that makes you give them a standing ovation?

Experience the feeling that says, "Heck yeah, you are *finally* here!" See it. Feel it. Witness it. Celebrate it. Say "Yes, yes, yes, there you are! I see you. You have arrived!" Allow yourself to be surprised and taken somewhere new. Notice. Dance inside the bliss and awe of creating something. Notice what arises. Allow this image to live inside of you, warm you, and tickle your soul.

Untangle Exercise: Role Model

Many things start with imitation. Behavior is learned from the environment through the process of observational learning. As you imitate, you start to learn ways to make new expressions, and then you start to do them independently. It is natural. We want to encourage an environment of play to help us learn. Often, we need to try on different versions of ourselves until we match deeply.

Even if you only learned that your Creative Self wears a pair of funky tennis shoes or a garment that says, *I am an Artist*, great! Start with where you are and build a practice of circling back over and over again. To believe something is possible is to make it possible. Moving a state from tangled to untangled is an art form. The process of breaking down and rebuilding with greater intelligence develops craft.

The more specifically you engage with the qualities you admire, stirring them and returning to them, the more you will spark vision and new possibilities. Remember, the zebra finches reiterated their love songs hundreds of times before they match.

We need to do the same.

Exploring attributes will help to strengthen your Creative Self. The more deliberate you are in clarifying how your Tangled Self embodies life versus your Creative Self, the more freedom you provide. We need to start small, find a little part that is willing to stretch into a bigger vision.

Think of an inspirational leader, a superhero, a mythological character, or a mentor who inspires you. It could be Martin Luther King Jr.,

Athena, Abraham Lincoln, Wonder Woman, the Dalai Lama, Albert Einstein, your grandmother, Meryl Streep, Picasso. If you struggle to locate inspiration from a person, that is OK. Sometimes one person is too rigid and doesn't seep into our creative pores. We can use abstractions, such as colors, nature, flowers, music, and animals.

❖ Pick one source of inspiration. Who or what is it? Be specific.

❖ What qualities do you admire most about this person or thing? Make a list with at least seven attributes—qualities such as power, grace, bravery, acceptance, unconditional love, flexibility, wit, confidence, creativity, enthusiasm, generosity, intellect, forcefulness, friendliness, honesty, optimism, badass-ness, commitment, passion, integrity, loyalty, warmth, or anything else.

❖ What are the top three attributes you most admire? Be specific.

❖ If your inspiring character is Mr. Rogers, and one of your attributes is love, how can your Creative Self embody this essence and express more love? Explore images specific to your circumstances. It could be at your son's soccer practice, with a difficult employee, or sharing hard truth with someone. Allow your inspired character to help you link its inspiration to a part of you. Dramatize it. Allow it to shape you into new creative forms. How can you take their essences and thread them into your life's expression?

Go granular. Zoom in, then zoom out to examine the bigger picture, helping you make a connection between things. We are stirring, mixing, and enhancing attributes into images, feelings, visions. The emotional brain works within images more than words. We want to endow one attribute at a time, strengthening imagery for the Creative Self. We need precision and a spirit of play. As we gather deep insights, we anchor a level of certainty in our system to support various new movements. The more specific, the more dynamic and fulfilling the experience is.

Close your eyes.

Return to the audience seat.

Feel the stirrings of an audience member's anticipation. Place your Creative Self on stage. Working with one attribute at a time, see how this attribute shapeshifts the Creative Self. What does bravery, grace, or love have them do, feel, express? See it. What changes? What actions do they now take? What vocal expressions form? What do they ask for, and what falls away?

Stay with the experience. Wait until clarity emerges.

Notice all of it. The colors. The actions. The declarations. The impulses. The perspectives. The more specifically you engage, the more you will spark vision. We are developing imagination in ways that strengthen clarity and build an active relationship with the Creative Self. Allow the picture to emerge.

After you circle through one attribute, do it again and again with two other attributes.

Untangle Experience: Pelvic Bowl

Our pelvis consists of six bones fused to create a bowl shape. This large structure attaches to the axial skeletal system—skull, spine, sternum, and ribs—via the sacrum: an incredible feat of biomechanics. Now, I want you to imagine your pelvic bowl as a structure that holds your creative and spiritual life force. Find a calm balance and come inside your home. Take the voices of others and ask them to wait outside. Close the door and allow yourself to root into this sacred space.

Place your hands on your hips. Let your hands drape over the crest of your bones to feel the support of your pelvic rim. Feel all its flexible connective tissue that holds your internal organs together. Travel into the darkness of your pelvic bowl. Sweep aside any dust. Open its windows. Peel the whispers off the walls and experience its energy. In some Eastern traditions, our pelvic area is known as the root chakra, where we ground safety.[79] And when we don't feel safe, it is a place we tend to "hold" fears, stresses, and collapses. Let's orient towards the place inside us that holds both constriction and opening—the sacred space of in-between fear and hope, white and black, birth and death.

As ferns have their tight curls, we have ours. As ocean shells have their rounded shape, we have ours. Our curls, contractions, and collapses are a natural part of our human cycle; they source preparation for emergent growth. We want to dance within all states of our being, embrace them, and awaken to their intelligence. Our constrictions have precious data for us to collect. As we gather this insight, we pull clarity from our murky waters to stand inside our lives more fully.

Shift focus and travel into your pelvic area. Explore its terrain. Notice the relationship you have with this area. For many of us, this area can feel like a dark hole. We may intellectually understand it, but most of us feel cut off from it. Take a moment. Explore its mystery. Travel into its cavernous space. Look around. Open its windows. Allow light to shine into its dark crevices. What do you see? Let your pelvic home receive this brightness. Take a moment to feel its vitality—travel in and out of this space. Stir the visceral feelings of creating a new home for yourself. Rest inside these bones that support your life.

Sit on a chair, and slowly allow your pelvis to move you back into a collapse, head down, and then guide you forward into an opening, face up like an ocean wave—spiral side to side. Swivel back and forth within this dance of rocking. Allow your body to slink back into a collapse. Feel into your round fern curls. Explore this state of being. Notice the sensations that arise as you reconnect with this part of your body. Notice if part of you rejoices, hides, or needs a break. Welcome it.

Locate the space beyond your perimeters. Let silence nestle in. Register the Earth. Register gravity. Register the field of energy. Now return to yourself. Notice how expansiveness is inside of you. Allow your body to circle back into its contraction, swivel side to side, and emerge forward, opening, extending, elongating, collapsing, containing. Don't repeat the movements but allow your body, not your mind, to drive them. Feel yourself become surprised by how the body wants to move you into a natural rhythm. Follow its lead. We don't have to know the map.

Now, explore the pause—the pause between movements. Notice your response to the pause, the space of not knowing where your body will go. This pause is the alchemy of the whole experience. We are collaborating a relationship with the space of in-between. We want to greet this space, acknowledge its creative power. Find your ocean wave and allow your body's wave to find you.

As we occupy our bodies more fully, we access sources of motivation that spark creative possibilities. Find communion as you travel back and forth inside this rocking rhythm of constriction and opening, the known and the unknown, receiving and letting go. Gather movements to bring you closer to your inspired truth, a truth you didn't even know existed, to realize your beautiful life.

The Untangle Method's Framework

The Organizer Self births a new structural way of being by housing the Tangled Self and the Creative Self. The circle is a universal symbol with extensive meaning, notions of oneness, wholeness, original perfection in all its imperfections.

The Organizer Self

The Creative Self collects the wisdom behind our struggles to assemble powerful inspirational pockets to guide our way. It holds a visceral understanding of life, one that travels below the trauma of circumstances to reconnect us with the magic of living. As we reclaim the Creative Self, we shift into a higher level of awareness. Energy shape-shifts. The Creative Self gains momentum to shape future outcomes. It is easy to keep it going once we reconnected with the life force energy of the Creative Self. It reclaims all that has been lost to us, and all that has yet been formed.

Untangle Exercise: Build a Relationship with the Creative Self

❖ Say out loud, "I have arrived!" Try it and see how it feels to celebrate this part of you arriving.

❖ What rituals, classes, activities, or practices return you to the experience of remembering and celebrating your life? Be specific.

❖ What colors does this part of you *love* wearing?

❖ What one attribute did you locate that inspired you the most? Be specific.

❖ How can you embody this attribute right now? What does it have you do, say, express, and create? Be specific.

❖ Write a poem that describes reclaiming this part of you, the Creative Self.

Here is mine, inspired by Ellen Bass's poem "The Thing Is":

the thing about life
is learning how
to love it

even when it
makes
no sense

even when you
have to crawl
towards it

study its emptiness
and collect its
pieces

to find
a part of you
that can say, yes

yes, I will take you,
and I will love you,
again

Chapter 10

Activate Your Inner Purpose

tangled eros: selfishly lusts for short-term pleasures.
untangled eros: seeks passion as a form of love and empowerment.

Many of us find it difficult to orient towards pleasure, and a common reason is feeling numb, ashamed, chaotic, or totally out of touch with our bodies. If the body isn't a safe place to be, there is no way for it to dig into passion and joy. These essential emotions help us greatly, not just by making us feel good at the moment, but by giving us the drive and energy to pursue our greater goals. So, we are now calling all parts of us home to access the Creative Self, which can help us unwind survival conditioning and motivate towards healthy pleasure. The Creative Self is rooted in grace, for it has an innate affinity for life and all living systems. And this affinity is based on a drive, a thrust that human beings possess to connect vibrantly with all of life. We deserve pleasure—in our moment-to-moment lives, our sex lives, and our overarching ambitions. In this chapter, we will explore ways of accessing the part of the Creative Self that holds the passion for realizing our purpose.

Imagine a Jaguar

Pale yellow. Dark swirls. Black dots. These beautiful cats embody their namesakes, the indigenous word "yaguar" which means "he who kills with one leap."[80] In ancient civilizations of Mexico—the

Olmecs, the Mayans, and the Aztecs—the jaguar was worshipped as a deity. Symbolically, the jaguar represents strength and beauty, having the ability to see and ambush during the night. As such, many Mayans believed that jaguars could move between worlds—a jaguar being of both the stars and the Earth. Traditionally, the jaguar has represented power, ferocity, and wisdom as well as protection from evil. Still today, the mystery and elegance of these cats inspire respect and wonder.

Humanity's modern state of existence has caged us in compartmentalized traps. We have trampled our inner wildness trying to maintain a role of "pleasant," "fine," or "good." We diminish our self-worth by fixing and attacking our broken parts. We become lost in the background of white noise, cut off from who we are and what we are here to do. Instead of asserting boundaries and mobilizing clarity of commitment, we abandon the deeper, authentic part that desires more from life. At one point, our impulse for desire may have felt dangerous, inappropriate, or confusing. Maybe it wasn't socially acceptable. We could have been humiliated by a teacher, parent, or group of friends. Somewhere along the way, we shut down the sense that it's *OK* to want more, and this loss separates us from the driving force of eros.

For untangling purposes, the jaguar represents healthy eros, granting permission to claim space, play loudly, assert boldly, surrender fully, be sensual, and receive pleasure. The Creative Self shakes and shimmies us into unbridled forms of expression. It will even show fangs and roar if need be. It is the part of us that embodies variety, novelty, and passion for engaging life. It alleviates pressure to "get it right" or "be perfect." And in doing so, it elevates our significance to reclaim our innate natures and join the world. We can stand our ground. We can assert what we need. And we can receive a lot of pleasure in doing so.

Power dynamics shift as we occupy our needs resourcefully. Limited paradigm structures that caged us into the victim, abandonment, ambivalence, and isolation structures can fall away as we restore impulses that shatter the unconscious narratives of "I can't." Healthy eros restores our instincts to move through challenges in ways other parts were too tangled to move prior. It unfreezes our life force energy to emerge stronger through the pleasure of living fully. Pleasure that heals. Pleasure that loves. Pleasure that tickles our souls.

The Creative Self runs on eros. It reclaims the language of pleasure to develop a new vocabulary, coordinating cues within our body, mind, and spirit to match our facial expressions, vocal tone, and behaviors. Holding more power in our bodies than we are used to can feel scary and like we are losing control. Healthy eros sounds like good sex—which it is. Part of the reason orgasm can be elusive is that it requires that we both build trust and lose control. That means making strange noises, facial expressions, and movements, as well as saying things that don't come from our logical minds. Learning to let the Creative Self take us somewhere new and trusting its impulses requires a similar mechanism of trust and letting go. Good *anything* in life requires more from us, but don't worry. Feeling uncertain or constricted can be a part of the process of building capacity.

The Creative Self opens our faces and moves our bodies into purposeful alignment. And in doing so, it restores trust and harmony. Sometimes it adopts an activating nature, like a jaguar, to assert desires and wiggle into higher levels of visibility. Other times it embraces the snake and creates a sacred space to shed skin and heal. It looks different for everyone. Restoring balance requires consistent fine-tuning. Shifting boundaries and roles are part of the dance of creation, both on the Earth and within our lives. Its rhythm is one of opening and releasing, shifting and emerging, expanding and constricting, running and surrendering. As the Creative Self becomes stronger, more shifting occurs and more healing arises.

Purposeful Belonging

Once you access the Creative Self, knowing who you are and what you desire is a fluid process of intuition. However, many of us aren't there yet. Declaring what we want can swirl overwhelm and disgust. Shifting from camouflage into vibrant colors is brave. The Creative Self reclaims the full range of our experiences. It recycles us into a deep knowingness to reclaim the part of us that can emerge into healthy eros, if only a little.

Check in with your body. Explore what sensations arise. What happens when you assert your needs and desires? Dread? Confusion? Pleasure? Pain? Welcome whatever arises. Listen to it. We are not rushing into somatic liberation. We are learning to dance within it, little by little. Listen for any voices that judge your desires as bad or dirty. Keep dissolving punitive self-talk and encourage your deeper nature to become known. You are part of this place, not a visitor. Touch into your wilderness and provide it a creative space to emerge.

The more we cultivate creative awareness, the more magical and fulfilling our "doing state" becomes. Creative awareness is a similar experience to meditation in that there is a deep focus on "being" with an experience. The Creative Self mixes the diversity of our experiences to leverage them into services, offerings, pieces of art. It repurposes all the crappy things flying around and makes them beautiful, unique gifts. It collects the wisdom of the chaos to make music, love songs, poetry. As we expand our "being state," it dramatically influences our "doing state."

When we were young, we encountered the world in this way of deep, full-body engagement. We would pick up a stick and imagine we were in the jungle battling a lion. We asserted, engaged, played, touched, and created without any struggles. It was our nature. As we grow older, we often undervalue our "being state" and focus solely on the busy "doing state." We stay stuck in our heads, yet we wonder why we feel disconnected. By encountering life with more visceral awareness, we are letting our bodies experience the world in a different, more natural way.

Have you ever witnessed a person embedded in purpose? A doctor, a nanny, a mom, a teacher, a lawyer, an artist—anyone? They occupy space differently, caring in ways others don't. They radiate aliveness, pride, joy, and excellence. They are not in a rote routine. Their bodies, hearts, and spirits move in purposeful harmony. They are present, falling in love with the tiny moments of exchange happening right before them.

In my town, there is a crossing guard named George, who works at the elementary school. Everyone in our town knows and loves George. Why? George commands his job like none other. He sees traffic patterns with joyful energy. When he whistles, you feel it in your spine. When he stops traffic, everyone wakes up. When he takes your child's hand, he converts stress into reassurance. Every part of George is alive, present, and alert. He embodies purposeful belonging. He loves our children into safety. He sings them into happy moments. His service of protecting children radiates through every cell of his being. It is vibrant, clear, purposeful.

We, humans, have an inner and outer purpose with life. As we become more internally present, our external actions will align with an empowered state of awareness. As we become more connected with our inner riches, our outer purpose with life aligns. There might not be a noticeable change in what we do, but this shift dramatically influences how we experience the world. Seeking only an external purpose, we can achieve success through sheer hard work, but there is no joy in such endeavors, which invariably end in some form of suffering. Purposeful belonging is about deep engagement between these two worlds. Learning how to collaborate with our inner being first allows us to match into an external way of doing that embodies the two, synchronizing their rhythmic movements.

We gain clarity when we have a vision of what to do in the world. Purposeful belonging means living in action; every part of us is engaged in action. Living in the world, asking for our needs, asserting our desires, and contributing are acts of existence. The Creative Self encourages integrated alignment with both worlds, inner and outer, as they dance together. Our inner purpose is the state of awakening. We share this with every other person because it is the purpose of humanity. Our outer purpose can change over time and varies from person to person.

The Creative Self restores trust and dignity. We want to hear all that has been lost to us and all that hasn't been formed—all the wind songs, spirit songs, birdsongs, and love songs we have yet to realize.

Untangle Exercise: Mix, Stir, Cook

Often, we lose pieces of ourselves or forget who we are on the road of a rocky life. We try to forget our horrible childhood, terrible divorce, financial disasters, or abusive boss. However, as we leave behind the "bad stuff," we also leave behind much of the "good stuff." Instead of empowering us, we let our histories revictimize us.

The work here isn't about cuddling up to negative memories. It is about acknowledging and valuing *all* our experiences. It doesn't mean we must like everything about our past; we may have suffered difficult lessons or great losses. But we can recognize that these experiences have shaped who we are today. We can have a structural shift in our identity and become blown away by the part of us that emerges.

In this exercise, we want to reclaim our histories' good parts, which may have gotten lost or swept away in our effort to clean out the bad.

All our successes. All our educations. All our good relationships. All the times we felt seen or supported. All our interests, hobbies, jobs. All our talents, assets, skills. All the obstacles we have overcome. Write a list of *all* your skills and experiences, however small.

Locate as many as you can in five minutes.

Your first reaction may be to think it's impossible, but start recording everything you can think of and see just how far you can go. Find talents you may have forgotten. Remember a person who inspired you from work or school. Remember taking the stage in 3rd grade. Remember your basketball team in middle school. The musical you did at camp. The card tricks you mastered or the art projects you made. Make sure you add hobbies, special interests, free services, educations, and travel experience.

List ALL of them. Then, pull the ten most important, salient memories that defined you or encouraged you. Memories have no forms except into the mind. We want to ascribe our memories to an object to layer within its particles. Draw and color the memories on paper. Or make a model of them or find tiny objects representing them to draw your attention to moments that connected you meaningfully.

We want to wake up and remember all of it. As we encounter all the little pieces of experiences, valuing all of them and stirring them together, our sense of self is in the process of becoming reshaped. Our experiences offer a valuable foundation. We want to reconnect with the courage of being alive. The Creative Self remembers all the learnings. Your first crawl, your first walk, your first word, your first kiss, your first experience with money, your first job, your first recognition of self. It remembers childhood encounters with nature, trees, bugs, flowers, love, awe, wonder, sky, stars, colors. It draws confidence from past experiences to shapeshift bravery in magical ways.

The Creative Self reclaims aspects of us that we have forgotten or lost. This is healing. We want to dig into the deeper part of us that says, "See, you crawled your way into walking, and you can do it again." "You trained hard in middle school, and you can do it again." "You felt worthy in that one relationship, and you can feel it again."

As the Creative Self strings together pieces of history and mixes them with inspiration, confidence emerges. It shatters the Tangled Self's language of "I can't" or "I won't" and reclaims the language of "Of course you can." Here we are no longer so rigid or pressurized. We are free to move. We quickly become in awe that in all the years of "working on ourselves," we hadn't touched on the simple tool of reaching the Creative Self and allowing it to greet the world.

Explore the prompts below. All journeys look different; make the Mix, Stir, Cook exercise work for you.

❖ Mix Experiences:

Mix into the particles of the past and retrieve experiences that could help you today. Explore how your childhood ballet training could twirl you into a marketing campaign. Or how your high school drama class could fire creativity in your romantic life. Or karate class can discipline your time. Be specific. Play. Explore. Remember.

Which past skills and experiences could help you today?

❖ Stir Medicine of Healing:

As you stir memories, inspirations, and experiences from the past, decide which ones you want to make stronger. Shifts and perspectives can happen. Put them into an imaginary medicine bottle. Our medicine helps us become stronger bit by bit.

It puts us in direct contact with visceral aspects of who we are, what we have overcome, and who we aspire to become.

For some people, the memory of being seen is their medicine of healing. Their medicine bottle contains memories of when they connected resourcefully and felt seen. It could be a first boyfriend, a teacher, an animal, or a family member. Others need access to more touch. They need to build a relationship with their sensual desires to help rejoin their bodies in healthy, satisfying ways. And other need to remember the grit of their gymnastics coach and how they could handle pressure well and perform well.

Mix your medicine. And take this medicine two-three times a day. Remember it. Feel it. Taste it.

❖ Cook the Elements:

The Creative Self cultivates an "ecology of mind," where we can change the nature of reality through our focused attention. It cooks new experiences by gathering visions, flashes, and hits of inspiration that tickle our spirit. Study nature. Is it a rare bird that opens your heart and provides you permission to play? Or the grace of a horse to embody strength and stillness? Or the power of the jaguar to assert your desires and surrender fully? Be specific. Find images and tend to them. Build a relationship with them to help you engage the Creative Self and transform your experience.

Return to the Enchanted Theater Space. Remember feeling, "FINALLY, here I am!" How does remembering an old skill help you transform? See it. How does remembering being seen help you heal today? Feel it. How does the spirit of a jaguar help you find the courage to become more assertive at work or in your home? Experience it. How does that tiny red bird permit you to unlock your heart and belong with the world? Dance it.

Mix, Stir, Cook. Allow yourself to be surprised. Allow yourself to say, "Oh, there I am. I remember you. You can do this."

Untangle Note:

Moving from invisibility into vibrant color is brave. We need to engage the part of us that can create pleasure with this new experience.

Five years ago, I hired a business coach to help me grow my business. She looked for me online and said, "I can't find you. You are invisible." Glee shot through my body. I am successful *and* invisible! However, shortly afterward, shame spiraled me into a depressive state.

I understood my reality was conflicted. I had achieved the invisibility I'd longed for as a child, but if I wanted to grow my business online, it was going to require marketing and becoming seen. The logical part of me understood this; however, the other part of me, my body, didn't. With each marketing video I recorded, I cringed with hatred and disgust. The sound of my voice, the way I looked—I couldn't stand to be seen.

After days of struggle, I decided to untangle my video camera. As I worked my way into Step Three, I soaked into the language of *safe enough* and explored my deeper nature, a branch, a flower, an itty bit part hungry for a new experience. I needed creative inspiration to transform my relationship with visibility. I needed to become more excited by a new experience to rupture the spell of my Tangled Self.

I started watching David Attenborough's *A Life on Our Planet,* and these tiny birds from New Guinea showed up, igniting my heart. Their ability to prepare, wiggle, jump, flirt, attack, and play provided me with unabashed permission. They meticulously clear their space from leaves, branches, clutter and wait patiently for an opportunity to arise. And then, with a sheer committed force, they jump into a dance routine with their entire heart to win a mate. Their eyes flash back and forth between yellow and blue. Their sidestep shuffle and head bob are captivating from all angles. They won my heart.

Whenever I do a retreat or speaking event, I share about these little birds, and the audience sees how they influence my performance. I needed to remember playful movements to let myself shift from invisibility to color. And these little birds helped me. I couldn't achieve higher levels of visibility without this source of creative connectedness. They swirl me into a committed, purposeful place in heart, spirit, and soul: no costume, just permission to play and wiggle myself into new experiences.

Untangle Story: Katie's Purposeful Job

Many years ago, I worked with a woman, Katie, who was riddled with shame and under-earning. Katie spent a decade in therapy, trying to figure out her confusing childhood. Although she gathered valuable insights, this knowledge hadn't helped her find purposeful belonging. Katie was working several part-time jobs, all of which she hated. She cleaned houses, took care of people's gardens, and answered phones. Her punitive, victimizing language sounded like:

"I have no time. I am too tired. I will never figure out my life. I am too exhausted thinking about it. I can't do it."

Instead of fighting her reality, she needed to embrace it. She needed to bring *more* to her jobs, not less. Instead of hating them, she needed to dip into her body's relationship and explore them. There was a critical reason she was stuck. Instead of plowing through each job by rote, she needed to slow down and pay attention to her sensory experience. This work became her "purposeful job."

Katie made a list of her experiences: hobbies, jobs, achievements, experiences, sports, arts, and more. The list was longer than she had expected. She wanted to skip over how she had played competitive soccer in college, but I stopped her. I wanted to understand. What position? What did it feel like on the field when she scored? Her eyes rolled as she said, "It was a long time ago." However, as she slowed down and reconnected with this part of her experience, something began to shift. It was an energy of calm and confidence. Her voice changed, and her posture strengthened. It was slight, but noticeable.

The soccer field wasn't complicated for Katie. It has been a place where she felt synchronicity. She remembered the joy of competition, collaborating with the team, and feeling good as she worked hard to compete at a high level. As she remembered it in this way, her body swelled with an intuitive knowingness. There was a part of her that did know how to show up and be successful. Even without encountering it for years or decades, the connection was still there, waiting to be remembered and become a resource. As she reclaimed this particle of history, it began to reshape her present state.

For the next few weeks, Katie wore tennis shoes that reminded her of this connection. She noticed her feet moved to a different rhythm, how they made contact with the Earth and wanted to spring high. She experienced her head tilting right instead of down as she surveyed her life from a different playing field. She noticed the jobs she previously hated, like watering her client's yards, became a thrill, reconnecting her with the smell of grass, stimulating the pleasure of soccer memories, ambition, and play.

Katie was learning to pay attention to these memories, recollections, sensations, and come home to herself. As she worked in this way, she reclaimed her thriving language of "I can." "I can handle a difficult situation." "I can handle a strenuous competition." "I can perform at high levels." One day, while watering, Katie accessed a life-changing insight. Her stomach swelled with pleasure, and her blood tingled with aliveness. In a flash, she realized she wanted her own house.

Katie shared with me, "I am so shocked. I had no idea I wanted a home. I always assumed I would rent. I guess I never thought I could take care of my own house. But now I know I can."

Katie discovered a treasure chest of committed energy. Her old world tore apart. She was encountering vision, and with it, a change in her identity. As she reclaimed healthy eros, she aligned with a deeper part that wanted more from life. It was starving for a greater challenge and more responsibility. Instead of overwhelming her, it acted as a stimulant, empowering her life. Committed energy rebuilt Katie's backbone to work differently. She was no longer exhausted, even though she took on more responsibility and worked longer hours; she was alive. She finished two years of undergraduate work in one year. She declared a career in financial services, and within two years, Katie purchased a home in Los Angeles.

Katie's body, not her head, gathered assertive confidence to move her life quickly. Meaningful success was Katie's willingness to show up differently—the bravery of attuning with her whole body, linking old and firing new. As she reunited with all parts of her experiences, she accessed connection and vision to reclaim purposeful belonging. And you can as well.

Untangle Exercise: A Pleasure Chart

Many of us gravely underestimate the capacity needed to receive healthy pleasure. We assume we can handle it; after all, look at all the "bad stuff" we have survived. However, when we build a life of surviving, receiving healthy pleasure is our blind spot. Surviving is a closed state, while receiving pleasure is an open state, a flowering. In a way, staying closed is easier. Instead of trying to jam pleasure into our system and then feeling ashamed that we can't handle it, let's build a Pleasure Chart.

As we build larger capacities to receive, we discharge and open to the world. We can metabolize pleasure without triggering a shame spiral. And we can start right now. Our senses receive stimuli from the world and build awareness. Your voice, on the other hand, is a device of response. We want to develop both. Your voice communicates as much about you as the words you speak. As you start taking in the world differently, notice and enhance your voiced expressions with joy. Make the sounds louder. Wiggle into your "yums," "ohh-hhs," and "eeeees." It is a practice that primes present aliveness. We don't want to close off but rather allow sensations to wake us up. I can't overstate how important this exercise is and how simple it is to put into our day.

Rest your attention on one sense at a time. Savor for one minute.

A Pleasure Chart:

Visual: Rest your eyes and contact a sight: find a leaf, a dancing branch, a bird, a pillow, or a crack, a color. Gaze softly, allowing your visual field to open and receive. Focus on one item and take in the pleasure of its beauty. Notice a little sensation that sparks joy from an unexpected thing. Expand the connectedness for one minute.

Touch: Open your skin and contact a sensation: cold air on your nose or hot moisture against your cheek. Notice the sun warming your eyelids or the softness of your shirt on your neck. We need to touch and feel the world. Savor the pleasure of touch and notice one sensation your skin can receive. Expand the sensation of receiving for one minute.

Smell: Open your sense of smell and contact a scent: lingering sweetness of primrose or pine needles. Smell the furrowed bark of an old oak or the dew-covered grass. Savor the world of smell with your eyes closed. Nudge your nose closer into the experience as we might approach a morning cup of coffee. Savor one scent and expand this connectedness for one minute.

Taste: Open your taste buds and contact a flavor: a plump blueberry, swirling sweet juice. Tomatoes. Cheese. Rosemary. The next time you eat, slow down and notice all the subtle flavors and textures on your tongue. Wiggle into delicious sounds and express them out loud. Say "yum!" aloud. Savor a flavor for one minute while saying "mmmm!"

Sound: Open your ears and connect to the hum of nature: the sound of the wind, birds chirping, the flutter of leaves. Listen for whispering songs of pine trees or wavelike hisses of streams. Notice one sound, from a sharp rhythm to the trickle of water, allowing it to swirl you into the music of the universe. Expand your ability to savor sounds for one minute.

Space: Locate the space behind your spine. Feel the unconscious threats that linger there. Allow your head to spin around and notice that nothing is there—bubble bath pleasurable sensations as you savor *safe enough*. Now notice the space in front of you, the vulnerability of your soft stomach. Expand this awareness of space for one minute—bubble bath gratitude.

Our senses invite us back to ourselves. Many of us overlook the subtle sensations of being alive and receiving pleasure available throughout the day. Add this exercise while brewing coffee, waiting for the subway, or standing in line. Our felt sense is always changing, sometimes vague, yet always complex. Through this experience, we can acquire new information, interrelate with one another, and ultimately know who we are. It is so integral to our knowledge of being human that we take it for granted and underestimate its power.[81]

Untangle Experience: The Untangle Dance

The Untangle Dance allows us to find music within our body's intelligence. We are gathering capacity to move into a new experience and join the world. We are a storytelling, singing, and dancing species. **Let's shake it up**, if only a little. If we want to embody a thriving life, we must bring *more* of ourselves to it—more silliness, more weirdness, more loudness, more rhythm, more desire, more commitment, more energy.

Return to your mismatched message and say it out loud.

As you do, allow your body to move into your Tangled Self's dance. Imagine you are in a silent movie. How does it shake, move, attack, hide, collapse? If you encourage your body, it will automatically proceed. It may have you duck behind your hands to cover your face, raise your fists to fight, freeze like a possum, or try to tap dance on a tin roof. Whatever the case, dramatize it.

What music captures this dance? Is it rock, punk, or white noise? Get specific.

Allow the Tangled Self's dance to be fully expressed, embodied, and realized. And then stop. Interrupt it. Shake it off. Like waking up from a nightmare, open your eyes. Look around. Orientate. Check out present reality. Stand up straight and free.

Imagine your mismatched message is GONE.

What does it feel like to step into freedom? Notice. What swings and sways occupy this space? Welcome all the sensations that arise. Let's bounce inside our legs and remind ourselves that we can handle all our experiences. Feel your natural rhythm, sway, and swing as you bring yourself into present aliveness. Notice. Greet the world with a warm hello.

Find your Organizer Self's dance.

Ground into your legs. Feel the strength of your legs and their ability to stabilize balance. Allow them to bounce, sway, and move you into the Earth. Find a rhythm that supports flexibility, adaptability, and openness. Pound them, stretch them, strengthen them. Feel this Stabilizing Floor of Okayness. Imagine it is a surfboard, and you are surfing. Feel the energy of the waves. Feel the Earth supporting you. Listen to its drumming. Feel the mystery.

What music captures this dance? Pink Floyd, taiko drums, Beyoncé? Get specific.

Find sounds or instruments that match you into this organic rhythm. Register your freedom sway, your freedom walk, your freedom dance. Explore its movements. Does it feel safe or dangerous to emerge from the Tangled Self's dance? Does it feel vulnerable or exciting? Be curious and gather your body's intelligence. Listen to it. Allow it to speak.

Find your Creative Self's dance.

Imagine standing inside your freedom. Full-spectrum color. Ground into your feet. And allow the Creative Self's dance to move you into new shapes and rhythms. Freedom to express, assert, and occupy your desires with *no* apology. Feel your aliveness. Feel your fangs. Feel your power. Allow your body to surprise you. What starts to open, move out just a little bit? It may be a twist in your hip, a roll with your shoulders, or a wiggle in your butt. Does it pop your heart out or move your hands in circles?

Instead of forcing it out, allow it to take you somewhere unexpected.

Feel the surrender as you allow your body to play and capture its essence. It may look like modern dance, a catwalk strut, or an Irish jig. Whatever the case, let it shape you and become shaped by it. As much as we have a Tangled Self's dance inside us, we also have a Creative Self. What music do you hear? What rhythms does it create? **Explore it. Shape it. Embody it.**

Enlarge the gestures of your dance. Indulge the movement. Allow your whole body to swing and sway into a larger experience. Move between each dance, swirl them together. Tangled-Organizer-Creative. Feel the transitions between each one. Notice the simple shift in your response from one dance to the other.

As you move in new ways, you discover parts that were dormant and parts that can access your spirit. Notice how it feels to embody more energy of movement. Notice how good it feels to move. Notice how much imagination can be ignited by moving our bodies into new dances.

As we differentiate our three dances, we help our brain understand what each part feels like in our body's felt experience. We can shift inside one, shake out another, and stand inside a third. We can facilitate our own transformation from a tangled state, into a neutral state, into a creative state. We can develop a new structure of engagement to return home to ourselves in all our visceral dimensions.

Dance your life into full bloom. Sing your life into full bloom. Kiss your life into full bloom.

Chapter 11

Join the World

tangled life: terrified to take risk and become seen.
untangled life: safe enough to embody a committed life.

People who have been made larger by suffering are *brave enough* to let their Tangled Self unwind, activating deeper parts of themselves to take on a broader meaning. Slowly, through steady dedication, we are transforming a central part of ourselves to harmonize with others and our authentic nature. Gradually, the Creative Self will overshadow the Tangled Self. In this way, soul formation and wholeness are not individualistic; they are relational, a dynamic interplay and exchange that pulls us into conscious contact and committed actions, synchronizing us within the larger world. The rhythm of oneness dances in a chord structure that links past, present, and future into a whole integrated system. As we complete Step Three of The Untangle Method in this chapter, we become ready to step forward and rejoin the world, rediscovering our oneness, wholeness, purpose, and mystery. Untangling becomes soul shifting—a homecoming to our deepest belonging.

Imagine Ceremony

A Jewish wedding is a tapestry woven from many threads—biblical, historical, mystical, cultural, and legal—carried from one generation to the next, forming a chain of Jewish continuity which goes back thousands of years. On a cosmic level, the sages teach that each marriage ceremony is a personal Yom Kippur—the holiest and most auspicious day of one's life, where the gates of Ne'ila are open for the bride to usher down blessings for people's health, happiness, love, and prosperity. The groom places a thick veil over the bride's face, and she can't see—she stands and walks in darkness as she circles and sways through the remaining service.

Being blindfolded in the Jewish ceremony is a purposeful ritual, dancing us into the great mysteries, the unknowingness of what will arise in marriage, and a willingness to embrace all of it. It is a reminder to partner with the deeper elements of what we see and what is unseen. A commitment is making a promise to something without expectations, unleashing a desire to lose yourself in something or someone. It changes who you are, or rather embeds who you are in a new relationship—a mission, a cause, a family, a community, a beloved, a life of purpose. Here, commitment moves you into a higher level of service, an act of surrender and self-transcendence.

The first encounter between the Organizer Self and the Creative Self is an invocation. It invites our innate spirit to become present for life. In essence, the Organizer Self marries our opposing parts of the Tangled Self and the Creative Self, helping all aspects unite and orchestrate the music of our soul. As we move into deep communion, we find ourselves integrated with our flowering consciousness. There is a universe hidden inside us, and we want to open to its mystery, not close it off. We want to greet each part of our nature, learn their languages, embody their spirit, and dance them into serving the world. Just as our mismatched messages can travel us everywhere, so it is with the union of our three parts.

Ceremony moves us from sadness to joy, from feeling numb to feeling alive, to being part of a connection instead of being isolated. A ceremony repeated over time gains powerful meaning by ritualizing it in ways that move us through dance, drum, or song. This spirit of rejoining oneness is fueled by happiness and beauty. Create or imagine an altar where you can dedicate yourself to this ritual. It could be outdoors or inside, large or small. It may hold symbolic items that embody qualities of beings that we want to invoke in the ceremony, such as stones, plants, feathers, or photos. You could include elements of earth, air, fire, and water. It could be an area at your desk or a place you paint. It is for you to claim, recognizing a way for you to come home to yourself, home to the Earth, and home with life.

Interdependence

As MIT systems scientist and author Peter Senge points out, a critical effect of having lost touch with the totality of nature is that we've lost the ability to perceive interdependence.[82] Most of us just don't see it. Plants happen to grow in these little universes called ecosystems, where a complex web of interdependency sustains them with fungi, microbes, animals, and other plants. And science shows us that it always comes down to connections: from the fungi in the forest that nutrify the soil to the trees that sprout and grow from that nitrogen, to those trees, exuding the very oxygen that allows you to find your next breath. Every entity has its place and its function. We are part of this exchange, not separate and alone.

Our living world, in all its diverse variety, is something to remember. The Earth is alive. It is breathing. All creatures visible and hidden have their own language. Many of us cling tightly to self-reliance, trying to forget how helpless and scared we are, but at what cost? Rigidity often becomes our salvation to buffer against the terror, but it also blocks us from experiencing our cosmic belonging. The rhythm of nature has complexity and intelligence much wiser than us. We need to marry the brilliance of the wild, the authority of redwoods, the lyrical sermon of birds, and the tolerant rhythms of seasons. The musicality of nature helps us harmonize balance, wholeness, oneness.

Our perspective expands when we realize that nature engages in a very big game of passing things back and forth—a mysterious ebbing and flowing and appearing and disappearing act once described by philosopher Neil Evernden as the rhythm of exchange.[83] Our bodies naturally align with this rhythm—one of touching and listening, one of tightening and releasing, one of inhaling and exhaling. One thing talks while another listens. One part waxes while another wanes. One thing dies while another is born. We might not understand these intricacies, but we can appreciate their rhythm and find predictability within their interactions.

We are more than our bodies and minds. We have spirits and sacred dwellings. The Creative Self realigns us to this "nature," offering wisdom to fall back in love with life and the mysteries of the world. It carries the divine truth of existence, understanding that we are not separate and distinct from the universe, but rather, we are part of the universe, and the universe is part of us. The migration of the birds, weather patterns, ecology, brain activity, heartbeats, digestion, and metabolisms are all part of a correlated symphony. The more we notice and partner with this knowledge, leaving us to feel just a little bit different than the previous day, the more untangled we become.

The Energy of Trust

The world unwinds in different forms of energy—chemical, kinesthetic, electrical, thermal. These energies are not mystical, but rather the driving forces of our physical universe. When heavy energy is converted into vibrant energy, it pulls you forward and unleashes movements. Perceptions fall away. The mind is quiet, and time slows down. Similarly, energy flow is also shared within relationships and expressed in tonal cues, emotion, pace, and perhaps most of all, trust.

Trust holds our relationships together. Its presence grounds relationships by allowing people to feel safe, work together, and belong. Trust is difficult to define, but we know when it is lost. We can feel it—we withdraw energy and levels of engagement. Without trust, there is no flourishing, vibrancy, or growth. However, when trust is intact, we operate at a higher level of exchange. We contribute willingly to what is needed and share our dedication, talents, energy, and honest feedback.

Trust is not some elusive quality that you have or you don't have, but rather something you create within a process of showing up. Trust shapes how we love, express, grow, and belong. It locates resources to meet needs and expand connectedness in ways that regain dignity, access confidence, and embody transparency. Trust affects the quality of every relationship, every communication, and every effort of engagement. Before disappointment and failure got the better of us, there was a part of us that had trust in the exploration of life. Rebuilding trust is a process of remembering, attuning, growing, and committing.

Without trust, we are trapped in the lower states of the Tangled Self. We can't repair trust and restore dignity if we don't take responsibility for our lives. For our work, we restore trust in ourselves, making it *safe enough* to commit and belong to life fully. The Creative Self can willingly surrender, letting go of fear and inhibitions, because it trusts in the world and in its own power. If you still aren't quite there yet, remember that trust is an ongoing exchange. Trust can be earned. Trust can be lost. Trust can be rediscovered time and again. Whatever has happened in your life so far to rattle your trust in the world or in yourself, know that it can be earned back.

Untangle Experience: Needs Completion

The Creative Self orchestrates precision, tweaking, and redefining a way to meet our needs. The more consistently we practice meeting needs, the more we cultivate mastery with restoring trust. Variety mixes new hues and energies. Pleasure swells, pushing us out into the world in new ways—significance remixes in the forms of intimacy. As the Creative Self reclaims the need for growth, it writes us into a new love song, embracing uncertainty to join the larger collective world.

We first explored the four principal needs, certainty, significance, love, and variety, in Chapter 5. There, we discussed how the Tangled Self over-prioritizes some needs while neglecting others. Now we want to review the four needs in the new light of our untangling journey, recall the feelings that they sparked the first time, and acknowledge the new sensations that arise now. You may want to review your answers from the exercise in Chapter 5, or you may choose to move forward with a clean slate.

The Untangled Method's framework is designed to secure a healthy relationship with certainty. The Tangled Self's preoccupation with survival takes many of us hostage, chasing certainty in unhealthy ways. Unlike the Tangled Self that leans too hard on certainty, the Organizer Self gathers a new framework to stand inside our problems, building clarity, calmness, and love. The Creative Self synchronizes with variety to elevate our value and contribute in meaningful ways to our relationships. Healthy variety shakes things up and rattles us in the best of ways to embrace the uncertainty of life.

Close your eyes.

Swirl all the particles of data you have collected to enhance clarity around your needs. Now let's continue to determine the areas you want to strengthen. Drill into your needs to see how we can meet them today in ways the Tangled Self could not.

Return to the area you are untangling.

Remember, we are untangling one relationship, not a result.

Place yourself inside the interpersonal relationship you want to transform. It could be the relationship with your voice, asking for a raise, giving a presentation, or setting up a dating profile. Close your eyes. Is it possible to allow yourself out just a little bit more? How can your Creative Self help you meet the needs of variety, love, and significance to restore trust within yourself in this relationship?

Variety: What does taking new risks and playing harder look like? If you could let go and trust within the experience, what arises? How does your Creative Self help you dance with uncertainty and surrender control? Register it. What committed experience does it want to create? What feelings does it enhance and share with others that are meaningful to your heart? Allow it to emerge.

Love: What does embracing love within yourself and with others look like? What opens? When you remove all expectations of outside forces, how do you show up for love? How do you receive healthy pleasure? What emerges? How does the Creative Self express love in a way that blows your mind? Wait for it. See it. Feel it. How does it embody self-compassion and joy?

Significance: What does elevating your significance look like? What talents or past skills does it leverage? How do you realize your value in a way you never thought possible? Get specific. How do you become more intimate and share with loved ones in ways you never have? What feelings does it generate? How does it restore integrity and up-level your life? See it. Feel it.

Contribution: Once you meet all your principal needs, you can access the realm of contribution. This is how you put more of yourself into your relationships and enrich the larger world. What does generosity look like here for you? Your work, your life, your love should have breath and touch people, few or many. Contributions should give height to our commitment, coloring us in ways that push us and satisfy our souls yearning. What vision is sparked? What actions do you take? See it. Feel it.

You are the creator of your experience. Ritualize a practice of returning to needs. Become more curious and stronger in your ability to fine-tune meeting them in new ways. When you receive a hint of inspiration, move into it quickly. If you are untangling money, schedule a weekly date night with money. If you want to write a book, block off five hours on Saturday morning and write. Engage fully. Make it joyful, colorful, and meaningful.

The results of untangling and having the Creative Self meet needs are deceptively quick, but the effects are powerful. As you repeatedly return to your needs, your experiences will circle you into greater learning. The more precise, the more we create inspiration for new possibilities.

Inhale. Exhale.

Feelings come and go, and eventually, you realize that you are not your feelings or solely the Tangled Self, but that the real "you" is collaborating in the complexity of a larger system. As you become more aware of how the three parts harmonize with each other, you begin to live within an integrated, whole system. You can start to see all the ways that you have been tricked by the Tangled Self and how you have underutilized the Creative Self. As you identify with higher levels of consciousness, you nudge closer and closer to your realized, authentic self. **You are free.**

Untangle Exercise: Go Public

To fertilize growth, we need to go public. Yes, we need to share and engage in feedback. Whatever we are untangling requires a level of new behavior that engages with the world differently. Whether it is sharing a design sketch on Instagram, going to the gym, playing an instrument for family, reaching out to ask for help, writing a note to a mentor, or getting feedback on a book idea, we need to take it public.

Our brains love a challenge if it is within an optimal zone of difficulty. Often, we make it too big, scary, or unrealistic. The Creative Self does the opposite. It removes stress, pressure, and perfectionism. It works within a new set of rules to mess our way into new experiences. Remember, we didn't move from crawling to walking without a million little falls. And we certainly didn't get there having someone scream at us to "get it right" or "do it better."

When we create our own environment of success, we engage our whole system with commitment and excitement. If we believe we can have fun putting ourselves out there, we create more opportunities to engage, touch, feel, explore, and ultimately thrive. To increase motivation and aliveness, we need to jump into new environments, if only a little. Too much will overload us. Too little will kill motivation. Just enough will allow us to discover the magic.

My local community has three swimming pools: a baby pool (a foot deep, surrounded by lifeguards), a middle pool (three feet deep and perfect for kids and beginners), and a large pool (six to twelve feet deep and designed for competent swimmers). As we put ourselves out there, let's start in the baby pool. "Baby pools" are bite-sized opportunities to jump into new experiences, knowing full well we can jump out at any time. We can safely feel this water and gather its valuable feedback. Without it, we become stuck in our heads, circling, swirling, spinning.

Here are some ways we can put ourselves out there and still feel safe enough to explore. Take a deep breath and step into the first baby pool. Feel the cool water and splash around. Remember, you can always step back.

❖ Locate "baby pools."

Drill into the easiest way to jump into a new experience. It could be playing your guitar for your partner or taking it to the park. If you want to coach, find your first client. If you want to write a book, hire an editor. It could be saying hi on Facebook, taking an acting class, submitting your poetry, or sharing your money goal with a trusted advisor.

What is the first impulse that arises? Listen for it. Wait for it. And schedule it.

❖ New Rules: make it bad.

Yes, you heard me. Make it the worst first draft ever. Draw the worst picture. Or film the worst video. Feel free from any pressure to do it "right," just go for it! There is nothing you can't do when you are feeling light and agile, ready to play and experiment.

Your soul wants to be creating and living *now*. We are building a life, a body of work, a body of meaning. What are your Creative Self's new rules? Make a list.

❖ Cultivate a new mantra.

"I am willing to look bad." "I am willing to mess up." "I am willing to look silly." Find your new mantra. Start saying it. Howl it. Sing it. Claim it.

Have it insist on your own needs, rhythm, quirks, and standards. Love your personality flaws. Kiss them, say hello. Embrace them, work with them. Fun is better fuel.

❖ Match into your No and Yes.

Return to your declarations of "Yes More" and "No More." What actions lead you into the "No More" and which ones take you into the "Yes More"? Our "Yes More"s requires us to push into new directions, sometimes called contrary actions. What actions drive you into your "Yes More" declarations, and which one takes you into your "No More" declaration? Be specific.

❖ Keep at it.

If you are willing to keep working, that is your best guarantee of success. But the only way to sustain that kind of stamina is not to grind and push hard all the time, but to have fun every day. Whether it is exercising into a healthy body, decluttering your house, or accumulating money in your savings account, create systems that encourage variety, play, and adventure.

❖ Embrace your Spirit.

Become a jaguar, peacock, or dolphin. Allow the spirit world to help you rise, assert, fight, declare, want, need, and become realized. Nature has beauty and it has fangs. It preys, kills, gushes, and grows things on top of old bones. We need to call on all forces of our nature to help us claim life, become stronger, and do hard things. We can embody our fangs and still keep our hearts open. We are nature.

❖ Make it attractive.

Our bodies want to work towards pleasure. We wired our mismatched message to seek relief in unhelpful ways. Now it is time to separate low reaching pleasure activities and push them into higher reaching activities—junk food versus amazing food. Choose a weight set or notebook in your favorite color. Play. Highlight. Declare.

❖ Listen.

Listen to your whispers, the birds, nature, the swirls, the inklings. Notice them. You may not completely understand what it's like to be a flower but have faith in your imagination. Listen to the world inside of you and outside of you. It is full of life and wonder.

❖ Savor little victories.

Wiggle your hips into excitement. Sink into a cat's purr of "Oh yes!" Soak into a bubble bath of gratitude. We must feel it through our bodies. Remember the little victories, and they, too, will become your medicine.

Untangle Experience: Fairy Tale Endings

Each step of The Untangle Method corresponds with an element of the fairy tale structure. We are utilizing this structure to offer ways of resolving a stranglehold situation that could seem insurmountable. Untangling inspires us to look beyond limiting circumstances and find resources to transform them. There is no end to generating new possibilities; the Creative Self never gives up, and consistently finds ways to capture the magic of rejoining the world.

Return once again to your fairy tale, and this time we will focus on the magical ending, when our mismatched message is transformed into a powerful, enchanted love song.

Nightmare: The Tangled Self holds onto unconscious mismatched messages. What is your mismatched message? When you believe this mismatched message, what spell does it cast over you to suffocates your life force? Be specific.

Something Unexpected: The Organizer Self interrupts the blinding momentum of the nightmare with the Stabilizing Floor of Okayness. What three resources did you discover from your fairy tale or The Untangle Method to help overcome your nightmare? Be specific.

Magical Ending: The Creative Self's magic spell rewrites our mismatched message into a love song. What falls away, and what gets stronger? It could be more color, movements, images, music than words. What are its essences, and how does it arrange a new chord progression to mobilize you into a new experience and contribute to the world?

Mismatched Message: "If I open myself to the world, I will be hurt, rejected, and humiliated."

Love Song: "When I open myself to the world, I discover love beyond my wildest dreams."

To write ourselves into a new love song, we must activate inspiration. It is not sufficient to merely string together the correct beats or phrases. How your music makes you feel is more important than the words exactly. The Creative Self is engineered to take you somewhere new that blows your mind and helps others along the way. See it. Feel it. Inspire it.

Your Bigger Why

Nature and humans love seeking patterns, mastery, excellence, and rhythm. It isn't burdensome work but soul synchronizing. As we expand our lens of perception, we connect the dots. A new picture of freedom emerges—a vision swells from our lower bellies to warm our faces. Sparks of pleasure, joy, passion, and harmony become available. As we reclaim the Creative Self and take our place in the world's natural rhythm, we may be greeted with a warm sense of purpose, a certainty of belonging.

The Creative Self ignites transformation from a deeply embedded place of *why*. A way of connecting that enhances the deeper truths of who you are and what you are here to do. Ask yourself, why move your life forward? Why open your heart to love again? Why forgive and let go? Why, why, why. The more specific you become with the details, the more imagination the body will create. Our *why* is the vehicle to embody our compelling visions. Allow your *why* to spiral through your spine, guts, heart, throat, and eyes to soak into the wonders of nature. Allow it to move you from tangled to untangled.

Inhale. Exhale.

It is all inside of you. Your *why* may surprise you when you are taking in the beauty of trees, stars, flowers, art. It might jolt you when encountering a poem or doing a challenging exercise class. Our *why* wakes up into early morning wonderings. It asks, "Where have you been this whole time?" As we look deep into this source of life, we begin to understand everything better. We realize that we don't want to die without shaping our lives into their full glory.

For some, it is scary to ask *why*, because we have come to believe our *why* must be huge or epic in reach. We pressurize it by associating it with money or astronomical goals. On the contrary, it is often the simplest things that imbue our life with meaning. A purposeful *why* is not about grandiosity, but rather, it vibrates with meaning. Right now, your *why* may be providing a nourishing meal to your family. It could be taking care of your elderly parents. It could be a courageous conversation you bring to your team or spouse or child. It may be writing poetry, healing a broken relationship, creating art, fighting fires, producing plays, creating jewelry, or coaching your son's soccer team. We need to listen. Listen to the whisper of our children, the cries of Mother Earth, the longings of our heart's deeper desire. Let the world help you locate your purposeful *why*. It unleashes energy to reshape life.

How does your *why* help your family, community, collaborations, or the Earth?

Don't stop until you locate it. Let it tickle you. When it comes, you will know it in your bones.

The Untangle Method's Framework

The Untangle Method provides an organizing structure to link the Tangled Self, Organizer Self, and Creative Self into an *integrated growth structure*. As all parts collaborate and work together, they form an organizing structure for oneness and wholeness.

A Structure for Integration

We have a critical role to play in our own healing. We are never finished with our development. However, each of us deserves to return to who we are. Wholeness can be felt by anyone. No matter your age, gender, race, background, or level of spiritual development, oneness is your birthright. We untangle to shift our worldview and emerge within interdependence. How to dismantle as things arise and stay in the moment is an experience with grace. Cracks of openings allow new life to emerge. There is always a part of us that can love fiercely and reclaim life. It is never too late to untangle.

Untangle Exercise: Write Your Love Song

❖ What is your love song? How does it tickle your spirit? What does it have you want to contribute? Be specific.

❖ Place your love song around your heart. Declare it. Allow it to travel you somewhere new. Dance inside it. Hum inside it. Wiggle inside it.

❖ What widening circles do you create embodying your love song? How does it have you rejoin the larger world, if only a little? Be specific.

❖ What ritual or ceremony would help you remember this deep partnership? Meditation, candles, vision boards, smells, colors. Endow this connection with a practice that engages your senses. Be specific.

❖ What will you do with all you just learned? What changes? How do you help others? What do you contribute to the world? What energy do you create? What battles do you release? Be specific.

PART V

ONWARD

we are nature, long absent but now returned,
we are plants, rooted in compost to seed majesty,

we are bedded into earth, we are rocks, seeds,
we are blooms which open side by side,

we are daisies coupled together in perfect harmony
we are a towering amaryllis of creative musings

we are flowers, the fountain of life
we are two bees cross-pollinating,

we are moss, the emblem of love, always there, always available
we are grit, coarse minerals, acid and salt

we are a white lily, grace of tranquility and balance
we are fields of lavender swirling a map for home

we are wildflowers, blooming vibrancy, and frequency
we are dandelions traveling like little parachutes

we have circled and circled till
we have rooted and arrived home

(Inspired by Walt Waltman's *Leaves of Grass*)

My Untangle Story:

The Color of Purpose

As the heat of untangling vaporized *whore* from every cell of my body, I could feel myself being remade. My body holds stories like the woods, and its branches interlace to make new nets, so whatever rises, they will hold me. All is captured, welcomed, and soothed under colossal oaks. My body roots me into channels of memories. Some good. Some bad. All important.

Every time I untangle, part of my psyche breaks apart, and there is an unwinding of pieces of myself that I never imagined would be gone. And then, without realizing it, another part snaps into focus. Love enters. The realization that this tangled part was not my entire existence. And there is freedom in acknowledging this reality. It deepens my understandings of the richness of being a human. A stronger, wiser human emerges.

As I deconstructed my relationship with money, space opened and allowed me to move freely in my own skin, reclaiming my desires and ambitions. I no longer needed to hide behind the distorted faces of a "good girl," "bad girl," "the rebel," "the martyr." Or drown in the chaotic waters of under-earning. I became alive, present, available, accessing the inner workings of my Creative Self. Untangling wrapped around me, unlocking my windpipe so I could breathe deeply. It turned burning shame into fluorescent orange—no, red—no, purple—no, every color in the world.

Freedom moves fast when we are available.

One summer afternoon, nudged into warm grass, my oldest son, who was seven at the time, asked me to take him to Paris for his birthday. It was a sweet, impulsive request. What color? Viridescent. Lush. Green fields. Vision lit my heart like a lightning bug. I felt the world tilt in a new direction, leaning up inside of me. No thought or language, just joy. One word formed its shape around my throat, mouth, and lips. YES! At that moment, I tore my old world into pieces and saw a new landscape emerge. I had no idea how to earn the extra money, but I could figure it out.

One request, one vision, one possibility embedded bright vision to locate my purposeful *why*. Paris. It swirled through my blood and connected me to a larger world. I felt like a withered tree, discovering spring again, able to drink in the sunlight rising east. It wasn't heavy, difficult, or complicated, but vibrant. It created urgency, rooting me into a willingness to work differently and travel somewhere new. Within three months, my money life was transformed. I earned my last year's salary in two months. My son and I went to Paris. Vibrant pinks. Yellow daffodils. Snow globes of joy. All ushered us to Paris. London. Amsterdam. And it continues.

My Creative Self demanded I ask larger questions, such as, what would I need to create to earn last year's salary in one month? It needed a larger canvas to see my smallness in ways that sparked creative inspiration, not self-hate. It needed me to register the dirty pain, the cost of living small to find self-forgiveness and spark motivation. It needed me to remember all my experiences and puncture the victim noise of "I can't." It needed me to study great artists like Picasso and Gaudi, allowing their work to melt my brain and bestow inspiration. It needed *more* of me.

As I worked in this way, memories returned to me to tell a new story.

Like the sharp squeak of a wheel from a child's wagon, memories catch me. The more I remember, the more I am pulled little by little, rattling and circling into images and visions. Forgotten things come back quickly, like when you visit a town you haven't been to in twenty or thirty years. And at first, it seems strange, but then you start to notice little things, buildings, colors, roads that pull together clarity and remembrance.

Memories infused new colors, interlacing creativity to birth my company, Untangle and Thrive. All the pieces of my history mixed within complementary forces—dance training, theater experience, addiction work, financial expertise, death meditation, Jewish studies, mothering, gymnastics, trauma treatment, Buddhist spiritual practices, somatic work, ballet training, clinical skills, divorce, neuroscience, poetry, Shakespeare, homeless cases. How could I help others leverage their past and elevate their significance to contribute powerfully? As I leveraged my experiences and intersected them with passion, I created The Untangle Method.

I remembered my tap shoes.

Click, click, click: memories of my childhood forest, its rising slopes, giant lump trees, perfumed evergreens are pointing heads of green leaves to welcome me home. When I was a child, my body intuitively understood her organic workings. So how can I build an untangling practice to remember the intelligence of nature underneath the trauma of circumstance to help us heal in ways the mind can't? As I did, I attuned to the inner workings of my creative nature to help others find peace and realize their potential.

Click, click, click: memories of tucking into the theater's velvet curtain, dwelling, erasing, rocking myself into a sacred, spiritual state of emptiness snapped into focus. This emptiness wasn't a black hole but an invitation for a new experience to emerge. How could I build an untangling practice that locates the part of us that connects with the larger, mysterious world and can embrace uncertainty to transform? As I did, I developed creative resources to wash away shame by taking more risks and contributing to the world.

Click, click, click: memories of feeling fuchsia pink hitting me in the chest when I felt met by others. Eyes that saw me, supported me, encouraged me. Eyes of dance teachers. Friends. Rabbis. Mentors. Therapists. Aunts. Brothers. Colleagues. Clients. Dogs. Birds. Eyes shining light towards me to burn away the residue of shame, pain, hiding, unworthiness. After I stopped focusing on what I didn't receive, I could remember the times I did receive. Memories of my mother's eyes and my father's eyes that were there for me, loving and supporting me. As one memory integrated, other ones snapped into focus. How can I build an untangling practice to retrieve positive memories and allow new memories to emerge?

Click, click, click: bit by bit, *whore* dissolved from my skin. A spiral of energy flowed up my spine and into my brain, where it created a sensation of pleasure. The Creative Self clicked into focus. It spoke a different language, and its thoughts were determining all that was happening, infinitely gentle and yet sturdy as a rock. As I united within all my parts, partnerships interlaced a dynamic network. My work expanded across the country. It wasn't that the type of work I did changed, but how I engaged with it. I was unburdened and free. I hummed with pleasure as I rejoined my intimate desires and created value for others. At last, I was embodying my innate love song.

I often ask, what is the music that my body wants to create? I wait for it to respond.

Chapter 12

Continuation

We are never "done" with untangling. There is no beginning or ending in this process, only circling, eroding, and becoming more fully alive with each passing step. There will be expansive growth, and there will be setbacks to test the progress. This is normal, natural, and organic. We are gathering skills to lead ourselves from darkness to vibrancy, as many times as we need to. Like jazz, untangling has a specific language and structure. If you learn that structure, you begin to discover new tempos, rhythms, patterns, emotions, and soon you can start to improvise with the music of your soul. In this chapter, we will discuss a variety of ways to iterate on The Untangle Method as you move forward on your journey.

A Day in the Life of Implementing The Untangle Method

The following is a series of directives to help you continue to strengthen your untangle practice. These suggestions are designed to be simple and easy to execute, inviting you into a regular practice. You decide what feelings, creations, characteristics, movements you want to bring into the world. This is what untangling is all about: the empowerment of being able to choose. Start with one or two exercises that fit into a routine you already have. Try them out, then keep going or mix it up with something different. I hope that all, some, or even just one of these exercises will be of help to you as you strive to make untangling practice a part of your new life.

Practice Your Creative Self

Start trying on words of the person you want to become. Artist. Successful. Vital. Show up to a mall, gym, or coffee shop as your Creative Self. Or go shopping to try on things to explore matching this aspect of you. For some people, this could mean putting on a favorite pair of jeans with paint splashes. For others, it may be a particular pair of sunglasses or a fancy scarf. Or wear a special perfume to help you remember your capacity to be with a new experience. We need to practice what it feels like to embody the world from the Creative Self's perspective.

Start doing it where there is no threat, where you can play and explore the world safely. Notice what life feels like without your mismatched message dominating your worldview. Notice how you walk, drive, and move in the world. See how you interact and engage with others. Allow space for the Creative Self to come out just a little bit. Notice the energy of feelings and movements. The more you practice this, the easier it becomes.

❖ What image calls to your Creative Self? Is it a painting, color, or a spirit animal? Be specific.

❖ How can this image help you create variety and connectedness? Be specific.

❖ What self-talk will help you? Be specific.

❖ What ritual, mantra, or prayer could help? Be specific.

Practice Your Organizer Self

The Organizer Self is your prediction machine. It is continuously tracking and taking in your surroundings and analyzing the information it comes across. We can't always explain it, but learning is happening all the time. We can choose how we treat our body, how to manage time, how we show up in relationships, how we create our realities, and how we envision our futures.

What shifts you intentionally into an Organizer Self's presence? Is it putting on a pair of glasses or sitting in a particular chair? Notice what connects you with this part. What ritual would help your Organizer Self anchor into the day? Maybe it is a 20-minute routine in the morning. Maybe it is an exercise. Maybe it includes daily reading, mastermind class, meditation, or writing projects. Maybe it is seeking additional services or therapies to your life.

Get specific with how your Organizer Self interrupts old, unresourceful behaviors and begins installing healthy routines—with self-care needs, food, sleep, time, money, activities, and exercise. Strengthening the Organizer Self requires we push into challenges just a little bit more every day. It is no different than an athlete or artist practicing their skills, building endurance, stamina, and flexibility.

❖ What foods make you feel good and maintain good energy levels?

❖ How much sleep do you need to perform at an optimal level? Be specific.

❖ How much movement helps your body dissolve stress and become energized? Be specific.

❖ What are some oppositional forms of exercises that you could explore? If you always do yoga, how about kickboxing? Be specific.

❖ What calming techniques, meditation, or breath work regulates your nervous system? Be specific.

❖ What therapies can you add to your life or business to help support an empowered day of joy and love? Be specific.

❖ What does 1% better today look like? If we focus on 1% a day, imagine the progress we have accumulated after thirty days, sixty days, or ninety days. Be specific.

Play a Game

Strengthen your resilience by putting yourself in a slightly uncomfortable environment. It could be taking an improvisation class or playing a board game. It could be playing your instrument in front of your family, or deciding to go live in an Instagram feed. Connecting fear with action, safety, play, and inspired pleasure is the work. Embrace your powerful jaguar and decide on one small challenging environment to engage your Creative Self.

Games and competitions are a great way to see the inner workings of your Tangled Self. One hour of uncomfortable play can provide you more information than one year of talking about your problems. Test it through trial and error. It isn't about getting something perfectly. It is about engaging, learning, and refining what worked and what didn't. What trips you up? What strengthens you? How do you convert dread into pleasure?

After pushing through and exploring one little activity, my clients come back to me with loads of essential data. They get visceral access to their punitive self-talk, and how this talk throws them into a noisy, chaotic experience where everything feels heavy and not fun. This is so valuable because we can see the gap—where inspiration is lacking, and our critical needs are not getting fulfilled in a way that liberates the experience. Working with these gaps is how we become stronger and more resilient.

❖ What is one activity, game, or competition that makes you uncomfortable? Be specific.

❖ How can you inspire meeting all four principal needs (Certainty, Love, Significance, Variety) within the experience? Be specific.

❖ Test it. What works and what doesn't? What hijacks you? What unleashes you? Be specific.

❖ What do you need to give up or allow to create more joy in the experience? Be specific.

Baby Pools

Put "baby pools" *everywhere*! Locate one "baby pool" a day.

Create conditions to get *safe enough* to jump into a new experience, if only a little bit. Enhance your needs of love, connection, and variety as you try new things. If you are quiet, explore making louder sounds as you eat something yummy. If you are closed off, explore how you can open and play with an animal or a garden. Try new things in your business. Reach out to one new person who feels safe enough to meet for coffee. Explore learning a new dance routine. Learning a new language. Going to a party. Speaking up in a class-room. Asking for boundaries.

Locate the part of you that is available to play, experiment, explore, and try new things. Pay attention to the way it tilts you in a new direction. Notice the part of you that can shake off rigidity by becoming more excited by the experience of aliveness. Explore being inside your body, inside your life, inside a new experience every day. Jump in. Splash around. Jump out. Keep exploring.

Practice Emotions

Many of us wake up overwhelmed with enormous fear and stress about the day. As we anticipate what might happen or what might not happen, we end up creating more anxiety and stress. If this is the case, set a five-minute timer and do a fear dump—toxic stress, worst-case scenarios, allow your dark emotions to vomit on the page. The more we create space to share, the more we allow new feelings to arise.

Actors train by memorizing and rehearsing feelings to access them freely. They build a repertoire of feelings: grief, tenderness, confidence, shame, disgust, surprise, sadness, joy, love, rage. Feelings help the actor locate the character's motivation—why the character takes the actions they do, or why they don't. We want to do the same. Let's explore our feelings, understand them, look inside their signifi-cance as we grow our capacity to access a full range of feelings.

Explore your emotional life by engaging in these questions to build a daily practice:

❖ What one feeling do you want to create in your day or week (joy, peace, love)? Be specific.

❖ What actions link you to this feeling? Be specific.

❖ What colors link you to this experience? Be specific.

❖ How does this feeling shift your relationships? Be specific.

❖ What do you need to let go of to feel more of this feeling? Be specific.

Bubble Bath Gratitude

"Gratitude lists" are popular wellness tools—for good reason. However, for many of us, they can start to feel colorless or become rote. Sensations of joy and wonder are often impossible to convey in language. Imagine how much more you may feel while looking at a mountain top bathed in an alpine glow, or feeling the ocean spray splash your face as its surf crashes on the rocks, or walking along a country road surrounded by wildflowers, than you could ever express.

Scan your day to focus on one thing that you did that made you feel good. Maybe the spirit of your business whispered for you to take a break, and you listened, even though your brain was screaming "NOOOOO!" Or it could be saying hi to a stranger, licking the sherbet off your fingers, listening to a song with complete attention, making an uncomfortable phone call, or opening your bills. It could be noticing a beautiful flower, playing in the grass with your child, or helping someone across the street.

Notice. Notice. Notice what happens when you allow yourself to feel love, beauty, awe, gratitude, calm, peace. Bubble bath one experience every day. Savor an imaginary bubble bath and allow your skin to soak up gratitude for thirty seconds, sixty seconds, ninety seconds.

Let the bubbles pop, tickle, absorb your skin with gratitude.

Allow your skin to soak and receive gratitude to its fullest.

Practice bubble bathing gratitude throughout the day, noticing one exchange at a time.

Punctuate Your Day

Transitions happen throughout the day as we move automatically through our many tasks. Developing inner reflective experiences with transitions helps us organize mindfulness and intention within our day. Often, we barrel through transitions without noticing our inner experiences. Practice mini-interruptions. Punctuating transitions help us slow down and develop an understanding of the balance between our inner experience with the outside world.

You can punctuate transitions by taking slow breaths, getting a cup of tea, or connecting with a tree for thirty seconds before you greet your home, your child, your boss. We are all cyclical beings. When things are too much at the grocery store, street, or concert, you can take a moment to regroup. Change your breathing pattern. Wake up mindfulness. Notice all the little transitions we move between throughout the day—from the sofa to the kitchen, from the car to the house, from one action into another.

Stimulate Your Learning Mind

Spend twenty minutes a day learning something new. Dive deeper into an interest or hobby. Learn how to speak a new language or study science, nature, art, or a sport. Building a learning brain requires daily focus and concentration. Ritualize the space with a candle as you commit to your subject with no distractions for twenty minutes. Get lost in pleasure, learning to travel just a little bit every day. It doesn't have to be logical, just answer those little inklings and callings to explore.

Often, we make learning a chore. We forget about the splendor of learning and how pleasurable this state is for us. You may have poor school memories or struggle with feelings of inadequacy. Or maybe you felt the need to overdrive school for validation and performance, and in the chase, forgot the deeper joy of learning. You are a powerful creator of your life. Your energies, thoughts, and focus shape the world around you. You can't control the outside world, but you do have power over the way you experience it.

Explore new environments internally and externally. Engage in new books. Travel to a museum, study Picasso, create a new garden, take a new dance class, write your book, or sign up for a course on yoga postures. Shake things up. Challenge yourself to engage in learning every day and gather the necessary support to help along the way.

Untangle Problems

While not everything you untangle will follow this exact form, most of our mismatched messages do. Each time we circle back through the chord progression, we find more space to improvise in ways that continuously synchronize our hearts, bodies, and spirits.

Just because one part of you digs into "No," "I can't," or "I won't," doesn't mean there isn't another part that can engage it differently. The Untangle Method gives us a process to separate multiple experiences, thoughts, and feelings to collaborate within one whole system.

Choose any troubled area to work The Untangle Method. Think of the three steps as gearshifts to an overall system. As we separate the three parts and have them collaborate, we orient within an integrated system.

Step One: Locate the Tangled Self

Notice the part of you that whispers "I can't" or "I won't." As you understand the inner workings of this part, you will gain awareness to rupture its spell.

Step Two: Strengthen the Organizer Self

Notice the part of you that can root into the here and now. It says, "I am here," "I am alive," "I can handle more." As you strengthen this part, you lay down a Stabilizing Floor.

Step Three: Reclaim the Creative Self

Notice the part of you that is hungry for a new adventure, no matter how small or large. It says, "I can," "I will," "I want to go somewhere new." As you reclaim this part of yourself, you will find pleasure and joy in overcoming obstacles.

Balance Your Nature

Harmonize with the nature of plants, flowers, stars, and skies. Wherever you are now, however urban or interior your life, nature is still there for you—anchoring, inspiring, and helping you become more of what it is you set out to be.

Study the workings of nature. Watch how a cicada swells and pulls itself into molting. As the shell opens like an unzipped costume, the cicada's fresh body wiggles out, its new legs kick, and its inky eyes shine. Wings unfurl themselves from the sides to push from its brown, stiff husk, left behind on the branch. We need nature to help inspire us. We need courage and permission to peel back the layers of defensiveness. We need to remember we are nature.

Crawl into the dark morning to find your patch of grass and align with cosmic belonging. Feel the magic of stars and the mystery of soil. Locate the space of in-between, the movement that travels us between stuckness and liberation, chaos and beauty, hopelessness and inspiration, tangled and untangled. Find friendly openings in a clouded blue sky to open your heart and capture unbridled freedom.

Find Mentors & Community

Actively seeking additional mentors to help you on your journey is critical. We need to expand our social engagement system and gather feedback from trusted people. We want to seek resources and view asking for help as a strength, not a weakness, knowing full well we can't thrive in isolation. Mentors can be teachers, coaches, friends, bosses, sponsors, parents. They arrive in many shapes and colors. You can read their book and imagine them coaching you. You can sign up for their classes or take a retreat with one of them. Or you could regularly meet with them to get guidance and advice.

Finding your community is not up to chance. You can make concerted efforts to find your community or strengthen the one you already have, but you must seek connection. You may have to spend time in new places, join new groups, make new friends, but I promise, you aren't alone, and there is always a place to be discovered that resonates with you. It can feel lonely going at it all alone. We need community and people who *get* us to thrive with life. As much as there may be a part of you that hates groups, there might be another part that would like to be a part of a group. Get curious about what matches your spirit and go from there. It is a journey and a worthwhile one.

Scan to see where your ambivalence arises in the face of the community. Explore what is needed to level-up your commitment, love, passion. Maybe take on a volunteer role, or start a community to help solve a problem that weighs on your heart, or become a welcome greeter to your church or community organization. Explore how you can become more visible within your community by contributing your time, effort, and love. Or look to find a community that inspires you to show up in new ways.

For guidance on seeking support from therapies or community groups, consult the Additional Resources section at the back of the book.

Chapter 13

Conclusion

Becoming more conscious is the greatest gift we can give ourselves and others. The teachings and the practices in this book are about becoming fully human, dropping underneath the surface of things, and touching the magnificent intelligence inside our bodies and natures to untangle. Complete absorption and engagement of the material presented have been shown to help raise awareness and enhance higher levels of consciousness. Through frequent practice, our stuckness can convert into truth gathering and awaken intuitive vision. Untangling embraces the art of rupturing "black and white" states to become more colorfully human. Though you have reached the conclusion of this book, your exciting journey with this material is just beginning.

Collective Healing

Since 1999, suicide rates have risen by 30%. Between 2006 and 2022, suicide rates for those between ages ten and seventeen rose by 70%.[84] Roughly forty-five thousand Americans kill themselves every year. Opioid addiction is killing thirty thousand Americans every year.[85] In the United States, 36.5% of adults are obese, which strongly correlates with increased risk of heart disease.[86] Addiction, obesity, and divorce are impacting over two hundred million Americans. We are living shorter lives today because of the increase in so-called deaths of despair: suicide, drug overdose, and liver disease. Internal isolation, social isolation, and alienation are costing too many people their lives every day. We are looking for connections in all the wrong places. In the process, we're losing our connection to ourselves, to one another, and to our humanity.

Depression is a disease that we are still learning to fight. Depression manifests differently in every person, but treatment can help lower or eliminate the risk of suicide, and strong social support has been proven to play a large role in preventing suicide. If you suspect someone in your life of being suicidal, please reach out to them. Please, talk about depression. Talk about other forms of mental illness. The act of talking about it *does not* increase ideation or risk, and actually can make a significant difference.[87]

Three out of every five Americans feel alone.[88] Whether we think of ourselves as individualistic or collectivistic, we all need other people to thrive. Each one of us has a unique personality and set of needs, and no one person can meet them all for us, nor can we meet them alone. We need the diversity of community engagement to help us learn and connect more fully. With the U.S. polarized politically, ravaged by hate crimes, and suicide rates climbing to record highs, there has never been a more critical time to help people learn how to connect in healthy ways.

We are built for community, and that means learning to connect with others in ways that synchronize our bodies, hearts, and spirits. We are not designed to thrive in isolation. We need touch. We need social engagement. We need to gather. Part of becoming whole is about learning how to return to the body and build greater capacity for present connectedness. You have everything you need to call all the parts of yourself to come home and into greater collaboration.

In *What Happened to You?*, Dr. Bruce Perry, a trauma neuroscientist, engages a conversation with Oprah Winfrey, outlining the pillars of traditional healing that helped our ancestors overcome difficulties and thrive as a community:

"Our species could not have survived if the majority of our traumatized ancestors lost their capacity to function well. The pillars were 1. connection to clan and the natural world; 2. regulating rhythm through dance, drumming, and song; 3. a set of beliefs, values, and stories that brought meaning to even senseless, random trauma; and 4. on occasion, natural hallucinogens or other plant derived substances used to facilitate healing with the guidance of a healer or elder. It is not surprising that today's best practices of trauma treatments are versions of these four things. Unfortunately, few modern approaches use all four of these options, focusing mostly on the cognitive-behavioral approaches, greatly undertaking the power of connectedness and rhythm."[89]

We have reached a point of urgency that calls into question power dynamics and healing itself. One-on-one consultation with a health-care provider, while desirable and necessary in many cases, is inadequate for the epidemics we face. And unfortunately, good options are simply not accessible to everyone who needs them. We need inner resources to discern between destructive impulses and healthy ones. We need help to see problems from different perspectives, peeling back the faces of victimization and reactivity to connect more resourcefully. The skills of untangling, directing awareness, landing in what is working, and building more resilience need to become available to everyone who wants them.

You have taken steps to strengthen your bravery by being here with me. You have accessed glimmers of hope by strengthening your ability to land inside your truth, look around, and decide the next right action. As you integrate a sense of self-acceptance, self-respect, and self-love, there is nothing you can't do. And your personal healing can fuel collective healing. Use your experience, good and bad, to help others overcome suffering. You can spend less time on your own pain and have more available energy to turn outwards. You can cultivate resources to embrace uncertainty and change. Through this awakening, you will find liberation.

Your Story

Your story will apply to many others. You can take your darkest period and turn it into vibrant color. You can form new expressions, share them, and offer them to the world. And yes, it can be uncomfortable to open the doors to rigorous honesty and become vibrantly visible; it has to be, at least a little bit. However, as you embody your story, you access pockets of energy to color your life force. You can exercise your soul's capacity to create something new and experience deep pleasure in the process. You can reclaim parts of yourself that have been lost, forgotten, or never realized along the way. It is organic, natural, rhythmic.

Once you tell your truth, shackles come undone, fundamentally and irrevocably. When you tell your story, you reclaim new and different memories, looking at life from all its angles. Part of you is no longer hidden, ugly, dirty, loathed, or rejected. Self-hate can finally dissolve. When our old world is torn apart, we see what arises from the fragmentation, reshaping the pieces into a new world. Our chaos can become medicine. When everything feels like it is coming apart, untangling feels purposeful. And through it, we can help others heal as we learn to heal.

Embodying your living story in everyday life is an art form. We are natural-born storytellers. We can share our stories through dance, painting, music, speaking, or writing. We untangle our stories, again and again, until we are standing inside their pages. Self-knowledge is key to finding all aspects of your authentic nature, from which your story flows. As you finish one story, you strengthen your level of learning. You can then see what works and what doesn't. There is more genuine learning from failures than there is with successes. And there is no way to do this wrong. Waking up to your inner world allows you to reclaim the outer world. Untangling invites more of you to come into your story.

The process of living is one in which you are going to screw up. Noticing certainty dissolving into a pool of mud or having your pride disintegrate into a pile of doubt is not evidence of failure. It is evidence of aliveness, complexity, and metamorphosis. Being gripped by fear is not evidence of a character flaw. It is evidence of your need to be nourished by the qualities of safety and belonging. Welcome it all.

Henry David Thoreau wrote, "I went to the woods because I wished to live deliberately, to front only the essential facts of life, and see if I could not learn what it had to teach, and not when I came to die, discover that I had not lived."[90]

At the end of our life, I believe we will not remember our thoughts or intentions. But we will remember the actions we took and the ones we didn't take. We will evaluate our life by how we showed up. By what we said, what we stood for, how we acted, and whether we performed to our highest level. The reality is this: one day, we will stop existing. We must wake up to this reality to make changes today. Imagine death is staring into your eyes. Ask yourself, what are you going to regret?

- ❖ You will *regret* not giving 100% commitment to everything.
- ❖ You will *regret* not staying with things that mattered to you because they became difficult.
- ❖ You will *regret* not puncturing denial and opening your heart to feel everything.

❖ You will *regret* not answering the call of your gifts and realizing them to their fullest potential.

❖ You will *regret* not being kinder to those who are suffering.

We are all born with an innate power to create change and help others. We have deep wisdom and intelligence inside us. When we languish in vagueness, we are hindering our ability to reach others, to make a difference, and to contribute meaningfully. We want to take our untangle literacy to locate our voices and activate them in directions to help others. By learning these skills, you have expanded your organizing capacity, and hopefully, the drive to help others. There is no greater gift than reaching out and shining a light for someone else.

Much can be done by reaching out to help one person. Lives change. Families change. Organizations change. Helping others connects us to the collective *we*. Give by donating your time, resources, or money to populations, causes, and communities in need. Build a relationship with organizations whose work resonates with you and that you want to support and see grow. Take a moment. Think about what more you can do to offer a hand, to be of service. Share your story or call an old friend. We never know how one action could help shift someone's life.

An untangled life will challenge you, and if you face it with openness and willingness, you will find yourself developing more confidence, harmony, and joy. You will develop a cosmic perspective that aligns with mystery, stars, flowers, and wonder. There is so much awe in the world, and the world needs you. It requires all of you to show up every day and contribute meaningfully. Whatever that looks like, it needs more of you now.

My Untangle Story:

The Color of Untangling

I am my father. I am my mother. I am both. I am a Tangled Self. I am a Creative Self. I am more than flesh. I am spirit. I am purpose. I am color. I belong to all, and at the same time, I belong nowhere. I am roots. I am seasons. I am a star. Like nature before me, I too am untangling, eroding, and rebuilding.

People often ask me how I constructed The Untangle Method. I say from the ashes of despair and an intense desire to taste freedom—the freedom to speak, move, love, belong.

I remember the exact moment I stumbled onto the vision for this book. It was twenty-five years ago. At the time, I was barely able to tolerate my burning skin. My freckles felt like scars. I had recently converted to Judaism and participated in my first Orthodox Passover, commemorating the Jewish people's freedom from their slavery in Egypt. At the dinner table, the Rabbi shared that "converts" see things that rooted Jews cannot. In his words, I was an "untethered soul." He leaned towards me and encouraged me to share what I was seeing. What are the Jewish people missing?

I felt jolted by the question—heart drumming as dark swirls gushed inside my stomach. It was extremely unorthodox for someone of his religious stature to invite such inquiry. I had a lot to say, but my voice was unsteady. I pushed down the hard knot in my throat. All attention was on me. As I unlocked my vow of silence, the warm air greeted me.

I shared my vision.

The method of cleaning "crumbs" from every corner of the house seemed disconnected next to the celebration of freedom in Passover. On the one hand, the cleaning seemed like a form of slavery. And maybe that was a point? To put yourself into a visceral experience of slavery, remembering the harshness of the past? On the other hand, the ritual seemed arbitrary, not integrating or linking the two worlds, the physical and the spiritual world. It felt like a recreation of the trauma, not an unwinding.

Passover's practice embodies home. Every room, every corner, every story in your house is being stirred through the process of cleaning, offering a spiritual portal to unwind trauma. Why not use the exercise to locate our "unconscious crumbs of slavery" and learn how to unlock them? Isn't our relationship with the kitchen different than the office or bedroom? Why not investigate enslavement in each area and develop skills to find liberation? Aren't there so many of us disenfranchised, orphaned, lost, looking to find our way home? Wouldn't this way of cleaning embody the spirit of Passover and have us rejoin the world powerfully?

I remember the Rabbi's eyes.

I lifted my head like a rising wave and, at that moment, felt met. I had stumbled onto something. I felt its significance in my bones. A butterscotch smear washed over me. I was dripping in uncertainty as his eyes read the deeper hues of color rimming my blue irises. Honeysuckle blossoms.

Sunlight. Wilderness. I tried to soak in the encounter, but it felt exposing, terrifying. His head shifted a little to his left.

And then he said, "You need to write a book."

Glimpses of hope poked through the cracks. Excitement was mixing the perfect teal color. Pieces were being rearranged, and my synapses were firing like mad. I heard a new instrument, a double bass, stirring from my feet and pulsating my heart. I circle back to this one exchange over and over again. As I do, my body can metabolize it. I didn't know how, when, or where. But I knew it needed to move through me. And it has.

Untangling has been a soul wrestle. There were tears of frustration and exhaustion, as well as harmony and peace. I find wisdom in juxtaposition—bitter and sweet. My triggers are the crumbs that lead me to the seeds of healing. Where there is brokenness, there is also timeless beauty. It is a continuum, all working together to capture the essence of my innate nature and contribution.

As my parts smudge, I refine my sense of self through iterations and rediscovering the rhythms of my soul. The better I know myself, the better I can be with others. As with all art forms, craft becomes fine-tuned through a process of engagement—a practice of learning to find inspiration through challenges and commitment. I gain genuine pleasure from making something, no matter the result—dipping into the joy of becoming one with its creation. Musicality is the only constant.

Vision pushes me, like the Earth grinding rock into the dirt, slowly breaking things down so new life can emerge. I work on opening like a flower into this vision, and as I do, I get closer to the mysterious energy that inspires me to try new things. Invisibility is no longer my escape route. I am more comfortable in my skin. I am an orchid. For decades, I fought my nature. I had to learn how to train my system to bloom. Vermillion swirls. My nature demands a highly tuned, not rigid, environment, and for this, I am grateful.

With untangling, there is an ineffable sense of being returned home—a place of authentic connection lurking beneath the sediments of rigidity and chaos. It is a place you return to over and over again—a place of worthiness and value. Even when I am miles away from it, a song or a smell can return me. Joy sparks inside me when I achieve something unexpected or unimagined. Senses of newness, change, and beauty shines forth in all imperfections. And love infuses every perception of the here and now. Separation dissolves. And everything becomes exquisite.

I ask every day, "Am I tangled or untangled?"

I have learned to trust my inner compass, rooted like a magnolia tree. Every morning I peek around new doors. Am I living the life I love? How am I trying to help the world? When it is all over, what do I want to be remembered for?

I keep learning to pray again. Not in the way I was taught, but in all the ways Spinoza and nature have taught me. I believe the task of humanity is to reunite with the scattered sparks of light and repair the broken world. I long to participate in the mending process of harmony. The only thing we know for sure is that we are here, we are alive, and our life is full of wonder. I dwell in the complexity of being alive. I want to remember it all—the way the world used to swallow me into black cracks and now springs me into action. As I remember living in this way, the pieces of my story glue together, and I see a new landscape.

As I find my way home, I can help others find their way.

I try to stay open to what is coming and life's endless spectrum of color. That uncertainty is the only way of the world. I try to find balance in this rhythm, how my walk shifts, my pulse beats, my head tilts. Every night I scan my day, noticing one thing, one glance, one smile, one exchange. I swirl like a bubble, popping into its nuanced subtlety of aliveness. What color?

Step outside and look up to the sky. There. That little speck of the world. At first glance, it might seem flat, dull, or colorless. But it's much more complex than that. There are waves, like in music, capturing a world. Squint. See the touch of violet—the streak of copper. See white blossoms interfacing with hues of blue and drops of sunlight, all swirling together. Breathe them. Let them tickle you under your arm. And smile. Laugh. Those are the colors of home.

Questions and Answers

I've received many questions regarding the application of The Untangle Method. This section includes frequently asked questions and answers from workshops and classes that have been given around the world in recent years.

How does untangling help with resentment?

Blame is the world's greatest excuse, but it comes at a steep cost. The mind would like us to think there is such a thing as justifiable anger. We might like to think we are right and the other person is wrong, but we must confront resentment's detriment to our overall emotional and mental health. Resentments are like weeds or poison ivy. Initially, they look harmless, but as they grow, they strangle, suffocate, destroy everything. We can end up managing old resentments for decades, or even our entire lives.

Resentments are a wake-up call for untangling. We need not forgive or excuse unforgivable acts. However, as long as we hold on to resentment, we are holding on to pain. We want to better understand the part of us that needs to hold on. Once we do, we often discover other resources to reframe the experience. Resentments become a key to spiritual and emotional growth.

Why do we need to drop expectations?

Expectations of others can be a form of emotional blackmail. When we stop pressuring others with our expectations, we allow space to see them as the person they truly are. We will see more clearly and be more available to be with what is in front of us. Many of us need to become more declarative with what we want and need. We want to build skills to become unavailable to accept invalidation from others or ourselves. Period. As we stand inside of our needs more resourcefully, anger dissolves, and expectations melt. We move automatically from the level of sacrifice to the level of love. As we acknowledge ourselves for this move, we drop our expectations which will dissolve resistance in others.

No matter how good I look, when I look in the mirror, I hate what I see. How can The Untangle Method help?

The most powerful of all human sensory abilities is vision. Given this, it is also our most cutting, brutal, and harsh sense. Many of us give our mirror the power to make us feel great or horrible. As we do, we drown in punitive self-talk. We get captured in spells of waiting, self-hating, or fixing.

Allow the trigger of the mirror to help you heal. Once you understand the part of you bonding with it destructively, you can find self-compassion and acceptance. You can form a new relationship with this part of you as well as the mirror. Empower yourself to claim a new experience. Engage the other senses to enhance a pleasurable experience. Scent and touch and sound are less bound up in the way vision is. Cover the mirror if need be. Or write Post-it Notes on the mirror that say funny things or messages of "I Love You." Bring music into your experience. Allow the space between you and the mirror to be one of healing and reclamation.

I am not a follower of any spiritual path, but I have my own personal path. How can The Untangle Method be helpful?

While many spiritual practices can view the destructive part of us as sinful, evil, or bad, The Untangle Method aims to shift this response by not seeing our Tangled Self as a moral defect. Our responses at one time helped to protect us, and they are neither bad nor good, but can be helpful or hurtful.

Untangling can enhance any personal self-development, for it is compatible with a humanistic movement. It entails no spiritual teachings of its own. Instead, it provides a framework so that self-understanding removes the blocks to creative and spiritual advancement.

How does The Untangle Method differ when it's used by members of different genders? Or, does it?

It doesn't. I have often described the different parts of The Untangle Method as masculine and feminine, which seems to help my male clients. I see the Organizer Self as the embodiment of a healthy masculine structure. When this part of us is stuck in punitive harshness, it becomes an unhealthy force that drives wounded emotional re-enactments. As the Organizer Self wakes up to higher states of awareness and consciousness, it embodies a healthy structure to build a foundation of safety, kindness, predictability, and generosity for all parts to come home. It accesses transformation as it reconnects with the Creative Self, the part of us that aligns with resourceful, creative energy. I view creative energy as healthy female energy. In my opinion, all genders need both healthy masculine and feminine aspects to thrive.

Can you use The Untangle Method for political parties?

Yes, you can use The Untangle Method to locate your unconscious bias with political parties. Political divisiveness may be repellent to many of us, but we are a country riddled with it. Polarization offers fake intimacy and toxic belonging by uniting hatred against "the other side." It operates from threat, revenge, fear, apathy, and victimization. One never learns by hating, shaming, and pointing fingers. The Tangled Self operates under a radical polarization of an unconscious threat, but as we pull it into greater awareness, we can see this part of us is confused and broken from present reality. Similarly, the political divide is an outward manifestation of inner polarization.

If I work a twelve-step program, how does The Untangle Method help or hurt this practice?

The Untangle Method does not replace the need for self-help groups, AA, or individual therapy. It can help facilitate success in recovery efforts, and it is certainly compatible with all 12-step programs. The obsession to drink is a compulsion due to a response. This can be understood and possibly weakened through the process of untangling. Drinking is also an escape from pain, therefore building a practice that helps emote feeling to create a new relationship with pain can help decrease the need for the escape.

The Untangle Method doesn't talk much about goals. Why is that? And what is the difference between goals and vision?

Goals are important, for they offer clarity, and clarity requires greater responsibility. However, focusing solely on goals can stick us into our head's marching orders. Many of us are lost with who we are and what we are meant to do. Vision anchors this intimate journey. Without embodying vision, the whys, the feelings, the impulses, the desires, the layers underneath our goals, we can get stuck in mental strategy and self-will. This can lead us to all types of problems and frustrations, such as aggressive chasing, giving up, and shutting down.

For example, we can declare we want to earn a certain amount of money each month a month, but if we are not connected with the energy of that number, the value we need to create to earn it, and the worthiness we need to receive it, the goal can become a tangled quagmire. The Untangle Method works within these delicate systems to help. It is about connectedness—how we partner with our own needs to receive good things in ways that elevate our value. Goals have an important place but shouldn't be our sole focus, in my opinion.

Will untangling cure sexual anorexia?

The Untangle Method doesn't cure anything. Learning to open yourself to a new experience requires tolerating uncomfortable sensations and allowing new sensations to arise. Anorexia is a statement of "I can't" or "I won't." There are expressions of conflict, blocking us from more joy, love, expression, and aliveness. However, these parts of us carry survival defenses from the past, and they deserve to be heard, understood, and treated with kindness.

Many of us need additional resources and therapeutic support to increase our inner capacity and feelings of safety to tolerate opening, allowing, and exploring. Sexual anorexia has complex layers unique to our personal stories. Often, it is an attempt to solve other problems with traumatic memories or feelings of chaos, shame, danger, or terror. There is hope and recovery. Many people who use The Untangle Method with their fears report an overall improvement within their sex life and ability to connect within their bodies. Whatever you are dealing with, I hope that it will help you understand these feelings and take steps towards the life you deserve to live.

Fear and insecurity drove my success and accumulation of wealth; if I let go of those impulses, will I still be successful?

Many of my top-performing business clients are insecure. Because of this, they are always stressed and frightened in their responses. They are afraid that if they let go of their impulse to chase external validation, things will not work out, or they will not be motivated towards success. Since they operate from fear, any change or recommendation will activate fear, for it runs their life—fear of missing out, fear of not belonging, fear of not being good enough, fear of being found out.

Once they neutralize their threat responses, they can convert negative energy into joy, love, harmony, realizing their innate value at last. It is a dance of intimacy. When a lower motivation of the Tangled Self has been brought into present awareness, the mind will automatically replace it with a higher motivation to meet needs in healthy ways. These types of people are often amazed that their greatest fear, becoming a failure or unmotivated, is not true at all. They begin enjoying their work and earning money from states of love and joy, not fear. The same activity continues but from a pleasurable space, and it yields many rewards beyond financial ones.

Remember that the mind and the body have conflicting motivations, and it is our job to separate and better understand them. One part of you may want to be free of the stress, anxiety, and tension, while another part of you believes that hanging onto it will bring about some desired change. Unless one is conscious and has mastered the untangling technique, the Tangled Self's survival nature will override and dominate.

How does The Untangle Method work with meditation practices?

Meditation practices provide two foundational skills that are useful in navigating our inner world: mindfulness and concentration. Mindfulness trains us to notice without judgment, whereas concentration develops a capacity to focus where we want our attention to go and hold it there. Similarly, untangling is about activating awareness to organize within a mindful, creative state to harness choice and focus. One of the vital teachings of The Untangle Method is how to separate from the part of us that holds onto the past. Unwinding the energy of the Tangled Self facilitates a similar goal as meditation: producing a state of inner peace and acceptance in the present moment.

Like mindfulness practice, untangling exercises bring the sensory field closer through active observation and somatic experience. As we elevate our level of exchange within our inner and outer world, we prime our system to receive more joy with living.

How does The Untangle Method build within a community?

Coming out of isolation is healing. One of the most inspiring experiences I have had is sharing and working these skills with clients and groups throughout the years. It has been an honor to watch people listen to their own hearts, access their inner steadiness, and trust their own knowing. This is the gift of practicing with others. When I teach groups live or online, people learn from each other, and their learning in turn, supports the healing of others through their struggles and triumphs. Holding strong intention, we become a community of support and authentic inquiry. The most important part is to find communities that create safety for you and others in it.

Additional Resources

Trauma Resources

Owning our story can be a struggle. However, running from it is more difficult. The degree to which we grow is directly proportional to the amount of truth we can accept. The scope of trauma-related topics is wide, and the implications of childhood adversity are pervasive and profound.

Adverse Childhood Experiences (ACE):

Adverse Childhood Experiences sections of the Violence Prevention Branch of the CDC (https://www.cdc.gov/violenceprevention/aces/index.html): This site is full of educational resources, research articles, and policy implications related to adverse childhood experiences. It is the most reliable resource for accurate information about ACEs.

There are four main types of abuse: sexual abuse, physical abuse, emotional abuse, and neglect. As the ACE study has shown, child abuse and neglect are the most preventable causes of mental illness, the single most common cause of drug and alcohol abuse, and a significant contributor to leading causes of death, such as diabetes, heart disease, cancer, stroke, and suicide. Finding your ACE score can be a helpful step if you or someone you know is just beginning to understand their story.

Take the ACE test at https://americanspcc.org/take-the-aces-quiz/

It is estimated that 70% of adults experience at least one traumatic event in their lifetime. And 20% of these people will develop PTSD. PTSD is a type of anxiety disorder that can develop after a deeply threatening or scary event. Symptoms include insomnia, flashbacks, low self-esteem, and a lot of painful or unpleasant emotions. You might constantly relive the event, or lose your memory altogether. The good news is that trauma is *not* a life sentence.

There are a variety of therapeutic modalities that help with unwinding trauma. Somatic-focused therapies (versus cognitive-behavioral or "talk therapy") have been proven more effective in treating trauma, but everyone is different. Body approached therapies rooted in the language of the body include trauma-focused therapy, EMDR (Eye Movement Desensitization & Reprocessing), Hypnotherapy, Somatic Therapy, Biofeedback, IFT (Internal Family Systems Therapy), EFT Therapy (Emotional Freedom Therapy), Gestalt Therapy, and Psychodynamic Therapy, Psychomotor, Feldenkrais, and Hakomi Somatic Psychotherapy. To learn more: *https://www.healthline.com/health/mental-health/ptsd-causes*

Additionally, there is presently a re-emergence for mind-altering psychedelic drugs that have brought the field of mental health to a new frontier. MDMA, psilocybin, and ketamine have shown promising results in the treatment of trauma-related disorders, some forms of anxiety, and depression. As this field of science grows, researchers are giving serious consideration to how these novel treatments can work in the context of social work practices and psychotherapeutic treatments. Before jumping into an immersive mind-altering experience, please consult with a medical professional and therapist to facilitate the process. While these experiences can be healing for many, without the proper support, they can be difficult for others. To learn more: *https://academic.oup.com/ijnp/article/23/6/385/5805249*.

If you are in crisis, call the toll-free National Suicide Prevention Lifeline at 1-800-273-TALK (8255), available twenty-four hours a day, seven days a week. The service is available to anyone. All calls are confidential. To learn more: *http://www.suicidepreventionlifeline.org*

Resources and Free Programs:

SAMHSA's National Helpline, 1-800-662-HELP (4357), (also known as the Treatment Referral Routing Service) or TTY: 1-800-487-4889 is a confidential, free, 24-hour-a-day, 365-day-a-year, information service, in English and Spanish, for individuals and family members facing mental and/or substance use disorders. This service provides referrals to local treatment facilities, support groups, and community-based organizations. Callers can also order free publications and other information.

NAMI: NAMI, the National Alliance on Mental Illness, is the nation's largest grassroots mental health organization dedicated to building better lives for the millions of Americans affected by mental illness. NAMI started as a small group of families gathered around a kitchen table in 1979 and has blossomed into the nation's leading voice on mental health. Today, we are an alliance of more than 600 local affiliates and forty-eight state organizations who work in your community to raise awareness and provide support and education that was not previously available to those in need. To learn more: *https://nami.org/home.com*

Twelve-Step Programs:

Twelve-step programs are mutual aid organizations for the purpose of recovery from substance addictions, behavioral addictions, and compulsions. Developed in the 1930s, the first twelve-step program, Alcoholics Anonymous (AA), aided its membership to overcome alcoholism. Since that time, dozens of other organizations have been derived from AA's approach addressing problems as varied as drug addiction, compulsive gambling, and overeating. All twelve-step programs utilize a version of AA's suggested twelve steps first published in the 1939 book *Alcoholics Anonymous: The Story of How More Than One Hundred Men Have Recovered from Alcoholism*. Here is a list of sub-set twelve-step programs for anyone suffering. Please visit their websites to access free meetings, evaluations, resources, and support.

AA - Alcoholics Anonymous

NA - Narcotics Anonymous

CA - Cocaine Anonymous

MA - Marijuana Anonymous

ACOA - Adult Children of Alcoholics

AL-ANON - a support group for the relatives of people suffering from alcoholism.

SLA - Sex and Love Addiction Anonymous

SA - Sex Addiction Anonymous

UA - Underearners Anonymous

DA - Debtors Anonymous

OA - Over-Eating and Under-Eating Anonymous

Smart Recovery: www.smartrecovery.org
SMART Recovery is an abstinence-oriented, not-for-profit organization for individuals with addictive problems. SMART Recovery
does not use labels like "addict" or "alcoholic" and relies on scientifically validated methods to foster empowerment and positivity.
Members are encouraged to volunteer.

Somatic Experiencing Trauma Institute: www.traumahealing.org
Somatic Trauma Institute is a global network of somatic practitioners
to help people heal trauma through the body. If you are interested in
training, the three-year, eleven-module training is an excellent foundation in somatic work.

Further Reading

When my clients ask for resources, these are the books that I point them towards.

On Trauma:

Body Keeps the Score; Brain, Mind, and Body in the Healing for Trauma by Bessel van der Kolk, Ph.D. (Penguin, 2010)

The Pocket Guild to the Polyvagal Theory; The Transformative Power of Feeling Safe by Dr. Stephen Porges (W.W. Norton & Company, 2017)

When the Body Says No; The Cost of Hidden Stress-Disease Connection by Gabor Matè (Random House, 2011)

My Grandmother's Hands; Racialized Trauma and the Pathway to Mending Our Hearts and Bodies by Resmaa Menakem (Central Recovery Press, 2017)

Born for Love: Why Empathy is Essential—and Endangered by Maia Szalavitx and Bruce D. Perry, M.D., Ph.D. (Harper Collins, 2010)

No Bad Parts: Healing Trauma and Restoring Wholeness with the Internal Family Systems Model by Richard Schwartz, Ph.D. (Sounds True, 2021).

What Happened to You? by Bruce D. Perry, M.D., Ph.D. (Pan MacMillan, 2021)

Waking the Tiger; Healing Trauma by Peter Levine, Ph.D. (North Atlantic Books, 1997)

It Didn't Start with You; How Inherited Family Trauma Shapes Who

We Are and How to End the Cycle by Mark Wolynn (Penguin Life, 2017)
The Drama of the Gifted Child; The Search for the True Self by Alice Miller (Basic Books, 1997)

On Addiction:

In the Realm of Hungry Ghost: Close Encounters with Addiction by Gabor Matè (North Atlantic Books, 2010)
Facing Love Addiction: Giving Yourself the Power to Change the Way You Love by Pia Mellody (Harper Collins, 2003)
Attached: The New Science of Adult Attachments and How It Can Help You Find and Keep Love by Amir Levine and Rachel S.F. Heller (Penguin Random House, 2011)
Drinking, A Love Story by Caroline Knapp (Dial Press, 2005)
Portrait of an Addict as a Young Man: A Memoir by Bill Clegg (Back Bay Books, August 2011)
Unbroken Brain: A Revolutionary New Way of Understanding Addiction by Maia Szalavitz (Macmillan, 2016)
The Biology of Desire: Why Addiction is Not a Disease by Dr. Marc Lewis (PublicAffairs, 2016)

Psychotherapy:

Mindsight: The New Science of Personal Transformation by Dr. Daniel J. Siegel (Norton, 2010)
The Developing Mind: How Relationships and the Brain Interact to Shape Who We Are by Daniel J. Siegel (Guildford Press, 1999)
The Healing Power of Emotion: Affective Neuroscience, Development

and Clinical Practice by Fosha D. M. Solomon and D. J. Siegel (Norton, 2009)

Intensive Psychotherapy for Persistent Dissociative Processes: The Fear of Feeling Real by Dr. Richard Chefetz (Norton Series on Interpersonal Neurobiology, 2015)

Getting Past Your Past: Take Control of Your Life with Self-Help Techniques from EMDR Therapy by Francine Shapiro (Rodale, 2012)

Internal Family Systems Therapy by Richard C. Schwartz (Guildford Press, 1997)

Flow: The Psychology of Optimal Experience by Mihal Csikszentmihalyi (Harper Collins, 1990)

Additional:

The Untethered Soul: The Journey Beyond Yourself by Michael Singer (New Harbinger Publication, 2007)

The Eight Master Lessons of Nature: What Nature Teaches Us About Living Well in the World by Gary Ferguson (Penguin, 2019)

A New Earth, Awakening to Your Life's Purpose by Eckhart Tolle (Penguin, 2008)

Power vs Force: The Hidden Determinants of Human Behavior by Dr. David. R. Hawkins Ph.D. (Hay House, 2014)

The Artist's Way: A Spiritual Path to Higher Creativity by Julia Cameron (Tarcher Books, 1992)

The Gifts of Imperfection: Let Go of Who You Think You're Supposed to Be and Embrace Who You Are by Brenè Brown Ph.D. (Hazellden Publishing, 2010)

Bird by Bird by Anne Lamott (Anchor Books, 1995)

A Path with Heart: A Guide Through the Perils and Promises of Spiritual Life by Jack Kornfield (Random House, 2009)

Acknowledgments

I have leaned heavily on others during the creation of this book. Before anyone else, I must thank my husband, Sean, and my two sons, Benjamin and Wolfe. Sean has played every role a person can play in making a book: partner, friend, fan, critic, editor, cook. Benjamin and Wolfe have been my biggest cheerleaders and my loudest accountability players. "Are you done yet, mom?" "Mom, are you done?" This book would not have happened without my love for them and their rhythmic drumbeats to finish.

Second, I must thank my family members, who have all been generous throughout this tedious process. In particular, I want my mother and brother to know that I love them. I am grateful for your unyielding confidence in allowing me to share selected pieces of my story. This narrative focuses only on a few aspects of my childhood experiences to illustrate how unconsciously trapped I was inside my response to the events that happened to me. I appreciate your support for my becoming visible on these pages. I am the person I am because of our family.

Third, it is no exaggeration to say this book would not exist without the insights and wisdom of many mentors, psychologists, psychiatrists, neuroscientists, artists, rabbis, spiritual teachers, and scholars along the way. Above all others, Lee Garlington single-handedly created a sacred space for my life to take root and thrive. You gave me my first taste of safety and why this work is so critical. I knew I was catapulted into a new universe when I first connected with you. You exemplified loving boundaries for my feral-ness to come undone. I will be forever grateful.

I take great pleasure in acknowledging the brilliant minds whose ideas have contributed to this work. Bill Wilson, the founder of Alcoholics Anonymous, was not a doctor or psychologist but a man who saved himself from addiction by understanding the selfishness of the disease. Buddha, who lived 2,600 years ago, changed my understanding of the unconscious mind. I continuously circle back to the teachings of the Four Noble Truths and the cycles of death and rebirth through the path of the middle way. Rabbi Carlebach, a Jewish rabbi and religious teacher, created a space for me to wrestle with spirituality. His teachings have greatly influenced my work and my vision of embodying Passover.

As for the content of this book, I have a long list of people to thank. To start with, there are several people from whom I have learned so much that it would be a crime not to mention them by name. Bessle van der Kolk, Daniel Siegel, Peter Levine, Stephen Porges, Gabor Matè, Bruce Perry, and Richard Schwartz have each influenced my thoughts on unresolved trauma, addictions, and stress responses. Their work and ideas can be found throughout this text. If you have enjoyed this book, I'd encourage you to read their writing as well.

Throughout the writing of this book, I benefited from the guidance of many fine editors. Thanks to Rachel Rosekind, whose initial notes during the early stages stirred a momentum to help me realize this book. I am indebted to Laura Yorke, who helped me see the book differently and arrange it in ways that spoke directly with the reader. Christine Van Zandt helped me tighten my first draft. And finally, Claire Cohen, who encouraged me to add my narrative. I could not have become so vulnerable inside these pages without your guidance. You walked me through, hand by hand, the long stretch of rewriting this final version. I am so thankful. Your discerning eye and creative spirit allowed this book to become what it is today. Thank you.

To the team at DartFrog, who made this book a reality: thank you. I have tremendous gratitude for my publisher, Gordon McClellan. I knew in our first meeting that you were the person to champion this book. Thanks to Katelynn, for her ability to keep us moving forward. To Mark Hobbs, my cover designer: thanks for your help in capturing a beautiful book cover.

I'd like to thank many others who read and reviewed various states of the manuscript, including Kerstin M., Jennifer Schneiderman, Darcie Baker, Emily Baldwin, Lee Garlington, Carolina McFarland, Nancy Goldman, and Doris Mugrditchian. Their feedback was instructive, and yet always affirming.

With deep gratitude, I acknowledge my clients and participants in the Untangle & Thrive community. I wish I could mention you all by name for you have taught me almost everything I know. Your bravery is a constant affirmation of the life force, which drives us human beings to create a meaningful life.

Thanks to my many friends, neighbors who offered a word of encouragement and asked, "How's the book going?" There are many dark nights in the writing process. I was naïve and lost many times during this journey. I am grateful for your kind, supporting inquiry along the way. I needed it.

Finally, to you: thanks for sharing your time with me. Life is short. And I appreciate it. If you are looking for more support in your journey, reach out or visit my website for additional resources and next steps. Thank you.

Endnotes

1   Michael Klesius, "The Big Bloom: How Flowering Plants Changed the World," *National Geographic*, accessed 2 January 2022, nationalgeographic.com/science/article/big-bloom, nationalgeographic.com/science/article/big-bloom.

2   W. Thomas Boyce, *The Orchid and the Dandelion: Why Some Children Struggle and How All Can* (Knopf, 2019), 12.

3   Ibid., 23.

4   Kimberly Ann Johnson, *Call of the Wild: How We Heal Trauma, Awaken Our Own Power, and Use It For Good* (Harper Wave, 2021), 21.

5   Richard F. Thompson and Jeansok J. Kim, "Memory Systems in the Brain and Localization of a Memory," *PNAS* 93, no. 24 (1996): 13438–13444, https://www.pnas.org/doi/epdf/10.1073/pnas.93.24.13438.

6   American Psychological Association. *APA Concise Dictionary of Psychological Association* (American Psychological Association, 2009).

7   Jane Stevens, "The Adverse Childhood Experiences Study- the largest, most important public health study you never hear of-began in an obesity clinic," *Paces Education*, last modified October 3, 2012, https://www.pacesconnection.com/blog/the-adverse-childhood-experiences-study-the-largest-most-important-public-health-study-you-never-heard-of-began-in-an-obesity-clinic.

8   Ibid.

9   Katie A. McLaughlin, Margaret A. Sheridan, and Hilary K. Lambert, "Childhood Adversity and Neural Development: Deprivation and Threat as Distinct Dimensions of Early Experience," *Neuroscience and Biobehavioral Reviews* 47 (2014): 578–591, https://doi.org/10.1016/j.neubiorev.2014.10.012.

10 Bessel van der Kolk, *The Body Keeps the Score: Brain, Mind, and Body in the Healing of Trauma* (New York: Penguin Books, 2015), 54.

11 Stevens, "Adverse Childhood."

12 Ibid.

13 Ibid.

14 van der Kolk, *Body Keeps Score,* 150.

15 Ibid., 55.

16 Etienne Benson, "The Synaptic Self," *American Psychological Association*, last modified November 2022, https://www.apa.org/monitor/nov02/synaptic/.

[17] "Goethe's Color Theory," *Web Exhibits*, accessed 2 January 2022, webexhibits.org/colorart/ch.html.

[18] Steven R. Vazquez. *Emotional Transformation Therapy*: *An Interactive Ecological Psychotherapy* (Rowman & Littlefied, 2014), 28.

[19] Steven R. Vazquez, "Color: Its Therapeutic Power for Rapid Healing," *Subtle Energies & Energy Medicine* 17, no. 2 (2007): 191-213, https://journals.sfu.ca/seemj/index.php/seemj/article/view/43/33.

[20] David R. Hawkins, *The Map of Consciousness Explained: A Proven Energy Scale to Actualize Your Ultimate Potential* (Hay House Inc., 2020).

[21] Daniel J. Siegel, "Daniel J. Siegel, M.D. on Mindsight, The Emerging Mind, Mindfulness and Neural Integration, and Interpersonal Connection, Self-Awareness and Well-Being," *Towards Life-Knowledge*, last modified August 7, 2016, https://bsahely.com/2016/08/07/daniel-j-siegel-m-d-on-mindsight-the-emerging-mind-mindfulness-and-neural-integration-and-interpersonal-connection-self-awareness-and-well-being/.

[22] Daniel J. Siegel, "Mind, Self and Consciousness," April 22, 2020, Pathways to Planetary Health, https://www.youtube.com/watch?v=y79ktPcWPdc.

[23] Rebecca Kochenderfer, "Discover Journaling's Positive Effects on the Brain, with Dr. Dan Siegel," *Journaling*, last modified August 9, 2019, journaling.com/articles/discover-jouranlings-positive-effects-on-the-brain-with-dr-dan-siegel/.

[24] Saul McLeod, "Carl Jung," *Simple Psychology*, last modified 2018, simplypsychology.org/carl-jung.html.

[25] John F. Kihlstrom, "The Self," *University of California, Berkeley*, last modified August 20, 2021, ocf.berkeley.edu/~jfkihlstrom/SocialCognitionWeb/Self/Self_supp.htm.

[26] "Yes Brain Parenting: An Interview with Dr. Dan Siegel," *Good Therapy*, last modified January 25, 2018, goodtherapy.org/blog/yes-brain-parenting-interview-with-dr-dan-siegel-0123187.

[27] Steve Wasserman, "Internal Family Systems Therapy (IFS) and Schema Therapy," accessed 2 January, 2022, stevewasserman.co.uk/therapy/internal-family-systems-ifs/.

[28] van der Kolk, *Body Keeps Score,* 54.

[29] David Brooks, "The Brain Isn't The Only Part of Your Body that Thinks," *The Irish Times*, last modified Dec 13, 2019, irishtimes.com/life-and-style/health-family/the-brain-isn-t-the-only-part-of-your-body-that-thinks-1.4099334.

[30] Bruce H. Lipton, "Epigenetics and Evolution: Bettering Yourself and Humanity," March 28, 2018, Neurohacker, youtube.com/watch?time_continue=3339&v=WqRHskK3wyA&feature=emb_title.

[31] William S. Meyer, "Bruno Bettelheim and His Window to the Soul," *Clinical Social Work Journal* 38, no. 3 (2009): 275-85, doi:10.1007/

s10615-009-0218-0.

[32] Cathy Malchiodi, "Creative Arts Therapy and Expressive Arts Therapy," *Psychology Today*, last modified June 30, 2014, psychologytoday.com/gb/blog/arts-and-health/201406/creative-arts-therapy-and-expressive-arts-therapy.

[33] Jeffrey Borenstein, "Everyday Mental Health Tips," *Brain & Behavior Research Foundation*, September 17, 2019, bbrfoundation.org/blog/everyday-mental-health-tips.

[34] Daniel J. Siegel, *The Developing Mind: How Relationships and the Brain Interact to Shape Who We Are*, (The Guildford Press, 2015), 307.

[35] Carol S. Dweck, *Mindset: The New Psychology of Success* (Ballantine Books, 2006), 6.

[36] Tony Kirkland, "How Structural Alignment Coaching Works," *SA Coaching*, last modified October 21, 2013, https://salignmentcoaching.wordpress.com/2013/10/21/how-structural-alignment-coaching-works/.

[37] Kendra Cherry, "The Role of a Schema in Psychology," *Very Well Mind*, last modified September 23, 2019, verywellmind.com/what-is-a-schema-2795873.

[38] Michael Corry, "Jean Piaget's Genetic Epistemology," *The George Washington University*, last modified 1996, home.gwu.edu/~mcorry/corry2.htm.

[39] Stephen W. Porges, *The Pocket Guide to the Polyvagal Theory: The Transformative Power of Feeling Safe* (Norton Professional Books, 2017).

[40] van der Kolk, *Body Keeps Score,* 65.

[41] Antonio R. Damasio, "Feeling Our Emotions," *Scientific American*, last modified April 1, 2005, scientificamerican.com/article/feeling-our-emotions.

[42] van der Kolk, *Body Keeps Score,* 17.

[43] Eugene T. Gendlin, *Focusing* (Mass Market Paperback, 1982), 4.

[44] Johnson, *Call of the Wild,* 43.

[45] Kenneth Bachor, "Watch These Courageous Penguins Cliff-Dive for Food in an Exclusive Clip From Planet Earth II," *Time*, last modified February 7, 2017, time.com/4660247/planet-earth-ii-clip-penguins.

[46] "Know Thyself," *Wikipedia*, accessed 2 January 2022, https://en.wikipedia.org/wiki/Know_thyself.

[47] Saul McLeod, "Maslow's Hierarchy of Needs," *Simple Psychology*, last modified December 29, 2020, https://www.simplypsychology.org/maslow.html.

[48] Tony Robbins, "Discover 6 Human Needs," *Tony Robbins*, accessed 2 January 2022, tonyrobbins.com/mind-meaning/do-you-need-to-feel-significant.

[49] Anna Borges, "9 Emotional Regulation Tips for Anyone Who's Struggling Right Now," *Self*, last modified May 21, 2020, self.com/story/

emotional-regulation-skills.

50 Joseph E. LeDoux, "Evolution of Human Emotion; A View Through Fear," *Progress in Brain Research* 195 (2012): 431-42, ncbi.nlm.nih.gov/pmc/articles/PMC3600914.

51 Leon F. Seltzer, "Evolution of the Self; You Only Get More of What You Resist—Why?" *Psychology Today*, last modified June 15, 2016, psychologytoday.com/us/blog/evolution-the-self/201606/you-only-get-more-what-you-resist-why.

52 Bryan E. Robinson, "The 90-Second Rule That Builds Self-Control," *Psychology Today*, last modified April 26, 2020, psychologytoday.com/us/blog/the-right-mindset/202004/the-90-second-rule-builds-self-control.

53 Sepp Kollmorgen, Richard Hahnloser, and Valerio Mante, "How Zebra Finches Learn to Sing," *University of Zurich*, last modified January 15, 2020, media.uzh.ch/en/Press-Releases/2020/Zebra-finch.html.

54 Ibid.

55 Ibid.

56 "The Art of Rewiring Your Brain," *Foundation to Sustainable Success*, last modified December 15, 2020, foundationtosustainablesuccess.com/2020/12/15/the-art-of-rewiring-your-brain.

57 Byron Katie, *The Four Questions: For Henny Penny and Anybody with Stressful Thought* (Penguin Books, 2016), 15.

58 Bruce Ecker, Robin Ticic, and Laurel Hulley, *Unlocking the Emotional Brain: Eliminating Symptoms at Their Roots Using Memory Reconsolidation* (Routledge, 2012), 7.

59 Ibid., 4.

60 Ibid., 13.

61 Ibid., 57.

62 Courtney E. Ackerman, "What is Neuroplasticity? A Psychologist Explains," *Positive Psychology*, last modified February 5, 2022, positivepsychology.com/neuroplasticity/.

63 Ibid.

64 Margarita Tartakovsky, "Therapists Spill: How To Strengthen Your Resilience," *Psych Central*, last modified May 17, 2016, psychcentral.com/lib/therapists-spill-how-to-strengthen-your-resilience#1.

65 Leslie Riopel, "Resilience Skills, Factors and Strategies of the Resilient Person," *Positive Psychology*, last modified February 5, 2022, positivepsychology.com/resilience-skills/2021.

66 Misty Copeland, "Misty Copeland Teaches Ballet Technique and Artistry," *Masterclass,* accessed 2 January 2022, https://www.masterclass.com/classes/misty-copeland-teaches-ballet-technique-and-artistry.

67 Ibid.

68 James Clear, *Atomic Habits: An Easy & Proven Way to Build Good Habits & Break Bad Ones* (Penguin Random House, 2018), 53.

[69] Sigmund Freud, The Psychopathology of Everyday Life (W.W. Norton & Company, 1990), 243.

[70] Jeremy Bentham, The Principles of Morals and Legislation (Prometheus Books, 1789).

[71] Debra Fulghum Bruce, "Exercise and Depression," *WebMD*, last modified February 18, 2020, webmd.com/depression/guide/exercise-depression.

[72] Matthew Walker, Why We Sleep; Unlocking the Power of Sleep and Dreams (Simon & Schuster, 2018), 12.

[73] "Chernobyl Accident 1986," *World Nuclear Association*, last modified March 2022, world-nuclear.org/information-library/safety-and-security/safety-of-plants/chernobyl-accident.aspx

[74] Germán Orizaola, "Chernobyl Has Become a Refuge for Wildlife 33 Years After the Nuclear Accident," *The Conversation*, last modified May 8, 2019, theconversation.com/chernobyl-has-become-a-refuge-for-wildlife-33-years-after-the-nuclear-accident-116303.

[75] Janine M. Benyus, *Biomimicry: Innovation Inspired by Nature* (HarperCollins, 2002), 11.

[76] "Unbelievable Facts About Human Body," *Times of India*, last modified July 31, 2017, timesofindia.indiatimes.com/life-style/health-fitness/photo-stories/18-unbelievable-facts-about-human-body/photostory/59844962.cms?picid=59845249.

[77] David R. Hawkins, Power vs. Force (Hay House, 2012), 46.

[78] Ibid, 73.

[79] SarahLou, "The Birds and The Bees: The Female Pelvic Floor," *The Living Pelvis*, last modified January 23, 2019, thelivingpelvis.com/2019/01/23/the-birds-and-the-bees-the-female-pelvic-floor.

[80] "Jaguar," *Wild For Life*, accessed 2 January 2022, wildfor.life/species/jaguar.

[81] Peter A. Levine, *Waking the Tiger: Healing Trauma* (North Atlantic Books, 1997), 69.

[82] Ingrid, "We Live in Webs of Interdependence," *Grit in education*, last modified 2015, gritineducation.com/we-live-in-webs-of-interdependence.

[83] Neil Evernden, *The Social Creation of Nature* (Johns Hopkins University Press, 2010), 13.

[84] "Suicide," *National Institute of Mental Health*, accessed 2 January 2022, https://nimh.nih.gov/health/statistics/suicide.

[85] Jeffrey Juergens, "Suicide and Substance Abuse," *Addiction Center*, last modified January 11, 2022, addictioncenter.com/addiction/addiction-and-suicide.

[86] "Obesity and Overweight," *National Institute of Child Health and Human Development*, last modified July 28, 2021, nichd.nih.gov/health/topics/obesity/.

[87]   "Frequently Asked Questions," *Crisis Centre,* accessed 2 January 2022, crisiscentre.bc.ca/frequently-asked-questions-about-suicide.

[88]   Elena Renken, "Most Americans Are Lonely, and Our Workplace Culture May Not Be Helping," NPR, January 23, 2020, npr.org/sections/health-shots/2020/01/23/798676465/most-americans-are-lonely-and-our-workplace-culture-may-not-be-helping.

[89]   Bruce D. Perry and Oprah Winfrey, *What Happened to You? Conversations on Trauma, Resilience, and Healing* (Pan Macmillan, 2021), 32.

[90]   David Thoreau, "Henry David Thoreau Reflects on Nature, 1854," *The American Yawp Reader*, accessed 2 January 2022, americanyawp.com/reader/religion-and-reform/henry-david-thoreau-reflects-on-nature-1854.

About the Author

For the past twenty years, Angela McKinney has been transforming people's lives—including her own. As an expert in the psychology of habit formation and addiction recovery, as well as a speaker focused on decision-making and continuous improvement, she created her three-step system of healing—The Untangle Method—using research on the neurobiology of trauma with a creative approach on how to improve one's quality of life. She has appeared in the *NY Times*, *The Fix*, Lifetime, Showtime, and CBS. Angela lives with her husband and two sons in New Jersey, and this is her first book.

Get connected:

hello@untangleandthrive.com

untangleandthrive.com

What does an author stand to gain by asking for reader feedback? A lot. So if you've enjoyed *Untangle: How to Create Big Possibilities Through Small Changes*, please support it by giving it a review on the sales platform of your choice. Your opinion could help potential readers decide whether or not they would enjoy this book, too.

Made in United States
North Haven, CT
06 January 2023

30659258R00195